Inside Music Therapy:
Client Experiences

Edited by
JULIE HIBBEN

Barcelona
PUBLISHERS

Inside Music Therapy: Client Experiences
Edited by Julie Hibben

Copyright © 1999 by Barcelona Publishers

ISBN 13: 978-1-891278-08-2
ISBN 10: 1-891278-08-8

Distributed throughout the world by:
Barcelona Publishers
4 White Brook Road
Gilsum NH 03448
Tel: 603-357-0236 Fax: 603-357-2073
Website: www.barcelonapublishers.com
SAN 298-6299

Cover design: © 2004 Frank McShane
Music Typesetter: Thomas Smith
Copy Editor: Katharine O'Moore Klopf

Ann, a mother of young children and a music therapist, writes of six sessions of in-depth therapy she began when she was being treated for cancer. In her sessions, Ann listened to music in a relaxed state. She describes the imagery that she produced and its relevance to her struggle. By mutual agreement with the therapist who supported her during these private sessions, she does not name the therapist.

T presents excerpts from the journal he kept during his year of therapy with Jenny. T describes highlights of the imagery he experienced as he listened to music in a state of deep relaxation. The insights he gained from processing the imagery with Jenny helped him overcome his fears of memories of sexual abuse.

Guilio, in his early twenties, writes about two important sessions that took place during his 7 months of therapy with Gabriella. Guilio describes using improvisation on xylophones and drums to learn to free himself from obsessions, to stay in relationship, and to balance his male and female parts. (Italy)

Rebecca, now a music therapist, writes about her experience as a client when she was in her early forties and felt herself stuck and not living authentically. She describes the imagery she experienced as she listened to music in a relaxed state.

TABLE OF CONTENTS

Part I: Clients Write About Their Experiences

1. When Words Are Not Enough   3
Helen Bowe, Mary Brown Mudge,
and Andrea Frisch

Helen and Mary write about using music improvisation in their individual sessions with Andrea. Helen's sessions in a psychiatric institution began when she was a teenager struggling with depression and continued when she was discharged. She describes using her flute. Mary tells about making sounds and music that helped her to open to her feelings.

2. Out of the Ashes: Transforming Despair into Hope with Music and Imagery   7
Cecilia Herzfeld Schulberg

Cecilia, a music therapist, writes of her experience as a client in which she, as a child of Holocaust survivors, encounters and integrates her "Holocaust shadow." She describes powerful images that emerged as she listened to music in a deep state of consciousness, aided by the therapists who worked with her over several years.

This book is dedicated to the people whose courage is described in their stories and to Ken Bruscia, who had the vision to ask for them.

The courage
To risk moving my body,
To let it be awkward,
Searching for grace,
Is like risking an unknown, perfect sound
To find my own music.

To risk,
To risk in front of strangers,
To risk letting strangers become friends,
Is like facing a new sheet of paper
Blank, intimidating whiteness
And daring, bold splashes of color
I can't erase.

I can't take back the sound or movement
I can't deny the experience.

Through the process,
Daring not to be perfect,
Giving myself a chance,
I can tap my soul
And set it free.

If I can get past the terror,
*I can be a rainbow.**

---

* The response of Marion Corbin in a creative arts workshop led by Ken Bruscia, Anne Riordan, Gary Barlow, and Lewis Shupe.

7. Chaos, Crisis, Development, Cosmos   **53**
Mark Nielsen and Torben Moe

Mark, in his late thirties, begins his story with his early music study and precocious entry into a music conservatory. He met Torben when he entered a psychiatric hospital after many years of substance abuse. Mark describes the imagery he created from his deep unconscious as he, with the support of Torben, listened to classical music and the importance of the music sessions in aiding his recovery. (Norway)

8. Experiencing the Music in
Guided Imagery and Music   **61**
Connie Isenberg-Grzeda

Connie writes about her physical and emotional experience of the music when she is in therapy, deeply relaxed, and listening to classical music. Connie is a music therapist, but she writes as a client in therapy. (Canada)

Part II: Clients Tell About Their Experiences
in Their Own Words,
Gathered by Their Therapists

---

9. The Quiet Soldier: Pain and Sickle-Cell Anemia   **69**
Joanne V. Loewy

Joanne presents transcripts of an interview with Walter after a session during one of his hospital stays when he began to vocalize and create a song. Walter, a teenager, suffers from the chronic pain crises of sickle-cell anemia. Walter tells of his experience of pain and of how he finds music helpful.

Diane presents words gathered from eight or more adult clients in her practice. Some of her clients struggle with histories of substance abuse, eating disorders, or abusive or disturbed parents. Three clients tell in interview, poems, and prose of their experience using improvised playing and singing and of the feelings and images that emerged in the playing. Diane also presents both a collage of clients' words about singing in therapy, taken from her journals, and several poems about her clients.

Eric presents Rachel's written responses to his questions about their 10 listening and biofeedback therapy sessions in a healing center. Rachel, a musician, suffers from Raynaud's disease, a condition of poor circulation to extremities, which become numb and cold. Eric includes graphs showing Rachel's physiological responses during various aural stimuli, such as her favorite music and environmental sounds.

Madelaine offers excerpts from an audiotape Lilly prepared for their last session together. On the tape, Lilly, a survivor of childhood abuse, presents songs, readings, and personal celebrations of their sessions during which she shared the imagery that she generated while listening to classical music in an internally focused state.

Colin presents Charles's words about his therapy and his experience of the improvisational piano duet in session 21 from the 2 years they worked together. Charles had human immunodeficiency virus. Music excerpts from the two improvisations in that session are included.

Sally offers Peg's words, both verbatim interviews and monologues constructed from comments she has heard Peg make many times. Peg is a 92-year-old nursing-home resident. Sally interlaces the narrative with descriptions of Peg's music experiences in the home; these include sessions in which familiar music is recreated to stimulate physical movement, instrument playing, singing, and conversation.

To write this narrative, Alison and William, a midlife businessman, reviewed Alison's transcripts from parts of four nonconsecutive therapy sessions (chosen because they contained imagery of William's relationship to his wife) that took place more than 2 years earlier. William's imagery (evoked during relaxed listening), some of his words during the discussion after the music in the four sessions, and his feelings on revisiting the material of his sessions are included. Transcripts of William's thoughts about the therapy taped at their recent meeting conclude the narrative. (Australia)

Part III: Client Experiences
Are Written About by Parents

Anna describes participating with her 3-year-old son John, who is autistic with severe learning disabilities, in the first year of sessions with Amelia. Anna tells the story of John's birth and development and describes John's reactions to the music and movement games and playful improvisations of the sessions in a developmental center. (Great Britain)

Christina recounts her daughter Franny's engagement with music over her 15 years. In the 3½ years of private sessions with Julie that were part of her individual education program, Franny sang familiar songs, role-played, and improvised at the piano. Franny has developmental delays and mild cerebral palsy.

Laura, Catherine, and Victoria write of their children's piano lessons with Mary Ann, a music therapist and piano teacher. All three children (two are teenagers and one is 10 years old) have struggled with learning disabilities. The parents describe how the music-making in individual lessons and periodic group classes harnesses the children's auditory strengths.

Part IV: Client Experiences
Are Inferred by Therapists
Through Multiple Means

In separate interviews, Suzanne asked Kelly's mother and her co-therapist to watch a videotape of Kelly's thirty-sixth session in a music therapy clinic. Suzanne transcribes their comments about Kelly's experience and includes descriptions of Kelly's engagement (humming, playing percussion instruments, and listening) with the music. Kelly's music, brought back from week to week through Suzanne's piano improvisations, is included in the narrative. In a further attempt to get as close to Kelly's own voice as possible, Suzanne intersperses the narrative with soliloquies that are her interpretation of what 9-year-old Kelly, who has had frequent seizures for most of her life, would say if she could speak.

Michelle asked the teachers, therapists, and a parent of the profoundly multiply handicapped children, teens, and young adults who live and receive instruction in a pediatric nursing home what meaning the songs and adapted instruments she brings to them weekly has for these students. Michelle's report represents many students' experiences of the music, inferred by the spokespersons who regularly observe their behaviors.

Barbara describes 4 years of therapy for Lisa, first in Barbara's private practice and then in a small group school setting. Lisa was between 9 and 13 years old when these sessions, in which they used familiar songs and movement and percussion-playing, took place. Interspersed with descriptions of Lisa's behavior during the sessions are short soliloquies Barbara wrote on Lisa's behalf, saying what she believes Lisa would say if she could speak her thoughts. Barbara also reports an interview with Lisa's mother, who participated in the early sessions.

Janice and Roia write about Pat's experience of therapy in which piano improvisation is the primary mode of communication and expression. Pat's sessions take place in his residence, a developmental center. Roia is his therapist and Janice is Roia's mentor and supervisor. Since 30-year-old Pat is developmentally delayed and nonverbal, the authors describe his behavior in the sessions and make inferences about his experience. Using the concept of parallel process, they suggest that Pat's feelings about the therapy are parallel to Roia's concurrent feelings about supervision.

Rika presents the study of 8-year-old Henry during an 8-minute individual segment of therapy in a group therapy school setting with three other autistic boys. During the segment, she and the co-therapist encourage Henry to sit on the piano bench and play or sing with Rika's improvised music. (Henry's melodies are included.) Rika reports Henry's behavior during this short segment and interprets Henry's state of mind in the form of imaginative soliloquy, since he is not capable of commenting on his internal experience. A component of Rika's study is a review of the videotape of this segment with Henry's mother and the co-therapist; their interpretation of Henry's experience is included with her own. (Japan)

MUSIC THERAPIST CONTRIBUTORS

Dorit Amir, DA, ACMT

Diane Austin, MA, ACMT

Jenny Martin Caughman, MA, ACMT, FAMI

Barbara Crowe, MM, MT-BC

Janice Dvorkin, PSYD, ACMT

Michele Forinash, DA, MT-BC, LMHC

A. Jeffrey Friedberg, MA, MT-BC

Andrea Frisch, MA, CMT

Mary Ann Froehlich, DMA, MT-BC, CCLS

Michelle Glidden, MED, MT-BC, LMHC

Denise Erdonmez Grocke, MM, MT-BC, RMT

Julie Hibben, MT-BC, LMHC

Sally A. Hough, MMT, MT-BC

Leslie L. Hunter, MT-BC

Rika Ikuno, EDM, CMT

Connie Isenberg-Grzeda, MTA, MT-BC

Colin Lee, PHD

Joanne V. Loewy, DA, ACMT-BC

Sally McKnight, MM

Eric Miller, PHD, MT-BC

Lynn Miller, CMT

Torben Moe, MA, FAMI

Suzanne Nowikas, MA, MT-BC, NRMT

Lauren Obstbaum, MA, CMT

Amelia Oldfield, MPHIL, RMTH

Gabriella Giordanella Perilli, PHD

Donna W. Polen, MT-BC

Roia Rafieyan, MT-BC

Mary Rykov, MTA

Cecilia Herzfeld Schulberg, MT-BC, MFCC

Alison Short, MA, RMT, MT-BC, RGIMT

Henk Smeijsters, PHD

Alan Turry, ACMT-BC

Madelaine Ventre, MS, MT-BC

Barbara L. Wheeler, PHD, MT-BC

PREFACE

I hope that readers will find the preface useful in helping them dig into this book. I have tried to make the book accessible to many different readers: music lovers, people who are looking for or are wondering about therapy, people who use music in their work, and people hoping to deepen their understanding of the therapeutic relationship or the role of music in therapy.

THE CHALLENGE

I took on this book because I wanted to change the imbalance I perceived in writings about therapy. In professional journals—not just music therapy but all psychological journals—evidences of or searches for clients' points of view are far outnumbered by writing about clients by therapists or researchers. Therapists typically write from the perspective of their own theories and techniques. In the last decade, the increased awareness of and regard for differences (of gender, culture, class, sexual orientation, age, and handicapping conditions) has led therapists and clients to look for and respect multiple meanings in the therapy room. In the professional literature, however, I find not much attention paid to the meaning that clients make of their experience of therapy. This book is dedicated to adjusting the balance by presenting the therapy experiences of the client.

The music in therapy sessions evokes many reactions, metaphors, and feelings. Therapists and clients engaging in music therapy expect multiple and sometimes ineffable meanings to emerge from listening to or playing or singing music. The enthusiastic response to this book by the writers may be due to the effect music has had on their awareness of the efficacy of individual perspectives. Clients and therapists have seemed eager to share their stories or their studies from inside music therapy.

I hope that the accounts presented here—the vantage point provided by this collection of information from and about the experience of clients—will enlighten potential and current practitioners and clients of music therapy. Even more, I hope the book will influence what happens in the therapy room and what is talked about in case conferences. At the very least, I hope that future writers will use these narratives as models for their own publications.

GATHERING THE NARRATIVES

I began gathering narratives from clients' points of view in the only way I knew how. I contacted practicing music therapists and asked them to invite their clients to describe their experiences. Since not all clients are able to write, I suggested to therapists that they put together a study of the experience of clients using words, behaviors, or other material from clients and spokespersons. I also suggested that music therapists who had been clients in therapy might write of their own experiences.

The result is a collection of 33 narratives written in many ways. In some narratives, clients or parents write a personal story of their experience; in some, music therapists present interview(s) of clients or spokespersons; in others, therapists and researchers compile studies from transcripts of therapy sessions, interviews, and various sources including clients' poems and songs. The authors are clients or parents (almost half of the narratives), music therapists, and researchers. People of all ages—from 3 years to over 90—are represented in these narratives. Some writers describe individual and some group music therapy. The narratives are primarily from the United States but are also from Australia, Canada, Denmark, Great Britain, Israel, Italy, Japan, and The Netherlands.

In asking therapists to engage a client in this project, I knew that there was potential for awkward, if not unethical, situations to arise. I was especially vigilant that clients were protected against any hint of coercion and that their confidentiality was safeguarded. I asked therapists to tell clients what support would be available if new and disturbing material was brought into awareness from therapy review or from the change in roles that such a project required. I prepared contracts for both parties to discuss and sign to ensure they were fully informed about the risks and benefits of participation.

A number of therapists contacted former clients who agreed to write or to be interviewed. Most of these reported that reconnecting to old roles and feelings affected them deeply and that new understandings emerged for both parties. In some cases clients and therapists met to review past therapy sessions and as a result of studying the experience of therapy, clarified the experience for each other. Some clients or spokespersons for nonverbal clients and therapists contributed a narrative as part of their ongoing therapy or as a conclusion to therapy. They found that the writing produced otherwise unavailable insights.

HOW TO READ THIS BOOK

Readers may want to start with the introduction, which summarizes how clients in the book have experienced music in their therapy. I suggest those who have questions about what happens in the music therapy sessions read the introduction. The introduction is not necessary for an understanding of the narratives, but it may help put them into context.

Each narrative has a short introductory paragraph or two so that the reader can quickly tell what the narrative is about and how it was written. The narratives are grouped according to the role of the writer(s). In part I, clients write stories of their experiences (narratives 1–8). In part II, therapists gather clients' descriptions of their experiences through interviews, transcripts of sessions, questionnaires, or review of sessions with the client (narratives 9–19). In part III, the experiences of clients who are unable or unavailable to talk or write for themselves are described by parents (narratives 20–22). In part IV, the experiences of clients who do not have meaningful language or whose words are unavailable are inferred by therapists through more than one means, such as observation of behavior, testimonies of spokespersons, client music, journals, or an imaginative representation of client thoughts and feelings inferred through long experience with the clients (narratives 23–30). In part V, researchers gather and synthesize the words of clients about their experiences (narratives 31–33).

The table of contents contains a brief synopsis of each narrative. Readers who do not want to read from front to back can use the synopses to select narratives of interest. For each narrative, the synopsis describes the therapy setting; gives the age of the client; tells whether group or individual therapy is involved; describes the role of the author(s), method of writing, and the predominant way the client experiences the music; and gives the narrative's country of origin.

EDITING DECISIONS

I have tried to guard the confidentiality of clients by deleting specific references to clinics and hospitals and not citing the city where the sessions took place. I requested that clients and spokespersons use pseudonyms, but I have honored and respected requests from clients to use their real names if their stories do not implicate people who would not want to be known. Readers should assume that a client is using a pseudonym unless it is stated otherwise in the narrative's introduction.

Since this book is about client experiences, I have restricted therapists' clinical or theoretical formulations unless they are absolutely necessary to the understanding of what the clients experienced. I have edited professional and music terminology when I thought it was too specialized for nonprofessional readers. The music notation that is included enhances but is not necessary for the understanding of client stories. Readers who have questions about sources can contact the American Music Therapy Association (AMTA) by mail at 8455 Colesville Road, suite 1000, Silver Spring, Maryland 20910; by phone at (301) 589-3300; or by fax at (301) 589-5175. There are also music therapy associations in other countries.

With the consent of the authors, I have made small changes in the material. I have edited writings and verbatim interviews where necessary to make sentences more readable. In the verbatim quotes, material that is left out is designated by ellipses (. . .) and inserted words are in brackets [ ]. I have not needed to make changes in clients' writing in most instances, since their narratives came to me edited by their therapist co-writers. I have left British spelling—which is different from American English spelling in some cases—in narratives that originated from Great Britain or the British Commonwealth countries.

THANKS

I am very grateful to the people whose stories are contained in this book. I know that in many cases contributing has been an emotional and taxing experience; I hope that it has also been affirming and clarifying, as it surely is for the reader.

I am grateful to the music therapists who responded so generously and risked taking on new roles in the effort to further the understanding of their practice. For some music therapists, eliciting and investigating their clients' perspectives was not a new experience, as some have published studies of client experiences before. For others, highlighting the client's point of view has meant a struggle to let go of traditional ways of thinking about therapy and about writing. The narratives, both in style and content, have surpassed my dreams.

I thank publisher Ken Bruscia for suggesting this book to me and giving me freedom to mold it. There are two people without whose help I could not have gotten off the ground: Cheryl Dileo, who clarified ethical questions and helped me put together consent forms; and my husband, George, who is my in-house technical expert, among many other good things.

Julie Hibben
September 3, 1998

INTRODUCTION

The experience of the music in therapy sessions as reported by clients can be summarized in four categories of activities: improvising, listening, re-creating, and composing. This is the simplest way to describe what clients and therapists actually do in their sessions. The four categories represent a therapist's way of looking at the range of experiences of music in sessions; clients do not talk about the music in this way.

IMPROVISING

When clients and therapists improvise music, what they are actually doing is spontaneously playing or singing rhythms and tones; they are making up the music as they go along. In improvisation in therapy—on drums and other percussion or melodic instruments or with voice—there are no right or wrong "notes," but there is the challenge to make the sounds meaningful or intentional and to shape them into expressive interaction or satisfying form as they emerge.

Several clients describe struggling to improvise freely at first. Their words show that they think the experience is analogous to life: you must take the risk, dig in, and try out your wings. Clients almost invariably feel that improvisation is a risk because, as one client puts it, it makes your feelings real. Of course, feelings surface in the playing and are important in the work of therapy.

More than one third of the narratives describe improvisation as the primary music experience. Clients, in improvising with therapists, speak in many different ways about how the spontaneous music making mirrors other patterns of communication in their lives. Improvisations are never an end in themselves, although clients sometimes describe them as something to hold on to, and they enjoy listening to playbacks of them. The improvisations create a context, not limited or controlled by language, in which self-learning can occur. Clients describe learning to trust, to let go, to make decisions, and other metaphors for their lives as the improvised music continues. Some speak of pounding it out with drums or loosening a lump of fear with singing. In the narratives describing improvisation in groups, clients talk about the lessons of listening to others and the give-and-take of forming relationships through the music.

Improvisations are sometimes simple physical or vocal attempts at communication in which observers can hear the joy or the frustration or the effort or the boredom—in short, the experience—of the client. Spokespersons for clients describe random tapping that becomes, as the therapist joins, playful communication.

In improvisation, the therapist often has the responsibility of keeping the music going, of providing musical support, of enhancing emotional expression or providing inspiration, of motivating the playing, or of copying and remembering the music of the client.

LISTENING

We have all experienced how music is used in businesses to encourage productivity and efficiency or in medical or dental offices to calm patients. Listening to music is known to influence people's behavior and feelings, but the same specific selections of music do not work for everyone; music cannot be prescribed like medicine. Each of us has a unique response (or nonresponse) to certain music. These different responses are demonstrated in the narratives.

Music listening is almost always part of music therapy sessions. A number of clients report how music of a certain period or ethnic origin or music familiar for other reasons connects them to memories, feelings, or new insights. In some narratives, clients hear music that catches their rapt attention or brings about physical change. A music therapist may choose or suggest or create music for a client, or the client and the therapist together may choose music for listening.

Sometimes music is listened to actively, as when the client listens to a playback of a recorded improvisation; sometimes listening occurs after the client has been helped into a relaxed or meditative state. When a client is relaxed and music is put on, imagery from the unconscious (as in dreams) and accompanying feelings are often evoked by the music. This experience of music and imagery is described by clients in 10 of the narratives; the imagery and feelings become the material that the client and therapist use later in the session for discussion. Clients say that the dynamic of the music evokes imagery, that the flow of the music makes the imagery move on, and that listening to music may magnify emotions and yet, paradoxically, help contain them.

RE-CREATING

The term *re-creating* means the experience of singing or playing a familiar or known piece of music, one that has already been composed by someone. Familiar songs are especially valuable carriers of meaning and are re-created by clients and therapists in these sessions for many reasons. Clients talk about songs that are like old friends, that represent a period in their life, that say what they want to say, that give an outlook or an outlet, or that change you. Familiar songs sneak up on you, a client says, because you forget that you feel so strongly.

Active re-creating of cherished music occurs in many of the experiences described in this book. Clients describe singing songs as a context for discussion of meaning or memories. Clients tell of the satisfaction of re-creating learned music or an original song. Clients re-create dances, instrument playing, and games that are evoked by familiar songs.

COMPOSING

When composing or song-writing, a composer diligently works out a composition—perhaps at the piano or with guitar—writes it down, and then performs it or, with luck, has it performed or recorded. This is not far from what the client and therapist do in music therapy. In composing in therapy, some kind of written document is made so that the piece can be played or sung again. One difference is that in therapy, the composition is often a spontaneous creation that grows out of interactive playing or discussion in a session and is created by people who are in a helping relationship and may not think of themselves as composers.

The differences between people composing in therapy and composing for commercial purposes are not necessarily apparent in the composition but instead in the roles of the composers, their intent, and in the nature of the interactions that produce the composition. In therapy, the therapist takes the role of facilitator, helping a client produce music that is related to or expressive of the reasons they have met together. The process of creating usually involves discussion about personal issues. Clients describe song composing as a means of expressing their feelings, of proving what they can accomplish, of telling a story about feelings during a certain time or place, or of sending a message. When clients write a song together in group therapy, the song often represents group unity or diversity around common themes, the group members get to hear the perspectives of others, and the song may be brought back from week to week.

Four narratives report experiences in which songs have been composed and written down by clients and therapists during sessions. The compositions begin during a spontaneous improvisation that produces words and music material that has personal meaning; then the compositions are repeated or worked on together, taped, written out, and shared with family or friends. Several other narratives describe improvisations (not composed music) that are taped during sessions and played back but not saved, written down, or shared outside the session.

CONCLUSION

It is easier to talk about music experiences by separating them into these four categories. In actuality, all four of these experiences may happen in one session; music therapists may draw from any or all of these ways of using music, depending on the client's needs. Some music therapists may specialize in one way of using music and thus attract to their practices people who want to try using music in that way. Just as therapists may prefer one or several ways of working, clients have preferences for or natural affinities to certain ways of using music. Music therapists have developed specific techniques and materials for their work with specific clients or client groups.

Part I

Clients Write About
Their Experiences

In these narratives, clients write about themselves, about what they experience in music therapy, and, in some cases, how music therapy affected their lives. At the beginning of their narratives, their therapists briefly introduce their stories. For four of the narratives, the authors are music therapists who write from their experience as clients of music therapy.

Narrative 1

WHEN WORDS ARE NOT ENOUGH

Helen Bowe, Mary Brown Mudge,
and Andrea Frisch

ANDREA'S INTRODUCTION

I am fortunate to have worked with Helen and Mary. They are separated by generations and circumstance but are both articulate about
their struggles. Their verbal abilities were a tremendous asset to the
therapy work. Interestingly, they were aware that their use of words
had often been a hindrance in verbal psychotherapy and a source of
frustration in their lives. Getting to their feelings in manageable,
productive ways was a core aspect of our work in music psychotherapy. We often followed our improvisations with discussions about the
analogy of the playing to life situations. They have each written a
short description of their experience, not using their real names.

HELEN

I was introduced to music therapy as a patient in a long-term
psychiatric institution. I was 18 years old and had been admitted
after a third suicide attempt. Verbal therapy was not new to me. I
had struggled throughout my adolescent years and had been in
and out of treatment for depression since I was 13. For some reason I never could tackle the everyday, very "normal" pressures of
life like others my age could.

Being in a high-security hospital and having no contact with
family or friends for months on end was enough to motivate me to
finally deal with the issues facing me. These issues were primarily
my poor self-identity (borderline personality). Feeling the pain I had
bottled up for so long was also a goal, I suppose. So after committing
myself to the program in the hospital, I opened up to other forms of
therapy, such as music and painting.

There was only one thing I ever was good at through middle
school and some of high school, and that was playing the flute. Somehow this came back to me after meeting Andrea. She encouraged our

improvising together; she played the piano and I played my flute. It turned out to be a very healing experience for me.

In the beginning, I was cautious and giddy, embarrassed and scared. It took time before I felt safe. As time passed and our weekly sessions continued, they were the highlight of my week. While the formal sessions of psychotherapy continued on a path of speech and talking, the music therapy followed another path. This path was more colorful and freeing than those very formal, timed sessions with my psychiatrist, where I knew what was acceptable to say and feel and what was not.

Colorful is a good word to describe it. In music therapy, I was more free. There was tension, too: sometimes I'd float right out of a music therapy session; other times I'd be heavy on my feet and in my head. Either way, there was something going on—call it progress.

My days in music therapy are some of the most memorable not only from the period of isolation during the hospitalization but from the postperiod as well. Support and trust were there in those rooms— with a piano always there, my flute close by, and Andrea. Some days I'd open up, feel, and let it come rolling out and other days I would be quiet and just be. The trust was phenomenal.

Music made things solid or real or "expressed." Music defined what I felt and thought, made my feelings real, or made me real. The piano supported and coached or trailed behind, but it was always there. There was consistency. I could be a person—that "terrible" person I knew I was. It was okay with Andrea and the music.

Having so many of my feelings from my childhood—my flute was also from my childhood and was an instrument that could trigger old feelings—was a very emotional experience for me. My flute was emotion for me; it connected me to the past and at the same time cemented me down in the present.

Improvisation was a new "mature" territory for me. In improv, there were no rules—no right and wrong, no black and white, no structure—as there were in my traditional flute lessons, family patterns, and school ensemble. In the improv with Andrea I was able to stretch my wings or try out my wings a little bit, sometimes flailing and sometimes soaring in the music.

The strong trust and bond I felt with her allowed me to feel and not be afraid to get those feelings out, to voice them if only in the music. I experienced a wonder in the music of music therapy; it could be so different from the talking therapy, where words state your feelings point-blank. Music cannot be interpreted like that.

My intellect was always ahead of my emotions, especially in therapy, but in music therapy, I had no control over that intellect;

emotions came first in the music we played. I can remember being so tongue-tied lots of times after a session. It was different and difficult for me to let my guard of words down and let the feelings come out. I felt more open and vulnerable in music therapy sessions than in verbal therapy.

During those days, it was very difficult to be able to totally connect to the music that was the product of my feelings. Music therapy opened up channels that felt way beyond my understanding and clearly showed my inability to connect my emotions to my intellect. I thought I should have been able to make progress, intellectually, after hearing our music on tape; I wanted to have the ability to analyze the music like I could analyze the talk in verbal therapy. I often tried to dissect and analyze the music after hearing it on tape, but it was beyond me. There was no intellect involved, only the feelings in the moment as I played.

Perhaps I didn't utilize music therapy to the fullest because I only used my flute and no other instruments. It was and is so typical of me—too scared to try something new. Maybe it would have broadened my therapy and myself if I had tried other instruments. But then again, maybe at that time I needed the security of something familiar and constant, which was my flute. Another gift Andrea and music therapy gave me was permission to be myself.

After I was discharged from the hospital, Andrea allowed me to continue to work with her, and the support was instrumental in helping me manage on the "outside." Even after the posthospitalization period, when I had stopped psychotherapy, Andrea and our music were there for me. It was Andrea I confided in; by then, our therapy had turned more into talking, with my flute on my lap or on the floor next to me. That was exactly what I needed then.

To this day, I don't understand the full impact or reason for music therapy's benefits. It is difficult to define or analyze its actual concept. But one thing I do know is that it helped me so much at such a difficult time in my life. I can never look back on that time without thinking about the impact that music therapy had on me and the contribution it made to my life. Learning how to express and feel creatively through music was healing and it was a way in which to grow emotionally. I am grateful to have experienced such things.

Music therapy made a huge impression on me. Ten years later, I remember and long for that kind of freedom of expression and acceptance and the trusting, caring environment. It added so much to my life and I miss it desperately. If not for the impossibility of continuing music therapy [because of] the geography that separates Andrea and me, I would have loved to continue and explore through music. The relationship we built through music therapy is something that I will always be grateful for and cherish.

MARY

Responding to your [Andrea's] invitation to share something of my experience with music therapy provides the good feelings that come with remembering the distance we came together so that I could find some central stability and emotional resilience.

All along, I appreciated your steadfast belief that I could find ways to ground the reactivity of my inner turmoil so that I could express my deep self. Through sound-making and occasionally music, I learned to trust a process that flows from a place other than my overexercised, ever-protective thinker. It was very important for me. My feelings of emotional vulnerability and my fear of opening to the shame of not knowing the unknowable found some resolution through the spreading of your musical safety net.

I continue to value essences of your supportive presence, Andrea. Staying true to the process and not swaying with my fragmentation took some doing on your part. I was more comfortable with learning and understanding than opening and feeling. It became possible for me to trust that emotional balance comes from much more than merely understanding any issue.

The experience of being supported to let go into the unfamiliar creativity of making different kinds and energies of sounds while being inside a moment-to-moment process (with my judgment considerably expanded) was deeply significant to my healing and growth. The inner knowledge that I could continue to be creative through my own strength allowed me to finish therapy with good feelings.

Narrative 2

OUT OF THE ASHES:
TRANSFORMING DESPAIR INTO HOPE
WITH MUSIC AND IMAGERY

Cecilia Herzfeld Schulberg

INTRODUCTION

I am a music psychotherapist, but here I write of my own experiences
with music therapy as the child of Holocaust survivors. These experiences are transcribed from sessions that began during my training in
the use of Guided Imagery and Music (GIM). During the sessions, I
was in a deep state of consciousness listening to specially selected
classical music that helped me face and work through the powerful
images of the Holocaust. I am deeply indebted to the music therapists
who helped me in this process.

THE TRANSFORMING

The first time I was ever able to address this legacy was in a
group GIM session. I was led into a relaxed state by the therapist who
then put on a classical music program. The descending bass melody
quickly pulled me into an experience I had feared my whole life.

> I smell the smoke and the stench of burning bodies. I hear
> the cries of the dying and the mournful sobbing of those who
> barely survived. I feel the heaviness and emptiness of death
> all around me. It is too real. And it seems like I am here for
> an eternity. A few remaining survivors are slowly, hypnoti-
> cally making their way into a burned, desecrated syna-
> gogue. I find myself among them, also in a trance. The
> chanting, moaning of the familiar liturgy grows louder as
> the walking dead fill the remains of this holy place. I am
> surrounded by these rocking, half-dead bodies, their heads
> covered with prayer shawls, and I become one of them. My

voice rises with theirs, crying, screaming, mourning. The sounds are filling a deep dark hole inside me.

As the music ends, I felt my spirit rising from this place into my own shell of a body. I drew a mandala (a circular drawing) to capture this experience, and my body became filled with me—my heart, my life, my spirit—and I was born. I was no longer that 15-year-old who survived Auschwitz: she was my mother.

It was in that music and imagery session that I was first able to look at how the Holocaust affected me directly as a child of Holocaust survivors. I experienced it with my whole being, from bodily sensations to psychic numbing. It was the ultimate death–rebirth experience: I was no longer my mother, a Holocaust survivor; I was reborn as me. The experience is as alive in me today as it was then, years ago. As a result of that session, I realized at a much deeper level how much I lived my life for and as my mother. I came in touch with loss, despair, and grief so overwhelming that I created powerful barriers of protection from the pain within myself and in the world. That GIM session was the beginning of breaking through those barriers, the beginning of my life.

My reconnection with music as a powerful source of life, healing, and spirituality enabled me for the first time to face, experience, and release some of the tremendous loss and grief I have felt since I was a child. This occurred in recurring death–rebirth GIM experiences. Although this first session highlighted the entanglement with my mother, following sessions intensified my lack of connection with her mother, after whom I am named; she was gassed at Auschwitz.

The image of my grandmother during my GIM sessions embodied for me all the losses incurred during the war. These losses showed up in various images of death in my GIM sessions: being in a grave and not being able to get out; being dead for a whole session; being in a death march to the crematoriums and not being able to do anything to stop it; being surrounded by dead bodies, half-dead bodies, and mass graves without markers. I experienced death in my body as nothingness, heaviness, coldness, or emptiness in a shell. It was not the actual death that was so painful; it was the inhumanity.

The image of my grandmother in my GIM sessions also provided me with the safety and protection I never felt in the world growing up, enabling me to work through and heal these traumas. In my GIM sessions, I experienced her comforting me as a child, rocking me in her lap. I felt safe in her arms while sirens were blaring and bombs were exploding outside her home. I have felt her presence with me throughout my life; but with the music, she helped to fill the endless void I had with the loss of her and everyone else. With the music and my GIM training community, I was developing resources for facing this "shadow." Whether in individual or group sessions, I knew I was supported and I no longer felt alone.

My first powerful encounter with my "Holocaust shadow" began in an individual session, with the music pulling me inward and upward this time.

The image of a smokestack is emerging in my groin, and the music is drawing it up inside of me. I feel the music wrenching everything out of me—my essence, my soul— ripping me open. I feel a cord of light from the heavens latch onto me and lift me upward. I feel I am going to burst as the swells in the music are squeezing everything out of me from many lifetimes—it's overwhelming! The violin plays on the strings of my heart from many lifetimes, everything of human experience—the joys, the sorrows, everything—it's so wonderful it hurts, but it's okay to feel that. The light now takes the shape of the smokestack and is so blindingly bright and powerful that I can no longer see the smokestack. The light is going through me and around me. When everything is squeezed out of me, all the heaviness, aches, and pains are gone. I become light and float up with the music. The violins are not gripping anymore. They are sweet. I am a transparent bubble, totally alone, but I do not feel alone. I am connected to the souls of the family I had lost, as we are all part of the light. However, I am starting to have feelings in my body again and float back down to earth; it is not my time to be there yet.

[*The music changes.*] I come down to fire. It is strange. I do not feel it but I know it is hot. I can feel its heaviness and hear its deafening roar. The fire is in the belly of the smokestack, the furnace. There is no enclosure; the furnace is immense and open. It seems like I am in Hell. I have to work hard to keep myself out of the fire, to reach back up into the light. I reach beyond the flames up to the level of gas. But I can feel fingers of fire—misery, pain, sorrow— pulling me down. I have to fight hard not to let them keep me there. I become filled with despair, feeling, "Why should I bother if I am going to lose anyway?" I am consumed by the flames and become crispy black embers. The fire wipes out everything without a trace. It pounds its chest in glory, boasting: "How dare you stand up against me? No matter how far you go (into the light), I'll get you!" I respect its words, but I cannot let it get me. With the help of the music, I return to the light with a hole in my chest to remind me of what was lost. Death felt cold, but the light and the music fill (the hole in) my heart with warmth and life. The strings play in my body. I am back on earth with the light, without the consuming fire.

The smokestack and light transformed into a powerful symbol of integration that I saw again later that year as the Jewish sanctuary in Dachau; I had never seen this structure before this GIM session.

The actual integration of this shadow occurred during a group GIM experience a few weeks later. At this advanced training, we were learning how to facilitate the mind and body working together with the music. As the client, I focused on the chronic pain in my left shoulder, where stress tends to accumulate in my body.

It is becoming a gray rock, which is there to store emotions. The rock spreads around my shoulders and over my head into a concrete prayer shawl to grieve, to say Kaddish (a Judaic prayer that is recited for the dead yet speaks of life). It continues to spread down over the rest of my body into a statue, as a memorial to those who were murdered in the Holocaust. And then, I become a smokestack. I can feel the flames coming up from my feet, roaring inside of me. I am horrified: I am killing all those people! It is the most painful experience. I am hysterical. All of a sudden, the smokestack and the fire are gone and there is nothing left but ashes. The pain in my shoulder is gone, too. The ashes are in a hole in my solar plexus, and I am Mother Earth. There is a new pain with this hole. It feels like a void in the universe, an emptiness; nothing is left. But then it becomes filled with dirt, which become people. I am Mother Earth and the people are my children, floating up into the light. I feel a seed planted in my pelvis, and a very powerful tree with one leaf grows out of it. The pain is gone.

Out of the Ashes
A flame ignited in the bowels of my groin,
Fueled with the energy and sounds of music,
Spread out through my limbs,
Sprouted into the wings of a white Phoenix
That rose out of the ashes, ever upwards,
As the music connected my many multicolored
Threads around the world,
Transformed into an angel, entering the heavens,
Connecting with souls and the light,
Tears flowing from the container of my soul.

In subsequent GIM therapy, I continued to have death–rebirth experiences as I continued to mourn the losses and to let go of the damaging constructions I erected throughout my life to deal with the pain. The most significant construction, or barrier, was that of control. The myth was that (unlike those who were enslaved or murdered by the Nazis) I could have control over my life. Unlike my parents, relatives, and family friends of that generation, I had the opportunity for education, freedom of choice, happiness, and life as I chose, so I was determined to make the most of these opportunities. I became a therapist, a social activist, and created a new family. But I also tried to control all the things I did not have control over (such as bad things happening) in an attempt to make my world safer than what my parents experienced.

The music had all the elements that allowed me to break through this strongly erected barrier of control and pseudosafety. The music provided the dynamics that evoked the experiences, a structure that provided the safety to have the experiences, a container expansive enough to hold all the experiences, and the integration of all of these that supported healing and transformation. The music allowed me to experience the despair and still have hope about the outcome.

Narrative 3

DEALING WITH PHYSICAL ILLNESS: GUIDED IMAGERY AND MUSIC AND THE SEARCH FOR SELF

Ann Newel

INTRODUCTION

As a music therapist, I had experienced Guided Imagery and Music (GIM) only as an academic exercise in a classroom setting, never as a means for my own in-depth therapy. GIM involves imaging in a relaxed state to prepared classical music. I had six GIM sessions, each about 2 hours long. My therapist helped me relax, chose the music, kept contact with me during my imagery, and helped me process the experience after the music.

In telling the story of my GIM therapy, which began when I was diagnosed with cancer, I have chosen not to use my real name. I have used as sources my journals and transcribed notes of my ongoing imagery that I spoke out loud to my therapist during the music; the notes were given to me by my therapist. By mutual agreement with my therapist, I do not name the therapist.

BACKGROUND

I never realized how important my relationship with music would be in my life until it seemed my world was falling apart. I'd grown up with music as my best friend all through childhood. The youngest child with much older siblings living on a farm with no playmates for miles, I spent many hours alone at the piano, playing and singing. My love of music continued through college, leading me to a profession in music therapy. As a music therapist, I made music with others and for others but forgot to take the time for my own expression; this pattern continued when I had a family to raise. Where did my music go?

When metastatic melanoma to my lung was diagnosed when I was 39, I felt as if my life came to a halt. I can still remember the empty, sinking feeling in the pit of my stomach as my doctor gave me the cancer diagnosis. I was paralyzed emotionally and physically and felt as if the floor had fallen out from under me. Depression seemed to be my primary emotion through this time period. When I was alone, I would sob incessantly. I wanted to be with my family (husband and two young children), but I couldn't cry in front of them. I was frantic, not knowing what to do. A friend suggested, "Do what you always dreamed of doing," to which I responded, "Play the piano." She suggested I write songs, but I was blocked by my critical self.

During surgery to remove the tumor from my lung, I asked to have taped music played, as I knew it would be a calming force (after all, it had aided me in two wonderful natural childbirth experiences). During recovery, I again experienced the power of music in pain management.

After surgery, I knew I needed some way of dealing with all my confused thoughts and feelings: what treatment to choose (since no traditional treatments were known to be effective) and how to deal with my work, my family, myself, and my feelings. I wanted a therapy that would help me get to my unconscious feelings, as I was having poignant dreams. I felt traditional verbal therapy would get me only so far and that I needed something that would help me uncover and express my unconscious feelings through symbols. I kept coming back to my experiences with music and the expressive therapies, knowing that there had always been so much contained in the symbols in my work with clients. I really wanted to deal with the hidden issues which I felt were putting me in this state of dis-ease. GIM seemed to be the answer, as I knew there were unconscious feelings and issues I was not addressing in dealing with my illness and that GIM could bring these to the surface. Other secondary (but important) goals I had were to find a meaningful direction for my life: What was I meant to do? What can I leave for others? I needed help in balancing family, work, and spiritual self, and in obtaining support, since I knew that statistically, those who express feelings have a better chance of survival.

SESSION 1: FEAR

I began GIM treatment 4 months after surgery, at a point that coincided with the beginning of my experimental vaccine treatment. I felt pulled in many directions. I wrestled with the question of how much longer would I have to live and how could I balance working and family and still take care of myself.

My imagery began in a field of flowers in the city where I went for treatment, a trip that meant being away from my family and spending time by myself to rejuvenate and be introspective.

The music takes me over a bridge to a green forest where the ground is covered with pine needles. I want to brush them away and see what's there. It's the earth. I feel resistance to look any further. I feel fear in my head. I begin looking up, curled up in a ball in the top of the tree. I am lonely but where I want to be. I want to hold on to the tree. I know I can't break it. I can squeeze as hard as I can. I am able to let go of the tree while still in it. I feel its textures. It's rough and difficult to get too close to unless I'm hugging it. It scratches. The only smooth part is on the needles. The tree is very tall and majestic. Floating above it, at first I feel propelled up. Looking around, I see the bridge. I'm trying to decide whether to stay in the city or go home. I feel pulled in each direction, by the idea of protecting myself or being with my family. My arms are being pulled in either direction. It's painful and lonely.

I want to go back and find out what's under the pine needles. It's my grandmother (who had passed away 4 years ago) with my ring on her hand. It's the ring she had as a young girl and the one I had worn since I was in college. The ring stands out. Is it on my hand or my grandmother's? It changes back and forth between being on my hand and her hand. It finally appears to be on her hand, and this leads me to make closure with her and relive all the good-byes we said in the past. It also makes me realize my own life is not yet over. I experience several periods of my life that had brought me joy and grieve their passing. I end in the present experiencing an intimate time with my family and realizing I don't have to die; I should focus on living.

The pine tree became a recurring theme, a symbol of connection between life and death and heaven and earth—life and feeling grounded on one end and heaven and the spiritual aspect of death as I went further toward the top. Fear was expressed in the need to "curl up" in the tree and "protect myself" from all the "rough textures" of life along with the desire to hold on to life with all of my strength. The only parts of the tree that were smooth were the needles, which represented to me needles used in the vaccine treatment, the one thing I was involved in that gave me hope. The ring also was an integral symbol representing a connection to others, but in this case a connection to someone who was deceased. The fear of my diagnosis and imminent death came to a resolution when I saw that it was my grandmother and not me in the grave under the pine needles. I was then able to make closure with my grandmother and find the energy to spend time with my family. My final statement at the end of the session brought reassurance, hope, and direction.

SESSION 2: DEPRESSION

By the next session, I was very aware of the stress my illness was causing my family. I began to ask such questions as: Am I worthy of healing? Am I putting too much burden on my parents, husband, and children? Would they be better off without me? My children say they hate God; how can I offer them the comfort I get from my faith? Although I had received positive test results, I began to doubt my body's ability to heal. At the same time, my life began to follow more of a routine: diet, exercise, yoga, reading, support groups, and spending time with my family—yet I was continually being distracted by my healing process.

I see a reddish purplish light. I follow it into a cave. It's cool, damp, dark. The rocks I'm stepping on are slippery. I want to stay inside. It's calm and inviting, a hideout. There are faint carvings on the wall. It's a stick person carrying a ball, a large ball, heavy. He's trying to find someone to hand it to. The ball is lighter now and other people are joining him, festive, joyful, pleasant, nurturing. (*Are you there?*)* I'm not sure if I'm part of it; I might even be the man.

---

* Throughout Ann's narrative, the words of Ann's therapist during the music are in italics and within parentheses.

The ball becomes a prop that everyone shares in the dance. But the man still is holding on to it. The music is pushing me toward the light. I discover a spongy shield of green vines. They become a trampoline. I'm doing flips. I feel like I could do anything. The rhythm of it feels good, like the rhythm of my breathing.

I'm aware of a tall tree each time I bounce back. A pine tree with a point on the top. I almost bounce that high up in the sky; light, silly, I feel it in my soul and heart. I feel strength emanating from my body except my head and wish I felt stronger there. My head needs security, surety, a knowledge of what is right. (*What message is your body giving your head?*) Connect. We'll share the strength if you'll connect with us. (*Another message?*) Follow your body; disconnect your head.

I picture my head up on top of the tree. My body is sitting at the edge of the trampoline. One can't move without the other. My head feels like it needs some kind of inspiration or spiritual strength and it wants to be up there to feel that strength. My body needs groundedness and playfulness. I'm jumping with a headless body. I'm trying to make it to the top to get my head. I can do it only with my head on; I'm more whole. My head is jumping with my body, trying to have the sensation of being up high and also [have] security and a spiritual sense. I want to climb the tree but am uncertain of whether to or not. (*Either is okay.*) I'm climbing the tree.

My kids and husband are at the bottom and I want to help them. I'm going back to help. They're not sure they want to go all the way up. We're huddling together halfway. Part of me wants to go the whole way. It's better for me to be with them awhile anyway. The top is closer to the stars and birds, an easier place to sit. They're willing to go to the top, but I'm really tired now. It's hard to pull them up. Maybe another day. (*What can you do to share the top with them?*) Take a picture of what it looks like at the top to show them. (*What does it look like?*) Tops of trees and vast blue sky.

I have a sense of being connected to the tree itself. It's strong and very tall, pointed at the top, with limbs you can sit on.

The theme of this session highlighted my sense of depression and aloneness. I felt a sense of calm in the dark cave and wanted to hide from the world. The music brought others into the picture and I discovered that I gained strength to deal with the weight of my illness by accepting support from others. I began to understand the need to pay more attention to my body and intuition as opposed to my head and cognition. The green vines and trampoline represented to me the joy of being alive (where my body wanted to be) and again the tree reappeared as the place to contemplate and withdraw from everyday life (where my head was). There was ambivalence between my head and body, between being involved in life and being more self- and spiritually centered. My body sat on the edge of life as my head longed for spiritual strength. The importance of movement and playfulness in my life was obvious to me once again. I told myself to be more impulsive, creative; don't hold back, let go, play, live!

Finally, the need to connect spirituality with my body as well as my family was apparent. I was very concerned that my family, especially my children, would not be able to handle the stress of my illness, leaving lifelong scars. I battled with how to balance this part of my life as well as share my faith with my family. The imagery allowed me to find a solution: "Take a picture and share it with them." I understood that all I could do was share with them the strength and hope I received from my faith and the rest would have to lie with them.

SESSIONS 3, 4, AND 5: ANGER

The next three sessions unveiled pent-up anger that I had not yet dealt with or been aware of. I became more in touch with the dichotomy between the messages my head and my body told me, becoming more aware of my body and less worried about my head. I began to have dreams and images of shedding my skin, represented as layers of old clothes and the pruning away of dead branches. I had also produced two nondominant-hand drawings in a support group that seemed pertinent. In the first drawing, I had drawn my chest cavity with emptiness on the inside and arrows attacking from the outside with a boundary of "protection" separating the two. I started the imagery for this session with the second drawing I had done to describe the healthy part of me, a bright red ball (my soul) with yellow surrounding it.

The red circle on the inside is soft and nurturing, like a heart with warmth. It's flexible. If you put a fist in it, it leaves a dent. If I push my fist in far enough, it wraps itself around it. It can engulf anything. There are many arms protruding from the ball: red, reaching out with hands on the ends, exploring the boundary. The hands are trying to pull at the boundary and pull it apart. It seems like it will break, but I'm not sure I want it to. It's breaking and I'm putting it back together; it's not quite as strong as it was. Now it breaks at times and some of the arrows get through, forcefully. The red ball in the center is getting very big, until the end, when hands direct arrows in and burst the ball. The hands and arrows are left. I feel like I was burst and attacked. It's painful, like there's nothing left. Betrayed, I feel cut in two. I feel it in my chest and gut. I feel angry, angry that I let people in and they hurt. (*How can you get it out?*) By talking. [*To the image:*] You promised me everything would be okay. You never listen to me. I hurt. I hate you.

The music urges me on to let it out. The therapist tells me to push some pillows she is holding and I begin pushing. I feel helpless sometimes and sad and angry at the illness. I feel like I'm displacing it on my family. I just want to change everything inside of me. I'm scraping everything away that looks unhealthy, mostly on my lungs, and wondering if I can scrape enough away and still survive. I've got my old red ball. I'm trying to squeeze some of the red into the tissue. I'm in touch with the sadness and anger about the whole thing. The anger is giving me energy, assertion. I haven't realized that anger before and how it can give me energy to fight. The music changes and gives me support and reassurance.

I feel it as peacefulness. It has the strength of the sun, but I have fear of the sun's rays. My chest feels clear, no garbage there. I'm afraid to let anything in that might be garbage. It needs peace. (*What color do you see?*) Green.

The music played a vital role in unveiling the expression of anger. For whatever reason—the belief that expressing anger is socially unacceptable or the fear of loss of control—I had not expressed or felt any anger up until this time. The therapist gave me permission to express my anger and the music moved me to do so. Green is the color of new growth. I need green and red together. Red is the healthy color of tissue; it was what I was trying to see while scraping. The healthy red part of me was being bombarded by the stress of the environment and the illness. I felt betrayed by my body and wanted to scrape away everything that was unhealthy and negative in my life. I also saw the need to change on the inside how I perceived myself and how I handled life's stressors. Although I was unable to identify who or what in particular I was angry at, I became more aware of the emotion being there and that I needed to not ignore it. It became apparent that I felt the anger as part of my soul and if expressed in some nondestructive fashion, it could free up energy to work in a productive direction, such as giving me the strength to fight for life. The therapist suggested that an outlet for anger is vital and we brainstormed about acceptable ways to express it. I felt much more tolerant of my family that week after I was able to release my own anger in the session.

Going into session number 4, I continued to wrestle with the idea of finding direction in my life and what alternative treatments to pursue. My heart tried to take the lead but my head often got in the way. I felt apprehensive about what might come out in the session after having such an intense experience the previous session. The imagery began with the image of the labyrinth that I had experienced during a workshop the previous week.

> I see the labyrinth path, calming, winding back and forth. I have a hard time focusing; I'm veering off the path. I'm dancing on the labyrinth, not following the path. It's freeing. My mind keeps wandering, preoccupied with what might come later. The music's calling me like angels calling me. I don't want to give in. It's scary. I'm amidst many angels; I feel sad, a cross between sadness and anger. (*Where do you feel it?*) In my chest.
>
> The music changes and I become anxious when I recognize the piece and know it will reach an emotional climax in the middle. I also realize the music will help me release

whatever I'm holding in. (*What do you see in your chest?*) Dark purplish, green color; the shape of my fist.

The object wants to tighten up. It takes a lot of energy. It doesn't feel healthy and needs to come out. I'm reaching in and grabbing it. It feels squishy, like a piece of liver, hot or warm. There's resistance to me getting it out. Wet and slimy, it's connected by tissue and won't come out. I have to get it out. I feel stuck; I know what I need to do is to pull out the diseased part of me, but it won't come. I feel the need to be physical; I need to push but I feel ashamed that the only way I can rid myself of the anger is to regress. Music is telling me it's okay, but I feel it's not. I'm in limbo, feel hopeless. It's just there. The music softens it. (*Can you have a dialogue with it?*)

[*Beginning the dialogue:*] What do you want from me?

[*The disease's voice:*] To pay attention to me.

[*Me:*] I am, but I don't know what to do to get rid of you. You're a force to be reckoned with. I'm afraid of you and angry, really pissed off that you changed my life.

[*The disease's voice:*] Maybe it wasn't that great anyway. Maybe it needed a change. What was so good about your life anyway?

[*Me:*] Maybe I wasn't that happy with it. (*How do you find that happiness?*) Stop being so serious and self-conscious, soften up.

My chest feels tight. I can imagine the blood flowing in. I feel very small, trying to relax and rest. I'm going to that spiritual tree to climb up, wondering why I can't get the lump out. (*What's the message?*) Try to look beyond yourself. Angels are there playing music.

The anger in this session was overwhelming as I acknowledged an inability to get rid of whatever it was that was making me ill, as if there was a magic key inside of me that had the answer and I couldn't locate it. I felt as if I should know what to do but couldn't grasp what that was. There was resistance to my pulling the anger/disease out and possibly ambivalence as to whether I wanted to recover or doubt about my ability to do so. Again I told myself to make a change, to let go, but what did that mean? This was my wake-up call to do whatever would fulfill me, but what was it? Again there was the message to focus more on my heart and less on my head: "Stop being so serious and self-conscious; soften up." Use a physical outlet to release the anger; express myself and not second-guess myself. The music helped me both to get to the anger inside of me and to find some answers of how to deal with it. It also helped me find a spiritual place to rest, grow, renew, and energize myself. At the suggestion of the therapist, I drew after the session but could only scribble furiously, filling the paper. I was then asked to do some drumming, which felt more fulfilling, as the air never runs out of space for sound, and the sound made some sense to me going in and out of an organized rhythm.

Before session number 5, I felt more aware of myself becoming angry and the need to release it in some acceptable fashion. As a result, I felt more freedom to be present in the here and now. I became more aware of letting myself be me, rather than being self-conscious and worrying about appearances. This felt positive and rewarding. I also began developing more musical outlets, playing by myself and with others, and using music with children both recreationally and educationally. This was an important part of my need to move on, to support the healthy part of me, and to find what was important for me to offer others.

Communication between me and family members was still difficult; I felt the need to communicate on a heartfelt level and I became frustrated when the response was on a more superficial level. I also would become stressed when I experienced my children's emotions. I felt responsible on some level for their emotional state, yet at the same time felt I could not deal with them effectively, which I was sure was detrimental to both me and them. Balancing life and finding my center began the session.

> There are many different pathways leading out from the center, like veins going out. I don't know where any of them go. I feel myself getting sad because I don't know where to go. (*Where do you feel it in your body?*) I feel it in my shoulders. (*Can you let the music in to help you?*) When I let the music in I get out of my head more, relax more.
>
> I'm thinking about my kids, watching them from a distance. If I'm with my kids they are more emotional and I get stressed. I'm keeping my distance; with music

it's okay to be with them. Three of us are playing together. I'm spinning around, dizzy. I feel sadness. It's hard to hang out carefree and light feeling. There's no whining, no worries. I feel anger for not being able to stay carefree, feeling anger in my chest. I want so much to stay relaxed in life, have some tranquillity. It's always turmoil. I guess I want my life to be ideal. (*What happened to the anger?*) It dissipated.

I'm trying to get back there. Why do I want to get back to anger? I feel something hard, solid. It feels immovable. It's gray, hard. (*What does it need?*) I can't say what it needs. It's a rock and can't move. It's a part of me. (*What do you want to say to it?*) I wish you weren't there. You're a part of me that I don't like. You make me negative and angry. You're ugly and I don't know how to deal with you. It scares me that I don't know how to live with you there.

I pop it with a pin. Steam or something is coming out, black. My chest feels more expanded. Everything surrounding the grayness feels like it's getting bigger and can grow over it. At first when I talk to it, it gets bigger and bigger until it pops. I keep having a feeling I need to get mad at it, let it get big and ugly. I need to do that in life. I'm yelling at it. I am given pillows to push and hit.

It's about the size of a pea. It's still there, still gray and hard, but smaller. I hold it in my hand, smooth and cool small gray rock, perfectly round. (*What do you want to do with it?*) Part of me wants to throw it across the room. But it's a part of me, that makes me who I am. It gives me energy. It feels like it's a part of me that needs to be expressed. It's so ugly and thinks negative thoughts.

It turns more green, gray green. I wonder how I can use it to heal. I guess by putting it back in the center and drawing energy from it to fight. (*Can you do that?*) I put it back.

It stays small. The area around it still is expanded. It feels very, very small, perfectly round. Before it was more cocoon-shaped. It's okay as long as it stays small.

How do I keep it small? But it has to stay there because it's part of my soul. (*What does it have to say to you?*) It says, "You need to deal with me. You can't ignore me. I make you human." (*What can you do to keep it small?*) I'll try to be more aware it's there. [*To the rock:*] Be ready to be popped when you get too big!

In this session, frustration was expressed and answers were found concerning choosing the right direction to take, how to deal with my children's emotions, and how to deal with my own anger, which was certainly a part of me that was not going to just go away. I found that the music was valuable in helping me to relax and find my way when balancing life became overwhelming; I let the music relax me and take me out of my head. Also it reinforced what I already knew: using music, I could interact with my children more joyfully, take the focus off the day-to-day realities we all became stressed about, and be more "carefree." Initially I turned the anger in toward myself, seeing it as a negative part of myself that would get in the way of interacting effectively with my children and causing stress in all our lives. I discovered that the anger was hard, solid, and immovable, a part of me that was not going to just go away, and when it was popped or acknowledged, the healthy part of me could grow and expand around it. I acknowledged that it was okay to get mad. This allowed the anger to remain a workable size that could then be used as a source of energy.

Letting go was a recurring theme I found over and over again. To find my direction, I needed to balance my heart with my head, choose a direction, and then let go and believe. I had to trust myself to listen to my inner soul.

SESSION 6: CLOSURE

This session took place after my final year-end evaluation by my medical doctor. The experimental treatment was to last only a year, and after follow-up tests, I had made it a year without any sign of recurrence. I felt successful and ready to breathe a cautious sigh of relief, as every year away from the illness meant a greater chance that something was working. I was anxious now that the vaccine would no longer be administered and my body would have to take over on its own. I was concerned about being too reliant on others for emotional support, the continued need to regulate the stress in my life, and the ability of my body to stand up to the cancer. The therapist and I also spoke about whether there was unresolved anger left from the previous sessions. The imagery began with a harpsichord, which I chose as a symbol for my body, relationships, and own neediness.

> The music reminds me of plucking on strings. The bass is vibrating. There is a lot of tension on the strings being pulled, being bowed; it is centered in my heart, very rich, intense, and warm. I like being able to feel the intensity there that is often lacking in life. Music is leading me down through a cave. The walls are shining and smooth. The music directs me upward, shoots me up in the sky, turning me around and somersaulting. It's great. I'm in the top of the tree. I'm able to sit on the very tip and balance with my arms outstretched, soaking in the sun, air, and fragrance. I lie back and begin to slide down the branches on my back. It is cool and smooth. I land, sitting on the ground.
>
> I'm sitting on a bed of pine needles. A small white goat comes up and puts its nose on my cheek. It's loving and wants to be nurtured. The music is leading me to a foggy field. I begin to get cold and try to get warm by hugging the goat, but it's wet, too. I get a blanket. A bear comes toward us. I think he's going to attack. I'm waiting, afraid. The goat's afraid, too. I remember you're supposed to yell at bears and run toward them. The bear is walking away. It gave up. I'm relieved but feel sad for the bear. He's a beautiful animal.
>
> The sun is coming out and I'm warmed up. I'm inside my chest, a small seed inside, moving with the music around my lungs. The seed turns into a little vacuum cleaner, housecleaning. I'm wondering if there is any anger here. It's finding a peaceful environment, a place to dance.

This session again underlined the healing force of music in my life. I was feeling the vibrations, getting in touch with the resonance in my body, and recognizing the positive energy that could be brought forth through music. It enabled me to be more in touch with my body and less in my head. I found myself balancing on the top of the tree, now able to balance both life and spirituality without the paralyzing fear and depression in the earlier sessions. In the goat, I met the needy part of me and of my children and was able to nurture and accept it. I also came face-to-face with my anger and fear when facing the bear and was able to face both emotions by using knowledge and self-assertion. Finally, the seedlike vacuum cleaner gave me a wonderful positive healing image to carry with me and use in visualization in the future.

CLOSING NOTES

The music was very powerful in supporting and magnifying my emotions, helping me acknowledge them, express them, and then find solutions for how to deal with them. I found I anticipated where the music would take me and could feel it drawing me into its core. Rarely did I feel hindered by it, but rather the music met me where I was and moved me to places where I needed to go; I might not have had the courage to continue if it hadn't been for the flow of the music itself. I was amazed that the same piece of music could be used during many different sessions without my awareness. Not only would I not recognize it as being the same music as the week before, but it would bring up different images each week depending on where I was emotionally on that particular day. This was empowering and gave me the awareness that I have "the answers" within myself.

The images brought forth in these sessions have stayed with me long after the sessions. GIM aided me in finding balance in my life, underlined what was important to me and what my priorities were, and offered me support in dealing with a catastrophic illness. It allowed me to see that all of the emotions and feelings that surfaced were normal and necessary in the process of grieving and healing.

Narrative 4

TOOLS OF REDISCOVERY:
A YEAR OF
GUIDED IMAGERY AND MUSIC

T and Jenny Martin Caughman

JENNY'S INTRODUCTION

In this narrative, T, a former client, presents excerpts from the journal he wrote as he engaged in music therapy. He had come to me to
address issues of sexual abuse. During the fourth session, I suggested
that we use Guided Imagery and Music (GIM), and he was open to
this. I explained that I would guide him into a deeply relaxed state,
choose music from classical music programs, and keep contact with
him as he experienced and narrated his imagery. As is often the case
in GIM therapy, there were also some sessions where we just talked.
In his excerpts, he uses the phrases *going under, came out, wake up,
visited,* and *hypnosis.* These are his terms that reflect his experience
during the music and imagery process. We did not use hypnosis or an
approach other than music and imagery. T had a total of 17 GIM
sessions. As a GIM therapist, I have the honor of entering deeply into
clients' worlds, witnessing their unique strengths, struggles, inner-
most feelings, and beautiful creativity. In this narrative, T invites us
all into his world.

T'S INTRODUCTION

What follows is a highly edited portion of over a year of my
journal entries during Guided Imagery and Music therapy. I
spare the reader a lot of detail about home and work, as well as
some of the more jargon-encrusted philosophical musings of a
relentlessly rationalizing mind trying to make sense of the experience. What are left are the sessions themselves, the highlights of
what was truly a life-changing experience for me.

When I began my course of treatment with J (the therapist), one of the first questions I asked her was if I was the oldest client she had ever heard of. I was assured that I was not. I would later recall that I was of prime age for the sort of Jungian insights that emerged. Early on, I exercised the convenience of labeling different aspects of my personality as I uncovered them. You will encounter references to the "controller" or "big guy" (my rationalizing instinct), the "middle guy" (my emerging emotional side), and the "kid" (the child that I was).

T'S JOURNAL

April 29, 1993

I thought today would be just another therapy session; I would make some progress, get comfortable with J, and learn about Guided Imagery and Music therapy. We had covered a lot of core issues about how I coped with feelings, intellect, anger, denial, and other related issues. She had said last week that when the memories came I'd be surprised. They might not appear in an expected form but they'd be there when I was ready. I wanted them to come. I really did. I just wasn't expecting them today. I thought I'd just do a little relaxation, free-association on a conscious level. The unconscious stuff slammed into me today like a sledgehammer and, 2 hours and two flashbacks later, I had drawn the first picture of my abuser on a shaky sketch pad. I still can't believe that for the first time I left something behind with J and no longer have everything buried inside me. Stunned, incredulous, scared, angry, sad, happy, and confused, I didn't lose control. Actually I lay there numb, cold, and tense while the visual memories just repeatedly slammed into the forefront and J gave me the choice of coming out of it or going back for more. She was there and I felt safe. I survived.

MY THOUGHTS ON SATURDAY, MAY 1. I was angry at the well-intentioned but thoughtless "put it behind you" talk that I get from others. I was confused at the "let's get it all over with at once" feelings. Here is a description of the session.

It began with me lying on the couch, adjusting the pillow, relaxing, closing my eyes and focusing on each part of the body from my toes on up to my head, and, in J's words, observing the state of each part but doing nothing about it. Quiet classical music was played. I was instructed to try to conjure up an image of somewhere I'd like to be. I tried to visualize an island in Canada and I was briefly successful, but the picture became cloudy almost immediately, swirling vortices of clouds. After a few minutes of clouds, I finally saw a stream and a tree-lined and sunlit embankment, not familiar but very pretty. The music was changing; it was getting fuller, swelling. I found myself walking in woods dense with foliage but still brightly sunlit. I looked up and saw the blue sky and indirect light on the tops of the branches. At ground level, I walked on a narrow dirt path not much wider than the width of my shoulders. Suddenly my field of vision was blocked by a sideways green face; it had little detail other than the eyes and nose. I was terrified, but it soon faded and I apprehensively resumed my wandering down the path. I was aware of a feeling of being led by someone to somewhere. The feeling grew and I reach the end of the path and saw a clearing with a little metal gate between two stone pillars. I was so apprehensive that I saw J's office take shape around me, my eyes half opened, and I was asked if I'd like to return now. I said, "No, I'll stay a little longer," and immediately I was on the path again, facing the clearing. I could not go on, so J's voice told me to turn around and retreat on the path, which I did. I came out into an enclosed valley with no apparent point of egress. I was momentarily puzzled as to how to leave, but then I remembered that I could levitate above the clouds, which I did. After a few minutes surrounded by clouds again, I gradually became aware that I was back in the office, but it was a full 10 or 15 minutes before I was sitting upright again, and my hands and arms felt strangely detached. I was shaky, confused, and elated. When offered a pad to draw on, I re-created the green face, and after staring at it for a minute, I realized I had drawn an impression of my abuser.

May 13

We talked about the May 7 session. The imagery was confusing to me; I had had unrealistic expectations of clear memories and I had merely managed to become aware of my two sides sizing each other up. I reordered my goals, placing first the necessity of unifying the personality over the recollection of memories. J was glad to hear me say this and told me that she was going to emphasize this if I hadn't brought it up. "The process is the important thing, not the immediate result," she said. She also said that she doubted my false personality thesis and reminded me that my one-sided analytical nature is a true part of my personality that has enabled me to survive by bolstering my self-confidence.

Then I went under again. I thought I was unsuccessful. Try as I would, I could visualize nothing, only darkness, diffuse geometric patterns, and an occasional glimpse as if by strobe light of a small portion of something recognizable as an ear, an eye, the shape of a head. It began to feel like a cave, and I was frustrated that this session also was going to produce nothing in the way of visual enlightenment. Then it struck me like a thunderbolt. I was being watched. It was a child, my inner child, and the reason nothing could be seen was that this was what he saw. This was his hiding place so far away inside me that it was a world unto itself, unrecognizable, detached from anything I thought of as real. He was scared that I had found him, yet he reluctantly had allowed me to find him. We talked without words, a thought dialogue: I want to help you; please come out; I'm sorry about what happened to you; I could come again to visit. Then, I swear, I felt him—invisible and small—hug me. When it was time to leave, to come out, a part of this child came out with me, taking me by surprise. I was fearful that I was not up to the task of introducing him to my world. We had about a half hour of hugs, tears, and promises to give him time each day. He even wanted to hug J and the stuffed bear.

This music and imagery is a most amazing tool. It seems to provide consistently in each session not necessarily what I want or am looking for but what I need for each new stage of growth. Although intellectually I know that the music stimulates the imagery, I am not always aware of the music in a session, and there are times when it feels as if the imagery is generating the music. Once again I am stunned by what is happening inside me and feel more real with each passing week than I have ever felt before.

May 20

After the preliminaries, I found myself in the usual abstract cave. I was then transported into a steamy shower room and found myself looking through a fogged shower door. I wiped a hole and saw through it to a bright green wooded scene beyond. I became angry, shouting, "Where are you, where are you?" I had a sensation of being confused, of being fondled, and of its feeling good. I remembered being slapped and a glimpse of a mean face, of mean teeth. I didn't like him. I told my mother I didn't like him, but I was ignored. I felt more uncomfortable and told the therapist I wanted to come out. After I slowly came around, I was struck by the fact that the anger was a little anger, not the adult rage I was used to. My biggest surprise, overall, was being able to handle the little anger.

May 27

I was asked to picture a child playing. Immediately I saw myself around four years of age, overdressed, playing alone in my room on the floor, very quiet and very alone as was usual. Quickly the image faded to be replaced by the familiar green path on which I was walking with a companion this time; my inner child was leading me to a deeper spot where I knew I would willingly be presented with further memories. When we got to the appointed place, he turned and faced me; he was waiting, looking at me, and ascertaining the moment when I was ready. After an uncomfortably long silence, I asked him to show me. Through the gloom, I was then presented with a series of freeze-frames, scenes of sexual abuse interspersed with long pauses. I didn't want to reexperience them as he did, for to do so would be to experience them alone, so I merely watched each moment, although for one split second I felt each of them. What came out of it all was the sensation of being sad and sorry he experienced it all alone. Again, upon awakening, the memory became clearer but more detached. The adult anger was back: anger at the wasted years, at the aloneness, at my mother for not believing me. For quite a few moments, I couldn't look at J because of my shame. I even asked her, "Why can't I look you in the face?" She said it was because she was now a witness. I was uncomfortable with that and so sad. It is real. It did happen.

June 10

J asked, "Why the ice cave?" "To hide, obviously," I said. "But," she reemphasized, "a *large* ice *cave?*" I entered the imagery looking for the ice cave and the kid. I found him, and he was angry and not interested in looking at memories. He told me I could do it without him today and promptly went to sleep. So I watched something get close, got scared, and stopped it on my own and I came out of it. I got the strength I wanted: my own ability to control what occurred. I also remembered stuff about [name deleted], the dirty records, and everything else questionable about him.

July 1

I went deeper into the imagery state, into a black hole, where the eye—which was me, the eye that saw everything—and the kid took me back to relive the abuse vividly and more violently. I felt the 6-year-old die inside and I let more of the anger out. There was still more. I told J that next time, I wanted to tear this stuff up. I drew a picture. It was a painful picture of a bleeding child being chewed by a large mouth, as in Goya's *Saturn.* I told her that losing hope for one's children was even worse than losing one's religion or even losing faith in oneself, because losing hope in your children was losing hope in the future.

The next day I asked myself if this was real. At first, I minimized it and said, "Well, something happened," but then I reviewed everything I've lived with and the something became more tangible. I was hit full force again by yesterday's experience: the anger, the depth of the imagery, the body memories, the shaking, the dissociation from my body, and the catharsis. Whatever happened with the abuse was becoming more and more real each week. No wonder I said that I died at 6. I must tear it up and expose every last bit of it.

July 15

I don't know how to write about the little one. Little Owl, I'll call him, though his name is mine, of course. On Thursday he came out and pushed the big guy (my rationalizing self) out. After 2 weeks without therapy (J was on vacation), it took about 40 minutes of talking to feel safe again in her office. After a few carefully chosen questions by J, out he came. He played and drew pictures and wouldn't answer big guy questions. He periodically looked over to where the big guy might be, like a kid who wants to play outside but is afraid of being called inside by his mother. The Little Owl was afraid because of the controller or big guy (my rationalizing self) and mad because he hadn't received any attention the past 2 weeks. He didn't want to talk to the big guy. This dissociation, if that's what it was, occurred without music, guided imagery, or hypnosis [with only art and discussion]. I found this somewhat disturbing.

August 12

After describing to J my current emotional exhaustion and my depression over future recovery, I asked her if I could go deeper into imagery to understand this middle guy, this bundle of undirected emotions. "It's not up to me," she said, and while I was wondering if this meant that she had to get some sort of permission from a supervisor, she said, "It's up to you." In other words, I could will myself deeper any time I liked. I was so upset that it took longer than usual to accomplish the entry or relaxation phase of the process. Then she asked me to visualize a knapsack and to reach in and pull out three objects. I pulled out, in succession, a child's rubber ball, a frog, and a feather. I immediately saw glimpses of an owl's face and felt as if I had a guide with me. J then asked me to go where I needed to go and to describe what I saw. I saw a deep, dark pool of warm, undulating water, and it was soothing and restful. I described watching the frogs, catching them, and then letting them go because it was their home. The ball gave me slight anxiety, and I figured it was a childhood memory of some sort. I then saw the sky through green treetops; the sky became clouded over with dark, moving shapes. I lay down, and the shapes surrounded me. They seemed friendly, nonthreatening, even caring. They looked like the light aliens from the movie *Cocoon,* and they were smoothing chunks of color on me, slapping and filling, adding stuff to me. I then went into an abstract wilderness I recognized as the cave. I couldn't find anyone, so I called out and challenged the abuser to appear. I saw snarling dogs, snapping snakes' heads, but no abuser. I realized he was afraid of me. I felt enveloped in a warm, powerful cocoon. Then it hit me. I felt anger, but it was my anger, mine, it belonged to me; the anger was a tool I could use, and I need not be afraid of it because it was mine to use to protect myself as I saw fit. I flew out of the cave, semiaware of the swelling, heroic music. I was laughing and crying at the same time, exhilarated with this new discovery. I had found another part of myself.

By the end of the week, I was feeling relentlessly uncertain. No sooner had I patted myself on the back for facing my anger and feeling strengthened by it than I felt an ominous buildup of something. It was like racing a train to an intersection or detecting an early tremor before a major earthquake. It was the real stuff, not just flashes and glimpses. I told myself to believe what therapists say: "It can't hurt me now." What they say is not true. It does hurt. It will hurt and it's necessary. God, I hate this.

August 25

I worried about the kid not being able to grow along with me, but J reminded me that he's a part of this process, that he's gotten to hear me say, "I'm sorry." This seemed pretty small and pathetically inadequate until J reminded me that the kid didn't hear it the first time the abuse happened. A cosmic "oh" came from me. J suggested that the kid has also shared his experience with me. This I doubted, since I had experienced him as having faced it alone. J pointed out, "But you now remember it." Another "oh" came from me. The kid was suddenly becoming as real as the memory. The old controlling side of me was becoming an annoying nuisance. J said I should treat the controlling side as I would the image of someone in a bear costume: "Oh, it's just that guy in the bear costume."

I asked myself, "Why did you hide in the cave for so long? Why is the cave so big? Why were you afraid? Why did you choose not to feel? What happened to you that made all this necessary?" It is now safe to remember.

September 10

I didn't know what J was asking me today. I didn't know the meaning of the imagery today. I was very confused. I visited a different cave today, one that captured my attention, an intense vision. It ended with a woman's face suspended above me. I longed for the face, longed to reach up and pull it down and to kiss it, but I couldn't. Was it a spiritual vision, a birth memory of my natural mother? Why did I have the irritation and anger about J's questioning my motives, my desire to examine memories of my father? What happened today? What was going on?

MY THOUGHTS ON SEPTEMBER 16. Instead of waiting to heal before I tried to regain my spirituality, I should work on my spirituality to aid my healing, especially since its loss seems to be a background issue that keeps coming up. I am thinking more and more about that car ride in New Mexico when I was a kid. I'm feeling powerful enough not to be afraid to follow the fear trail. I'm beginning to get a clearer picture of what happened.

September 22

My body was traced by a ray of soft light. The ray shone on a box. I opened the box, taking out a grapefruit-size lump of black crystal with sharp edges. It led me to the path and the cave, to a state of no fear and the realization of oneness: the smooth face, the old face, the mouths, the teeth, the patterns, the light. The imagery showed more strongly than before that everything—the fears, pain, personalities, memories, longings—is one vision. It is not to be analyzed but to [be held], to return to, to project with, to commit to. The imagery was wonderful, but it is a strain to think about it. I can't analyze what was really an imaginary experience, but I can't let it out of my sight either.

Later at home, the memories were very close; I could touch them. In my own relaxation session, I looked into the box again and took out a dirty rag. I had the choice of burying it or washing it, but I chose to carry it around. In the dark, I saw the teeth again, once sudden and clear, once more hazy.

I was thinking that I have the choice to move forward with healing or look back for more memories to reexamine. This choice will always be there. Shame seems to be one of the emotions there today. I know I am depressed, feeling powerless and even afraid. I am afraid that, presented with the chance, I would end it quickly. I'm not in good shape. I'll call J. [I did make the call and extended the contract with her not to hurt myself.] What does it mean that this is the first time I've ever had this thought? Do I have to remind myself that I have the power to take care of myself?

October 8

Today I decided it was the kid who's been slighted this past week. I found him, asked him about the teeth, and told him I was ready and not afraid. He was reluctant but not afraid and called me stupid. I told him I knew what it meant, but what did it signify? He showed me how it wasn't fear of the actual abuse but of the repercussions if I told anyone what was the origin of the fear I'd been living with all this time. After examining it a bit, I decided it was time to leave. I'd had enough for one day, but then the kid went spinning off on a wild visual ride that was fun but heading back toward darker matters. I had to remind him that I had already decided to call it quits for the day and to take him firmly back. It was a matter of control and parenting. Considering that loss of control was one of my issues this past week, this was another interesting development. It was more than a minor insight and a little less than a major breakthrough. The lesson was to work with my kid and to not leave him out. He's the smart one. Together we analyzed fear without being afraid, and he showed me something important: be firm but not authoritarian. We must work things out jointly.

October 29

Today I experienced a feeling of falling, spinning, disorientation, and then rapid flight into the cave. It seemed uglier than I had remembered it and not wondrous at all. The kid let me know that there were still things I didn't understand about the cave, not memories but connections. He said that he would show me more, teach me more at a later time. It felt good to be with him again. He also seemed to let me know that the cave wouldn't go away, that it shouldn't be forgotten. J materialized, full face and beautiful, and the kid then drifted over and curled up in her lap and went to sleep.

After I awoke from the imagery, J and I discussed transference. I wondered why the kid had what I didn't. I felt jealous that he could get the nurturing but that I couldn't—the grownup me couldn't. J has nurtured this kid. He feels safe with her and he trusts her more than me. He trusts my wife now, too. This jealousy is the first sign of real transference, anger at my mother for not being there to nurture and accept me. No matter how much I can detach and analyze what's going on, the emotions are real and strong. I'm glad I trust J to understand this complicated state I'm in.

November 10

I visualized a table with a box on it. I pulled out three objects once again. The first was a ball, but a small, hard, blackened one. The second was a feather. The third was a piece of embroidered cloth. I clutched them tightly and I was nervous. I didn't want to let them go. The ball is the abuse, the feather is the guardian or guide, and the cloth is the church. The Owl called me to fly. He wanted to take me aloft to a high place and have me drop the ball. I reluctantly went along. He said that after the ball was dropped, I was to drop the other two objects and that I would not fall. He said that I would become the Owl. Reluctantly, I did as he asked. I did not fall, but I did not become the Owl either. That, apparently, was for later.

I thought that maybe the child would have a better idea of how to do this than I [did]. Then I was given a demonstration. The Owl wrapped himself around me like a coat, and I flew. I soared. I no longer had hands to carry things, but I had wings, a new life, and a new environment, the air. It was a complete change. It made me apprehensive, this newness, but I can't go on living the old way.

When I awoke from the imagery, I was irritated that I must wait for the child to figure this out. I didn't want to leave the session room. I wanted to relive again and again what I'd just experienced. I thought that I must become my very own hero. I wanted to clutch a very powerful sword. I wanted to hear the music again that led to this vision.

December 8

We talked about my son, and about grief and spirituality. Afterward, when I was asked to name my good qualities, I couldn't and I was very uncomfortable. I got a homework assignment to ask my wife to write a list of my qualities and to name two on my own.

As soon as I went under, I sensed that the light people were waiting in high spirits for me and were eager to see me. They told me that they wanted to show me something and escorted me into the cave. Their positive energy illuminated the ugliness and it was more like a picnic or a visit to a museum. They told me there was another center of power within me, not creative power but a stronger, different one that I was as yet unaware of. I could see it, a hard, green crystalline orb giving off rays of light, very strong, very powerful. I didn't know what it was, but sensed it was spiritual power. They kept asking if I saw it. Soon I did see long filaments of light streaming from my fingers, dancing in long arcs out of control but not dangerous, rather harmless and untrained. They said I was beautiful, and I was uncomfortable with that comment. I felt extremely tired, so they let me go to sleep. I woke up aching, as if I had a bad night's sleep.

March 17

This is the 1-year anniversary of this therapy. We talked about the progress I feel I've made over the last year. During the relaxation phase of the imagery, I was asked to describe an object I found in a small box. I saw a bunch of keys on a ring, the many keys for many doors in my possession, to be used whenever I wished to. I then saw the eyes and beak of the Owl, which caused me to giggle. He kept getting closer and closer, and I could see every detail on every feather; I could feel the feathers. Then I realized I was merging with the Owl, becoming the Owl. We/I flew to a dark place. I felt myself being sodomized and felt the anger, disgust. I waited for it to be over and then I left my body and rapidly rose upward, higher and higher, until it was cold and the air was thin and it became harder to breathe. I felt so numb, so separated from my body, that I wanted to come back. Even the rape was preferable to this feeling of total separation and numbness. When I opened my eyes, the light in the room was blinding. Mentally I woke up, but I still felt very detached and had a difficult time regaining the sense of my body.

March 24

I visualized a childhood campsite at Deer Island in Ontario. I was alone, in the present, exploring this site of an early childhood experience. It was overcast, deserted, with no resonances of past experiences. It was not frightening but merely sad, a wistful dead memory. I left it by flying above the clouds. The scene faded into close-ups of pine needles and branches pulled back to light a path on a mountainside; it was a different path. I was alone on it, but it felt safe. The turns led around flanks of the mountain, with a brilliant glow always just around the next corner. Transparent, ghostly images of J and the kid appeared, there and yet not there. I knew I could still fly, but that tool was only to be used on special occasions. I belonged on the path on the ground in normal day-to-day life. I was suddenly aware of my physical body during the visualization. I felt it; I was not detached. My body was warm and comfortable. I woke up in J's room, this time body first, with my mind lingering.

T'S CONCLUSION

When I first started therapy, the issue of memory seemed of paramount importance. I had a wall of fear separating me from memories of the abuse I sensed had taken place. Now, at the end of this process, the issue of memory is not so simple. I did indeed confront and overcome most of my fears. I did reclaim quite a few lost memories, some of specific sexual abuse. The specific memories came almost always after an imagery session. I reexperienced feelings and images of sexual abuse during the session itself, but they were rarely clear and often of a symbolic nature. I have doubts as to what happened and by whom, yet the process has led to new intrapsychic awareness and insights, and finally to a reintegration of personality. More important, an agenda that had remained unspoken at the beginning, the recovery of spirituality, revealed itself as if by happenstance halfway through the process. In the end, the vision of wholeness supplanted the need for clarity. In the deepest sense, I received not want I wanted but what I needed.

It's now been 3 years since I concluded therapy. I've stopped holding my breath. It's not enough to state that these changes have taken hold. I seem to be an entirely new person, but not a stranger. Everything feels different, but very comfortable. I handle day-to-day stress differently. I enjoy not feeling compelled to analyze things to death, but instead reacting simply on an emotional level to things and letting them pass. Reason seems merely a helpful tool for occasional use, instead of a fortress to hide within. I find myself saying "it doesn't matter" to a surprising number of external influences on my life.

I still get upset easily when confronted by reminders of sexual abuse, but I can simply feel these reactions and let go of them. I still prefer the company of my women friends and I feel no need to change this. I am increasingly comfortable around men. I no longer feel a twinge when reminded that I am an adult. It's now safe to grow up. There do not appear to be separate compartments for the various elements of my personality. There is no separate little kid, no controller, no muse. Instead, there seems to be a well of energy that has a new focus. I've learned to access almost at will a creativity that interprets what's going on inside and then allows me to project it into writing or play or work or meditation. It seems that the imagery I awakened in therapy is now just below the surface of my everyday life; in a way I am living on the level that I so recently had to dig deep to investigate.

The anger is not gone and the losses are still here, but they are a part of the whole. They do not block off that inner self that used to hide in fear of them. The greatest gift of all is the realization that my new spirituality now consists of feeling the connections between my day-to-day living and the whole that I am a part of. The whole contains past, present, and future, joy and sorrow, the presence and absence of loved ones, growth, loss, anger, and inner peace. It is all part of the same fabric and this fabric is more than just my life. It contains all relationships, the world that I know and the world that I don't know. Everything seems a part of my life and my life is a part of this greater whole. It is this awareness that feels, once again, like prayer: a source of deep peace and contentment and an acceptance of how strange and wondrous life really is.

Narrative 5

FREEDOM, EMOTIONS, TOGETHERNESS

Guilio Romano and Gabriella Giordanella Perilli

GABRIELLA'S INTRODUCTION

Guilio Romano, a 20-year-old man, writes here of how improvisation on simple instruments in therapy with me helped him to understand himself. For a year after his father's death Guilio suffered from obsessive thoughts. His father died after a very long and severe illness during which he lived at home. Guilio's mother was preoccupied with the illness and always demanded that Guilio be perfect. An only child, he was not allowed to play at home with other children out of respect for his profoundly sick father. When his father died, Guilio began having obsessive thoughts: "I must postpone my pleasure in any way; I cannot express who I am, my emotions, feelings, and thoughts." Guilio avoided any social interaction and spent his time listening to music.

During his father's illness, Guilio was treated unsuccessfully by psychoanalysts for problems associated with his family situation. A year ago, he started psychotherapy with a transactional analyst along with weekly music therapy. The music therapy lasted for 7 months. Guilio has chosen to write of two music therapy experiences that he feels give an idea of some of the meaningful steps during his healing process.

GUILIO'S EXPERIENCES

I have known music therapy for only a short time, but when I am engaged in music therapy experiences, it seems as if music therapy already knows everything about me. It is unbelievable all it can do for me. Music therapy is a friend! I am thankful because it has given me the ability and permission to block my obsessions and to express myself with freedom. It is exceptional because it doesn't hurry me up, a terrible thing for me. Music therapy has given me permission to know myself. My feelings, wishes, and memories have become clear through playing instruments, hearing famous compositions, or creating improvisations.

Previously, I had forbidden myself to relax. I was trying to control my emotions completely because I feared they would endanger me. This conviction was pushing me to obsess. My obsessions were so inflexible that they didn't allow me to concentrate on anything else and thus it was impossible for me to participate actively with other people. It seemed that I would never have joyful interactions with other human beings. Two particular experiences lowered my anxiety and transformed me deeply.

My music therapist asked me to create a composition on the xylophone with her. I was perplexed, but I made an attempt. My obsessions took over immediately, and I couldn't pay attention to what I was doing. In fact, I was playing by myself without interaction with the therapist. This was very evident when we listened to the tape of the improvisation. It had happened once again: The others—usually it was people, but this time it was sounds—wanted to get into my world and I repelled them. In this improvisation, a sweet melody wanted to become my friend. I was compelled to escape this intruder who had broken into my obsessive thoughts. I played something swift and loud. I felt quite happy listening to my performance, since it was concrete proof by which I could understand my unhealthy behavior. Previously, I had known I was wrong—I was suffering a lot—but now I was beginning to be aware of when and how I behaved in such a way. I didn't know what I could do to modify my behavior. I decided to take a risk—never mind the outcome. I would try to play with the music therapist and not with my obsessions. Although I felt confused, I succeeded in creating a melody with my music therapist. What a meaningful success it was for me! I realized that if I succeeded in playing with a person without succumbing to my obsessions, then perhaps I could stay in a relationship with a person without obsessions. I could perhaps find attunement and not have to control the person or my emotions. This attunement happened in our second session; a melody was born and it was a very special one.

A commonly shared idea is that each individual has both male and female parts. I was convinced that I could not express myself completely; my energy, which I associated with virility, was completely blocked. I allowed myself to express only those characteristics I considered to be exclusively female, such as sweetness. I suffered deeply because I did not express my male characteristics. I felt like an alien toward myself. I knew who I was and what I liked, but I showed only one side.

Music allowed me to express both sides of myself. It happened this way. I decided that creating a composition using two instruments—the xylophone for sweetness and the drum for strong rhythm—would help me show both female and male sides. In practice, I could not play the two instruments at the same moment, so I performed them alternately, with the therapist taking the alternate instrument. At first I focused my attention completely on the sounds that were springing from my drum-beating. I listened to their depth without remembering that I was playing with someone else. Later I started giving more attention to the music interaction with my music therapist, listening to the xylophone as I improvised drum sounds. The therapist matched my strong rhythm with a clear melody. When we changed instruments, I played my simple and sweet melody and she supported it with a powerful rhythm. Listening to the tape, I felt satisfied. I had found a balance between male and female parts, strength and sweetness, in the blended improvisations. Equally important, my experience happened with a woman in a creative, cooperative way. I had unblocked myself and I could feel like a complete person. I thank my exceptional new friend, music therapy.

Narrative 6

EMERGING THROUGH MUSIC:
A JOURNEY TOWARD WHOLENESS
WITH GUIDED IMAGERY AND MUSIC

Rebecca Buell

INTRODUCTION

I decided to try Guided Imagery and Music (GIM) therapy when I was in my early forties. I had been trained as a psychotherapist, but I was working in an administrative/clerical position. I was experiencing an underlying sense of dissatisfaction with my professional life. I was tired most of the time and had frequent colds and other minor illnesses. I was paying the bills, something that had been a challenge for me most of my adult life, but there was no sense of satisfaction in my daily work. I wanted to start a practice in psychotherapy, the work I had been trained for, but I was terrified of leaving the financial security of my job. I felt terribly stuck, trapped by my own fear and tortured by the knowledge that I was not living authentically.

I was drawn to GIM because I had experienced the power of imagery through my studies of Jungian dreamwork. I sensed that it could be very helpful to have a therapist to help me into a relaxed state and to be present as my imagery actually unfolded, rather than relating the imagery at a later time, as I had done with dreams. I am also a musician, and the idea of using classical music to evoke imagery was very appealing to me.

I am a music therapist, but in this narrative, I speak as a client. The descriptions of the imagery from my GIM sessions are taken from a journal I kept during the time I was involved in this therapy. I have chosen not to use my real name and, by mutual agreement with my therapist, I have not identified my therapist. The imagery descriptions are written in the present tense (a technique that I found helpful in working with dream images) and indented. Between session 7 and 8, I have described a dream that seemed to relate to the process I was experiencing in my GIM sessions. For each session, I have also given my impressions of what the imagery represented to me, including insights I gained from discussions with my therapist.

THE SESSIONS

Session 1

I am in a beautiful old house. I go upstairs to the bathroom and begin painting it an ugly shade of sick green. I don't want to be making it ugly and I realize this is someone else's idea. However, I feel like I must continue the project. Eventually an old woman comes to the door and tells me to stop painting and come with her. I am relieved to be able to abandon the project.

It was clear to me that painting the bathroom represented my job. I was carrying out someone else's plan. I did not even like what I was creating, but I felt obligated to continue. This is very familiar to me. The old woman seemed to be a Wise One. Perhaps she is the part of me that knows I must stop this work. Maybe I can learn to listen to her and trust her more.

Session 2

A black woman in a white dress with a red sash shares a drink with me. After [I drink] it, my body is filled with streaming energy. I see brilliant colors radiating from the energy centers in my body, especially my heart center. I have an experience of a sensation throughout my body of joy and power. I have never felt this fully alive!

This session was certainly a peak experience. The black woman seemed to be another Wise One. She showed me a part of myself that I had not experienced before. This part of me is very alive and very powerful. The strong emotions and body sensations that I felt were unlike anything I had previously experienced. It has been difficult for me to believe that I am worthy. This session seemed to be a confirmation that I am a strong and worthy person.

Session 3

> I am walking in deep sand on a barren, endless beach. Walking in the sand is very difficult. I am tired.

This session felt like the opposite of my previous session. This is how I feel during much of my day-to-day life, going on and on with no purpose and becoming very tired.

Session 4

> I am in an underground room. I have a sense that it is both a womb and a tomb. An old woman (perhaps the one from my first session) puts me in a fire that doesn't burn me. A dragon comes out of my solar plexus and eats its own fire.

The underground room could have represented my unconscious or my inner self. The fire that does not burn could have been a form of purification or transformation. The dragon that ate its own fire was an unsettling image. Does it mean that I put my energy out into the world, but then I quickly swallow it back up, afraid of what it might do?

Session 5

> I become a white wolf and howl, giving voice to my frustration, sorrow, and anger.

This seemed to be a continuation of the previous session. This time, however, I did not swallow my fire. This time I gave it voice.

Session 6

> A huge vine is wrapping around me and constricting me. I do not want to kill it by uprooting it. I finally free myself by spinning out of it.

The vine felt like my job, confining and constricting. I want to leave my job, but I do not want to destroy things when I do. This imagery seemed to be showing me there is another way out.

Session 7

I am in an underground temple. People in white tunics are nurturing me. They put me in a small boat, which carries me downstream to the sea. I find a trunk on the beach. I open it and find a small photograph of my grandmother.

I was underground again. This time, people were helping me. It is often difficult for me to accept help or to notice that help is being offered. The boat that carried me to the sea was also moving with the flow of the water. No effort was required. This is a contrast to my daily life, in which everything seems to take tremendous effort. My grandmother meant a lot to me. She was a creative, free spirit. Seeing her picture in my imagery was a surprise. This picture exists in ordinary reality. It is her high school graduation picture. I had not seen it since moving from Boston in 1982. After this session, I went through my things and was unable to find it. I did not mention this imagery or this picture to my mother; however, she sent it to me several weeks after this session with a note saying she found it among her things and thought I might like to have it! Is this synchronicity?

Dream

Later that week, I had the following dream.

I go to a trash can and lift off the lid. Inside the trash can are the bodies of two kittens. They are my kittens. I wake up with a jolt, feeling intense emotion.

This was an intense, shocking dream. I love animals. I was devastated to find my kittens dead and to find that their bodies had been disposed of like trash. No respect had been shown to them. How had I let this happen? The kittens seem to represent my own creativity; it is still in its infancy, and I am allowing it to be killed. I am not even showing respect for it. This feels like a wake-up call.

Session 8

I become a snake. I have a very palpable sensation of what it is like to be a snake, to crawl on the ground, feel my strong rippling muscles, and "taste" the scent of other animals with my tongue. This is a very different, almost alien form of life energy I am experiencing.

A snake had appeared to me in a dream I had about a month earlier. In the dream, I was too fearful to engage with it, so my ability to become the snake in this session felt very significant. It seemed to represent a willingness to accept a way of being that is unfamiliar, to experience life from a different perspective. This is what I must do if I want to move beyond my habitual way of being. Maybe I am breaking through my fear.

Session 9

I lie in a stream and let the water flow around me, nurturing me and restoring my energy.

This session was simply restful and nurturing. I feel like I need more of this in my life right now.

Session 10

A young prince appears as my guide. He leads me behind a waterfall to an underground passage and tells me I must go on by myself. When I emerge from the passage, I see myself as a dismembered skeleton surrounded by glowing green light. I feel free, fresh, and renewed.

This seemed to be a death–rebirth image. Seeing my dismembered body actually gave me a huge feeling of relief! I have a sense that I do not have to try to hold it together any longer. Even if it looks like everything is falling apart, it will be okay. Things may have to fall apart before something new can emerge.

Session 11

Several days prior to this session, I gave notice that I would be leaving my job.

> I climb down a ladder in a dark chute that leads to an underground sewer. There is a strong feeling of sadness here, but it is not my sadness, and I know it is not my responsibility to stay here and fix it. I find a way out by crawling through the water until I come to an opening.

This seemed to be about guilt for giving my notice. Sewers represent guilt to me. Even though I feel sure I made the right decision, I feel guilty about the situation I am creating by leaving. This imagery shows me that it may not be easy; I may have to crawl through sewer water, but I will find a way out.

Session 12

> I am in an underground cavern. There is a bright fire burning here. I take a burning stick from the fire and go out of the cavern. I start a new fire from the burning stick. A crow emerges from the smoke.

I was underground again in my inner world, my unconscious self, and there was a fire there. Perhaps this fire represents my energy and my creativity. It seems as though it is time for me to take the fire into the outer world and let other people see it. The crow is an omen of change. It feels like a good omen.

Session 13

> I am walking down a road with an old man on one side of me and an old woman on the other. They tell me, "Look ahead. Don't look back." I am suddenly surrounded by a blinding, bright light. I feel powerful emotions of simultaneous sorrow and joy coursing through my heart center, my body becomes very hot, and my back arches involuntarily. I join hands with the man and woman and move up a column of energy and constantly changing color. I emerge in a place of wondrous emptiness and stillness. I have no sense of boundaries and am unable to determine where my body ends.

This was another peak experience. It was very different from the previous experience in which I contacted my own power. This was about something much bigger than myself. It is very difficult to describe this state in words. This was a profoundly moving experience, and as a result I will never have quite the same perspective on my life that I had in the past. It is as if I have suddenly seen my life in the context of a much greater whole and I can trust what unfolds for me.

Session 14

> I am a young girl. It is night, and there is a celebration going on. I am dancing. People follow me and I show them a bright star. I am relaxed, playful, and unselfconscious.

This was my final session. It was much less intense than my previous session, but it felt like a confirmation of the choice I have made and a readiness for new beginnings.

A few weeks after this session, I received a phone call from a friend I had not seen in several years, asking me if I would like to become a partner in a psychotherapy practice with her.

CONCLUSION

As I reflect on my experience with GIM, what impresses me the most is how changes in my outer life were foreshadowed by changes in my imagery. As my imagery changed, the outer world responded. Many of these responses were not initiated by me. Part of me knew what needed to happen, but I was unable to access this knowledge through normal, logical thinking. Imagery was a channel through which my inner knowledge became accessible. The music invited my imagery to flow more easily and helped sustain and support some of the strong emotions I experienced during the sessions.

I am also grateful for the insights I received that came from what I consider to be a spiritual perspective. This was not something I had expected. I came to therapy looking for the courage to let go of a limiting job. I left with experiences that changed my fundamental relationship with life. Through this work, I was able to uncover the strength and trust that allowed me to become a more fully realized human being.

CHAOS, CRISIS, DEVELOPMENT, COSMOS

Mark Nielsen and Torben Moe

TORBEN'S INTRODUCTION

I first met Mark in March 1995. He had endured 15 years of drug abuse. He was shy and insecure and believed that he was impotent. Two months earlier, he had entered, in miserable condition, the psychiatric hospital where I worked. In 1995, Mark had 16 sessions of music therapy. We used Guided Imagery and Music (GIM), meeting weekly and later twice a month while Mark was an inpatient. Therapy came to a close a few months after he was discharged in September 1995. Since then, I have had follow-up contact with him every 6 months.

Mark (not his real name) was able to use GIM almost from the beginning. In our therapy, I helped Mark into a deeply relaxed state and put on specially chosen classical music; Mark verbalized his imagery and I kept in contact with him. After the music, we processed the experience. Every person who experiences GIM has a characteristic imaging style. Mark's style was characterized by a myriad of symbolic images, often multisensory. Mark will tell his story and give an example from one of his sessions.

MARK'S STORY

My name is Mark. I was born in Denmark on January 12, 1959, as an afterthought in a family of four children. We were three boys and one girl. My father was an independent master artisan and my mother was a housewife during my childhood, but in fact she was educated as a hairdresser. I would describe my childhood as being very secure. I was brought up in a loving atmosphere in a typical middle-class Danish family of the sixties.

Music was always an intrinsic part of my life because my father was rather good at the violin; he played it often. My two elder brothers went to a music high school, and my sister played the piano.

I began my musical career at the age of 4 with a little violin through instruction and playing with my father. But the violin was not my instrument. My parents' attitude toward music was that it should be learned in a playful and pleasurable way; therefore, I changed to the marching drum, which I loved.

This relationship to percussion instruments lasted and became an important part of my childhood, youth, and adult life. I went to an ordinary basic school, but at 15, before my second year in high school, I left, in defiance of my teacher, and was admitted to an excellent music conservatory.

Music Study: Teenage Years

I studied for 5 years, but I did not take a final exam. In the same year that I was admitted, I began my career as a professional musician; I became an assistant in one of the most famous orchestras in the country. Obviously, this was possible only because of the intense experience I had gained from playing in several amateur orchestras since the age of 12. In 1978, I was an exchange student in Moscow. During my stay, I took part in the recording of the ballet *Spartacus*. Later in the same year, I had my London debut through several recordings with the London Symphony Orchestra. These were great experiences for me.

This period had negative consequences, however. During my adolescence, I was mostly surrounded by men and women who were older than I and who treated me as a contemporary, for better or worse. This, of course, made me mature extremely fast on certain levels, but in other areas of my personality, there were—and there may still be—shortages of some building blocks, although hardly any of the essential ones.

Because of the facts mentioned above—the unorganized structure of my everyday life and my lack of self-discipline—I started to virtually play Russian roulette with my life. First, I started to drink large quantities of alcohol and ended up with a serious case of pancreatitis and great pain. Next, I developed insulin-dependent diabetes and I started to receive controlled medicine containing great amounts of opiates (morphine) and various benzodiazepines. I was never high on the medicine, but because of my biological makeup and many other things, I quickly developed resistance to the various medicines.

For a couple of years, I took gigantic doses of medicine—with and without recommendation from a doctor—to ease the pain and to damp down my whole emotional life.

It is obvious that I could not maintain any sort of occupation in this condition and certainly not one demanding the precision of a percussionist in a symphony orchestra. My physical and social decline commenced.

Seeking Help

In October 1994, I realized that I could not continue to play; at that point, getting out of the hotel bed in itself was an effort. I was resistant to and fearful of going into professional treatment. In January 1995, I was removed to a psychiatric hospital and put on an open ward.

Four months later, I had recovered enough that I was able to commence my first session with music therapist Torben Moe. Below I shall attempt to describe some of the highlights of the music therapy sessions and their importance to my new life.

Before going into professional treatment, I was very close to having a physical and psychological collapse as a consequence of my medicine abuse. I sensed I had precluded all future possibilities of a professional career. I was so insecure that I thought I would never play music again.

While listening to the wonderful music flowing out of the loudspeakers, I learned to relax my body and started to feel myself as "the real thing, all clean." The imagery initiated a chain reaction of impressions, of visions, scents, flavors, and feelings, and on an emotional level, strange things happened.

At first I withdrew a little from the ungovernably beautiful scenarios (the images) that came from my inner self, probably because I feared I could not contain them. I struggled to relax and give in to the unknown. After the first few sessions, I was able to relax so much that a lot of images came up. I remember conducting the music, being a sun, having an incredible sense of relaxation, and having a body experience of being very heavy and very light at the same time. I sensed vitality in my images and my fear of being impotent disappeared gradually.

In the sixth session, I had a feeling of victory which I intuitively interpreted to mean that I somehow mentally had survived my drug addiction. Listening to the end of Mahler's *Fourth Symphony*, I imagined myself standing on top of a hill with a view of a beautiful landscape that contained all the elements I had met during this session: a remarkable intensity of the sun and a landscape with white ancient columns decorated with gold ornamentation.

Images During a Session

The following are excerpts of my experiences in session 7 during Vaughan Williams's *Fantasia on a Theme by Thomas Tallis,* followed by his *Fifth Symphony: Romanza* and *The Lark Ascending.*

There is a dark blue light around me, with thin light blue stripes in it. It is rather elegant. In front of me is a lot of light blue steam with golden spots in it. Now I see it becomes a very beautiful rainbow. I can look very far from up here in the air; it is as though everything stands in a faint haze. The landscape and buildings remind me of a concentration camp: barren, evil, and deserted. My legs are whirring. I feel pain. The colors change into blue and red and black, something blazes and flames—yes it flames— right next to me; it floats away, blows away, comes back, and disappears. I feel anger. My own body is red and violet blue in the lower part. At the same time as a powerful prickly feeling occurs, I feel weightless, free, and heavy at the same time. Something faint yellow appears; it is the white columns very slender and tall, one for each of my legs; I walk through them and on the other side an eagle awaits on my left. I start to fly and it draws me along. The colors vary between light gray and red—a brilliant combination— and I feel a wonderful fluctuation with the strokes of the eagle's wings. It would be nice if it weren't for that salty burned taste I have in my mouth. Never mind, I will defeat it because now I am in the middle of a lovely hardwood forest with the most beautiful golden colors.

I am still very sore in my left side. I fly with the eagle; it is sunset now. There are strong beams of light coming into my solar plexus, and at the same time I feel I am stretching out in my body, as if somebody had a hook and pulled my head. Everything is dark red now. I feel the color coming into my legs and I am falling and falling until I land at the bottom. Yes, I think it is an old volcano and I am very deep down. I have a very salty taste in my mouth. Now it is as though heaven is coming down to me. I think I have been far away; my legs are gone and I am moving up again. I am goosefleshy all over.

What stood out for me in this session was the view of the concentration camp, the eagle, and the volcano. The camp and the anger and pain I felt there were like all the pain I have gone through as a drug addict and in the treatment of my pancreas inflammation. On another level, the pain reminded me of a very traumatic "falling in love" experience I had when I was very young and was playing in Russia. I had very strong feelings toward a ballet dancer. The relationship was impossible in many ways, mainly because of the East–West situation at the time.

The anger I felt was somehow connected to my former teacher at the conservatory, whom I felt had let me down; I realized how ambivalent my relationship to him had been. It was very satisfying for me to get in contact with this feeling that I now also sense was a feeling of strength—like a readiness to fight for my life.

The eagle image is a very powerful symbol for me, since it is an animal with strength and a breadth of view; it can connect me to the unknown and perhaps to repressed areas of myself. Finally, I think that moving down into the bottom of the volcano symbolized the expanding potentials of what I can be—by myself and in relationship to other people.

At this point in therapy, I had regained more control of my body. I had lost about 10 kilos of weight [22 pounds], my diabetes was totally under control, and I had begun to play a bit of music again in an amateur orchestra.

Reflections:
Looking Back and Forward

The reflections that I reported above are from notes I kept of each session. During music therapy, I had a lot of unexpected exceptional experiences; these we analyzed and worked with immediately after the music listening in each session. Sometimes the material had to lay and mature a bit in the afterthought universe; we took up these afterthoughts the following week.

Another very important, almost archetypal figure that came up in my therapy was me as the jester-clown. This figure provided entertainment in a creative manner and had a light on each finger. The positive part of this image was the creative way he appeared and the negative part was that he never seemed to stop offering entertainment.

Music therapy has given me new life. It has been part of my transformation (as the title of the chapter suggests): from chaos to crisis to development to cosmos. I will outline this idea. The chaos period was my drug addiction ,and the crisis was when I lost my job and stopped playing music. The development stage was when I decided to seek help at the hospital and began my music therapy, and the cosmos is what I have gained from GIM therapy and, in a more spiritual way, how my view of life has changed.

Here is an example. My taste in music became broader. I started to enjoy listening and playing a lot of different kinds of classical music that I was never able to take in before. Some of the softer romantic pieces from the Romantic era now came close to my heart. Most important for me was that I began to enjoy the silence! For as long as I can remember, I have had an almost manic obsession to have sounds around me day and night, but now I enjoyed quiet periods during the day and I stopped trying to escape from myself.

When I left the hospital in the end of 1995, I returned to my apartment, which was in poor condition. A lot of crap was carried out from the place. With my renewed belief in life and renewed energy, I changed my drug addiction cave (my apartment) into a nice flat that reflected my new self: masculinity and musicality. Later, a famous Danish home magazine came to take pictures of the apartment.

During that period, I sometimes experienced all alone unexpected moments of happiness: tears of joy and goose pimples. My daily music practice went so well that the ambitious idea of a solo concert started to take shape. The big day came and the concert was a success. I have regained my old job as an assistant in the orchestra and I am usually the first person they call whenever they need a large crew. About 13 months ago, I met my current girlfriend and I believe we can create a future with lots of shared moments of happiness.

Thus, I am back in the labor market as a musician and I also work part time as a teacher in a youth club. I keep up with daily instrument practice for various music competitions in which the winner obtains employment on a permanent basis in an orchestra.

This practice helps me to keep up my solo repertoire. I have also started to take lessons in the marimba and this will ease my preparations for new and complicated music.

Summary

The scales fell from my eyes, and suddenly I could see and—more essential—I was aware of the beauty and grace of every atom of this world and the rest of the universe. You have to dare to see it and acknowledge it with open eyes and open mind; you have to be receptive and open to all the events of day-to-day life. Events can either become trivial repetitions or they can become new, wonderful happenings and experiences. It is your own choice. If you have physical and psychological energy, you can go very far in personal development with music therapy. Such development can be on many different levels and therefore useful throughout life. Music therapy can certainly open doors!

Narrative 8

EXPERIENCING THE MUSIC IN GUIDED IMAGERY AND MUSIC

Connie Isenberg-Grzeda

SPEAKING AS THERAPIST

I had intended to provide a forum for a client to share his or her experience of the music in the Guided Imagery and Music (GIM) process. This felt safe. The client would disclose, thereby sharing the internal emotional experience, and I, the therapist, would move into my intellect to reflect, comment, question, analyze, synthesize. I could thereby share my thoughts, in writing, about someone else's internal process. I could remain the therapist! I have decided, however, to contribute differently. I will share with you my own experience, from the perspective of client, of the music in the GIM process.

I will briefly describe the GIM process. While in a deeply relaxed state, I listen to classical music selected by the therapist and I verbally share with the therapist the imagery that is evoked in me. The therapist, in turn, takes notes and verbally supports and encourages the deepening of my experience when necessary.

The aspect of this process that I will focus on is neither the imagery nor the therapist, but rather the ways in which the music acts on me during these sessions. The examples that I present do not constitute an exhaustive list but represent some of the ways music has acted on me. I do not intend to complete this list because I believe that the complexity of GIM and of the relationship between music and the human psyche precludes arriving at a complete, neatly compiled list. Nor is it my intention to attempt to explain why the music acts on me in particular ways, or which music is most apt to act on me in specific ways, or how the music and the therapist interrelate in this therapeutic process. To struggle with these questions is to put myself back into the position of therapist. What I want to share is the experience of a therapist in the position of client. I notice that I use the word *position* rather than the more commonly used word *role*. I think that this is because the word *role* implies to me a part-self, whereas the word *position* implies a fuller use of self. A change in "role" leads me to temporarily close off certain aspects of myself, but a change in "position" involves movement into and out of different internal and external spaces while maintaining access to other spaces. I try to maintain open communication between my own internal therapist and client as I speak now from the position of client.

SPEAKING AS CLIENT

As I think about the music in the GIM process, I think of the way in which it acts on me, at times holding me, touching me, filling me. As I think about the therapist in the GIM process, I think about my longing for her to act on me. "Hold me, touch me, help me feel better," I plead silently. I plead, all the while knowing that what I long for is not necessarily what I need at this time and perhaps not even what I really want. The physical touch of the therapist or the physical holding may be too painful, too little, too much. It cannot feel right. And yet I long for it. I am disappointed when it is not there. I would probably be enraged if it was there. I do not need to act on the music to get it to act on me. It simply acts on me. The therapist, however, is a different matter. I must act on the therapist to get the therapist to feel, to understand, to respond. Or so it has seemed.

How does the music act on me as I listen to it in a state of relaxed preparedness? Sometimes it envelops me, holding me, caressing me. I sink into the music as a baby would sink into its mother's arms and I allow it to rock me, to cradle me, and to help me feel safe. The more I let go, the closer I get to a state of blissful fusion with the music, a sleeplike state of total repose. The music is now all that exists for me; the therapist recedes into the background. Memory fragments sometimes emerge for me in this state: memories of early but verbal life, memories of preverbal life, muscle memories, visceral memories. Whereas I can verbally share the memories from the later developmental periods with the therapist, I find myself able to experience the earlier memories in the presence of the therapist but unable to share them verbally.

At other times, the music acts in a far less nurturing manner. It sweeps over me in turgid waves, engulfing me, scaring me, and threatening to drown me. Barely able to breathe, I seek to fight it, to escape, or, alternatively, I succumb to the power of the onslaught. I do not consciously choose which of these paths I will follow—it feels, rather, as if the chosen response just happens. If the choice is to fight, I might find myself physically attempting to push the music away as if it had a material or corporeal presence. The inevitable lack of success might impel me to attempt to escape. How do I escape? One way is to create images that save me from the threat: for example, seeing myself as a lifeguard, reducing the body of water to a tiny puddle, imagining that someone saves me. Another form of escape is to block out the music. Although I continue to hear the physical music, I somehow manage to deaden its emotional impact on me, to quiet its resonance with my internal state. How I do this, I do not know. What it is that is closing off inside of me, I do not know. How it is that I am only sometimes able to do this, I do not know. I do know what happens when I cannot escape—I succumb or once again I fight. When I succumb, the waves sweep over me, submerging me, crushing me. Since they meet with no resistance, these waves may "flatten" me, numbing all affect. At other times they may manage to lift me up and carry me with them; my emotions merge with the intensity of the waves and pull me at once further into myself and further out, almost obliterating any sense of boundary between the inner and the outer reality. I thus feel as if I have become one with the music, one with the turbulent, intense, dynamic movement. And where is the therapist for me at these times? As I struggle to escape from the intensity of the music, I wish for the therapist to save me by reducing the volume, by changing tapes, or by turning the music off entirely. If I feel myself being carried away by the music, the therapist may once again recede into a seeming oblivion, ceasing to exist for me, momentarily. There are instances, though, when the therapist accompanies me on this journey, carried within my images. Yet there are other times when the therapist's voice serves to ground me as I yield to the pull of the music; this grounding renders the experience less frightening.

What are some other ways that the music acts on me? Sometimes it penetrates my being, infusing me with its energy, moving me both emotionally and physically. When I am moved emotionally by the music, I feel myself being filled with the beauty contained in the music and I feel this beauty resonate with my internal state, with a preexisting internal beauty and with deep emotion. At times there is a concurrent physical process, albeit different in nature. It consists of a physical response to the music. The physical movement of my body parts, largely restricted to my upper extremities, is not volitional. Arms wave in the air, arms that have a seeming life of their own, as if part of me and yet autonomous—my arms. Who is moving my arms? Is it I or is it the music? Who is moving my arms? I do not know. Can I stop the movement when I desire to stop it? Not always. Can I control the intensity of the movement, the amplitude of the arc traced? Not always. What force is this that seems to overtake my will, rendering me helpless in the face of my own bodily movement? I do no know. I feel helpless but fascinated as if in the presence of something new, something to discover, something that surely is linked to other aspects of my life, my being, my past, my memories, and my fantasies. Perhaps this movement is a reenactment. Did my arms ever move like this before? Was there ever another force as strong—as compelling but perhaps more sinister or more playful—making my arms move? I do not know. Why only my arms? Why is this the only physical part of me to dance to the music? Is it a result of the recumbent position or is it linked to something else? I do not know. What is the role of the therapist as my arms, barely in my awareness and seemingly out of control, dance their own synchronous dance with the music? The therapist helps me to be aware of this movement, to be aware of how it appears in the external reflective glass; the therapist helps me to claim it as my own. Together, once the music has left us, the therapist and I weave our connection through our joint effort to arrive at intellectual understanding, to link the emotional and the physical; together we revel in the enchantment and wondrous grace of the "arm dance."

There are moments when the very structure of the music acts on me. It is as if the music lends me an internal structure, an organization, a psychic-affective map. Just as a mother can help to bring order to her child's chaos, so can the music bring order at times. If it is the music that brings the order, what is the role of the therapist at these times? I think that for me the work of the therapist at this time is to recognize my internal disorder and the need for a structuring container and to select from among the music programs one that could provide the containment and organization. This heightened empathic response I have found more often to be a wished-for ideal than a reality. What is magical is the way that I have sometimes managed to use the empathic failures equally effectively. In fact, I have often found that the same music acts differently on me at different times. Music that can soothe me during one session can stir up rageful feelings during another session. Music that can feel not sufficiently "holding" in one session, can provide a tight container in another. I feel that this lack of predictability speaks to the complexity and the richness of the relationship between music and the human psyche.

Part II

Clients Tell About
Their Experiences in
Their Own Words
Gathered by Their Therapists

In these narratives, the words of clients about their music therapy experiences are gathered by their therapists in these ways: through interviewing, by requesting written answers to questions, by transcribing client words from video- or audiotapes, or by jointly reviewing therapy sessions with the client. Some of the narratives contain examples of client music, lyrics, or poetry.

Narrative 9

THE QUIET SOLDIER:
PAIN AND SICKLE-CELL ANEMIA

Joanne V. Loewy

INTRODUCTION

On a quiet morning in July, Walter and I had just concluded a musical interchange. On this particular day, Walter began to use his voice. We began the session playing the d'jimbe drums and eventually started to vocalize. At that point, I moved to the piano and we worked into a vocal dialogue (much like scatting) and then into a song. Walter called the song "The Pain That Ain't Nobody's". *Pain* was a term that had significant meaning in almost every context of Walter's life.

Walter, like many teenagers suffering from sickle-cell anemia*, appears to have a high threshold for pain. Staff have noted that in his numerous hospital admissions, his pain scale has rarely been reported to be higher than a 5 (on a scale of 1 to 10). Many of the therapists who have worked with Walter believe that he is experiencing a much greater intensity of pain than he is reporting. He often seems to be holding in the terror of the pain that his body seems barely able to endure. This could be the reason that music has served a role in the treatment of his pain and has been a part of Walter's plan of care for the past several years.

Walter began to talk after finishing an improvisatory song. I asked if I could audiotape the (interview) remainder of the session; he agreed. The following interview, which lasted 30 minutes, is a rare glimpse into the life story of an incredibly brave 17-year-old young man who has suffered the anguish of many painful crises.

WALTER'S INTERVIEW

My Life with Sickle-Cell Disease

From what I know, I've had sickle-cell since I was 3 months old. I knew I had it, but not until I was 3 months old did my father

---

* A description of sickle-cell disease appears at the end of this narrative.

know that he had it. And then, that's [when] his whole side of the family . . . realized they had it 'cause he never knew that he had the trait, whatever—he never knew. On my mother's side, they knew. After they found out that I had it, they knew, you know, that there were gonna be some big problems.

From what I can remember about when I first went to the hospital when I was real small . . . the pain was really at that time just in my joints. I never really had the terrible leg pains I have now. It was just in my knee or wrist back then; it wasn't ever in my chest or lower back or anything of that sort.

So when I was smaller I would miss a lot of school, and that was a problem. It was hard. You know, from what I remember, it was hard for me to catch up, but I guess I do okay catching up. My friends were okay. My cousins, they helped; they'd tell the teacher why I was out. Back then, I went to the doctors maybe four times a year. I'd go home and be told to drink a lot of fluids, fluids and folic acid. Back then, I had an enlarged spleen. Actually, I remember I wasn't allowed to do sports. I couldn't play gym or nothing 'cause they didn't want me to rupture my spleen.

I can't play basketball even now. As I got older and moved in the sixth grade, things changed. At the end of the fifth grade, I stopped going to school. My fifth-grade teacher, Miss Bardon, she was real nice; she came and brought me cards that the class had made. She was really nice, you know; she took the time to make that effort.

Back then, I went to another hospital. I liked that place; they knew me. It was my first hospital. I started going to here when we moved to [name deleted]. I think it was when I turned 12. I got my spleen and gallbladder removed and that was really painful. The pain from that lasted about 45 minutes. There wasn't anything they could do initially, so I just would be waiting in the bed for the stones to pass and that was really painful.

Then we moved out here and it was hard to go [back to the old hospital] every time I would get sick. So then at 12, I started coming to this medical center. It was really hard to change hospitals. I would complain to my mom a lot. I had been at the old hospital a long time. They gave me great care 'cause they knew me. This medical center was hard to get used to; it felt so new.

When I first started coming here, I had much less admittances. Like last year, I think I had 21 admittances. I didn't come when I was young as often as I do now. Already I have been here, for example, so many times this year.

School Loss and Painful Episodes

*Why do you think that is?**

I can't really explain or tell you that because I don't know. Now I come here more often and I miss much more school and everything. This time I'm here is bad. But the last time—was it 3 weeks ago?—when I had my chest and lower back hurting . . . it was, like, that time and the time before that my father had to help. You know, it's not easy for my parents.

Every time I come here it's like this routine: like, my mother gets out this extra thing of clothes—expecting—just in case they admit me. We always have to prepare everything, getting ready like I'll have to stay there that night. So then I come here and now it's, like, 3 weeks ago when I came here. I remember having pain like I've never had before. Never quite that horrible. I never had pain like I had that one time. I just remember it was, like, the worst time. I remember even now, in thinking back on it, that it was an 11 [referring to the pain scale]. I remember sitting in the bed just crying and everything because [*hesitates*] I don't usually cry, but I had such pain.

When was that?

That was 2 years ago, maybe. I never had pain so bad again until about, like, 3 weeks ago. That's why I was so surprised because I usually just don't say 10. When they ask, I might not always tell, you know, because I never have been like that, you know. I figure that when they ask, they only want to know your pain in comparison to the worst you ever had, and that's what I compare it to.

I was in such pain. It was the worst I ever had. I thought that I was dying and I would never make it to the hospital. When I got there, I actually got angry waiting for the nurse to come. When you tell the nurse to come, you know, it's like, all right, you know they're gonna get something for you. And someone like me, I'm thinking, *Oh God, please, oh please, just get up and go; just give me something for the pain,* because it seemed like it just took forever. I was getting mad. And my father was getting angry a lot. He doesn't like seeing stuff; 'cause, like, once before when I was younger, the pain I got was so bad that I lost my sight. I had tem-

---

* Throughout, Joanne's questions are italicized and in separate paragraphs from Walter's comments.

porary blindness. The pain was so great and my father started going off because I couldn't see. He was so angry—that's how he gets when I get real sick. And now [*hits cymbal*] when I come to the hospital [*hits the cymbal*], I hear this pulsing school bell [*hits the cymbal*] and I think, *I might as well get it over with now.* I think, *If I go to school, I'll be in pain the whole time, taking pills, and then at the end of the week I have to go to the hospital anyway—so why don't I just go and get it over with anyway?* When you have pain like that, you just want to go to the hospital [*hits the tom drum*]. You don't think about nothing else. It's just whatever anyone can give you; it's just hurry up and have them give it to you; it's just hurry up and have them give it to you and that's it. And eventually when you calm down, you'll be thinking more rationally. So I can think rationally [*hits cymbal with more energy*], but I miss school and everything, you know; I don't have an excuse, but I still miss class even though I'm there. I fall asleep 'cause I get so tired; my body is still resting from having been so tense. I crave relief and it's like [*models breaths by showing rapid sounds with long, emphasized* HHuuuh, HHuuuh]. I try to sleep.

After a lot of rest, I learn to get up early to get ready to get back into school. But in school, I doze off and then the biggest problem is the teacher not getting it and finding out that I can't take summer school. I just get mad sometimes and it causes me so many problems.

Do you ever express that you're mad?

To who? [*Hits cymbal.*]

To the teacher—[say] that you are dozing because you are still recovering?

The teachers look at me like someone who doesn't care, who never comes to class and [who] sleeps. I never tell her. I get my adviser to tell them. One time a teacher gave me something I like to read to try [to] get me to stay awake, but the other teachers didn't see it that way, even when I was in pain.

The Worst Kind of Pain

What was the worst pain you ever experienced?

When it—when it was deep in my lower back—it was deep, way inside. It's a pain that was always there.

What did it feel like?

There's nothing to compare it to. I just know; it's like I can't even walk. [It's] the back, legs; all I know is that I'm headed down that terrible road again. It'll be, like, 2 in the morning; we'll be looking for a cab, bus—whatever comes first. My father found a cab for us; he had it waiting for us and he explained to the driver, "My son is sick."

In the cab, I just hold it in when the pain is so bad. I breathe, like, a fast breath [*silence, gasp, silence*]; I breathe and then I pause. The pause means I'm straining, trying to hold the pain down. I do that 'cause I can barely breathe. There's the strain of the pain and then the search for oxygen. It's constant [*gasp, gasp*] and then I strain and strain, and when I strain, I'm not really breathing; I'm straining to match the pain so I'm not hurting. I'm holding so it won't hurt as much, and then I tense up at the end. I don't get enough air; I can't breathe right [*gasp, gasp, gasp, gasp*].

Oxygen can help. When I get pain, I breathe irregularly. It's as if I was accounting for or taking up some of the slack for the pain. I feel the pain [and] tense up. [I] account for the pain by tensing. The oxygen really helps. It alleviates some of the strain.

Music Therapy

When I was playing the recorder yesterday, I was only playing, like, one short note [*blows quick amount of air*]. But the deeper the air that I was taking in, the longer I was blowing out. So when I was breathing in, I took in and let out a long breath [*blows and tones whwheeeeee*]. I pushed out for much longer; that's what I was trying to do.

At first when I played, it was short [and] there wasn't much effect, but the music helped me blow out longer and then the rhythm encouraged me. Actually, the space in between the piano that you were doing suggested to me that I take more air in so that I could breathe out. The recorder helped me to pick up the slack for the air I might not have taken in.

What else has helped you or not helped you in terms of the music?

The cymbal really helps. Actually, since I was young, my mom taught me ways to encourage myself to take my mind off the pain. Computer games, movies . . . would help my mind go somewhere else. You know, if you just sit there focusing on pain, it's all there. But if you do some playing, like making music, your mind goes somewhere completely different.

When I play the chimes, which are actually the sounds that appeal to me the most, I am reminded of how many times [*tinkles chimes bottom to top*] they've helped me. The chimes offer pleasure in a world of pain. Every time that I hear them, I am reminded of some time or another that one of you has played them. I hear them and I start imagining. I go to different places; my mind goes way off the pain. Maybe the pain is still there, but if your mind ain't on it [*he trails off*]. 'Cause that's, like, the main thing I know about pain. Actually I do it with you. . . . Like your brain works in signals, and if you're not thinking about the pain [*he trails off*]. I think about the music I'm hearing and I really don't think about the pain.

The chimes take me [and] the guitar will carry me off. Certain instruments that vibrate: those bell things [Suzuki tone bars] that you move around my body. . . . Well, like, long after you play them, the sound isn't gone; they go *chingggg*. And then you touch it and it stops. But if you don't, you keep hearing the vibration, and the way you move the sounds around, just feeling it feels intense. I don't know why. It vibrates.

Does your pain vibrate?

Sometimes it does. It [*he sings* hmmmmm, *then hoarsely growls* chmmmmmm, chmmmmm]—it does. As my body contracts, the sound goes in and I hold onto it. I feel it contract. Sometimes it's continuing like that. The pain is there vibrating continuously and when it vibrates. . . . [I] start breathing irregularly because I begin to try to catch the vibration and then [I] go "hhehhh." I tense up, expecting the next one, trying to hold it before it comes. I breathe irregular and then I can feel when the cymbal is working with my vibration. The chimes then really remind me that I need to put the air to it. They're like refreshment sounds. It's really about using the sounds to push the air and the vibration back into something that is in my control.

It's similar to the pump.* When I first start pressing it, I hear it go off, but I don't feel anything. I fuss and race for the doctors to give me a bigger dose. It doesn't help until my parents make a fuss.

What would happen if you made a fuss? Did you ever think what it would be like if you were the one to let it out? Why are you more apt to hold it in?

You know, you're right. Most of the time my mom or dad will even notice a look on my face and I'm quiet, and they'll say, "Walter, what's that look?" And I'll think, yeah, I'm in pain. But

---

* Patient-controlled analgesia (PCA) pump.

lots of times it's not even really till they ask that I'll realize I'm in pain, because most of the time I'll be used to not saying anything or not doing anything about it. It may be that I don't want to bother anyone or it may also be that I don't even realize how much pain I'm in until someone mentions it.

During the nights, my mom has noticed that I'm in pain, but I'm so used to trying not to think about it that my body just automatically at times will forget to press the button [the PCA].

What about expressing it? Could that be useful, [such as] yelling and screaming yourself? Like when you play the drums in a fierce way?

Well, the d'jimbe drums do help. I can let out my mind's tense things—from my head and out through my joints and hands. Like when I'm angry, maybe rather than blame it on someone or tell them "you don't know how terrible this is," which might make them feel sorry for you—at those times I can just pound it out with you or one of the other music therapists.

I do play rhythms, too, but it's not always when I'm thinking about the pain. . . . At times, I think it's another thing that can take my mind away from the pain. It's more physical and involves my body. When we do it over and over again, like at the jams, I can go off, like, into a vibrating whirl. The rhythms can have my head spin in another groove that doesn't have to do with pain. But there [are] times when I feel at the end of my line, and rather than cry, I can pound the drum and the cymbal real hard and get some satisfaction out of that.

The real truth is that no one should ever have to go into pain as many times as I have. For real, I have had to learn about ways and things to do for my own self. Music has been really helpful, especially during times when I didn't necessarily think anyone could give me anything. At times, the sound of a soft, mellow voice has helped me to go to sleep. Sleep is a good option for times when I get exhausted and get too restless to stay awake and, you know, just think about the pain. I am thankful for all the therapists that know how to sing me off—you guys know my favorite tunes or whatever—just singing whatever you feel is there for me. When you and the music tune into someone, they know it. It's another way that can be helpful.

Thank you for describing some of the pleasant and not so pleasant parts of your experience with pain and with music therapy, Walter. . . . I am looking forward to future sessions together.

ABOUT SICKLE-CELL DISEASE

Sickle-cell disease is a genetic disorder that compromises the red blood cells. The disease weakens the cellular walls and causes a sickle deformation. The red blood cells cannot pass through the small blood vessels easily. They break down or clog the blood vessels, which results in anemia, poor circulation, and, at times, internal hemorrhaging. Common symptoms of sickle-cell anemia include poor resistance to infection, jaundice, damage to internal organs, and extreme pain in the abdomen and joints. In the United States, about 10 percent of African Americans carry the allele for sickle-cell anemia. Typically, a patient admitted to the hospital in sickle-cell crisis receives hydration, oxygen as needed, and a narcotic or analgesic. It is not uncommon today for school-age patients to receive a PCA pump, a relatively new system of pain management that encourages patients to monitor the analgesia according to their experience of pain by pressing a button that releases a prescribed dose at the moment pain is experienced.

Narrative 10

FAMILY DAY:
AN INTERVIEW WITH A FAMILY

A. Jeffrey Friedberg
and Lauren Obstbaum

JEFFREY AND LAUREN'S
INTRODUCTION

We interviewed this family (they use pseudonyms for first names only) as they entered their second year of music therapy at a community music school. At the school, each family member participates in a weekly music therapy group and also chooses to have a therapeutic music lesson before or after the group. The adolescents are assigned to a group according to their gender and age. Each group has four to seven members. There is one parents' group made up of foster and biological parents. In the groups, improvisation on simple percussion instruments, group song writing, sing-alongs, and verbal discussion give members the opportunity to express themselves. The two group leaders guide members in setting the musical and verbal agenda and ensure a safe and trusting environment. The individual lessons may include learning an instrument, developing a trusting relationship, and talking about issues related to the group.

The family was interviewed in one 45-minute sitting during an overnight retreat. Alfonso, age 14, and Carlos, age 12, are both in the younger boys' group; their sister, Tai, age 16, is in the older girls' group; and Tracy, their biological mother, is in the parents' group. We co-lead the younger boys' and the older boys' groups and teach some of the individual therapeutic music lessons.

The family was reunited 10 months ago after having been separated for several years. In the interview, the family members were asked to describe themselves as they would like to be introduced and understood by the readers of this book. They each chose their own pseudonyms. From the transcript of the interview, we have regrouped the family members' words under topic areas.

THE INTERVIEW

Introductions

ALFONSO. My name is Alfonso; I'm 14. . . . I'm a Gemini. I was born the year of the monkey. Life has been kind of rough for me, but I guess whatever doesn't kill you makes you stronger. . . . I guess you could say I'm a freewheelin', free-spirited kind of guy. To be honest— to be on a serious trip—I'm kind of close-minded about certain things. I'm sweet; I like to take long walks on the beach. [*Laughs*].

TAI. My name is Tai, okay, and I'm 16 and a senior in high school. . . . I told somebody this the other day: If you live to be 70, let's say [it's] the average age, and you're, like, 16 now and you say you had a bad life, you . . . [are wrong] because . . . [you have had] just a small percentage of your life. . . . And not only that, but this part of my life has not really been up to me to determine. It's been up to my foster parents [or] my family to determine. So once I get, like, out of my mother's house, it's up to me. You know, I just decide how I live. I make sure that I'm okay.

CARLOS. My name is Carlos. I'm a Gemini and I live in [name deleted]. I go to [name deleted] school. I'm 12. . . . [Life's been] hard and good. . . . I'm sweet and sensitive.

TRACY. I don't know if I can talk about me without [including] my family, but I'll try. I'm a widow. I'm HIV positive. I'm an alcoholic and an addict in recovery. My children were returned to me in December of 1996. . . . It's been a learning process. I'm glad that my children feel that the past hasn't hindered them and that they can't use that as an excuse. You know, I'm glad that they see that. About myself, it's just [that], you know . . . I made bad decisions . . . I made some good decisions. I never had anyone to tell me the difference between good decisions and bad decisions, so I had to learn that on my own. And I'm trying to be . . . there for my children so that I can give them . . . some of the [lessons] that I've learned from the decisions that I've had to make. And I'm learning how to make better decisions.

About the Family

TRACY. I'm grateful to have my children in my life. I'm grateful that I have an opportunity to make a change . . . in their life, that I don't have to rely on someone else to . . . have control over what happens to them, [and] that at night when I lock my door . . . they're all in their beds. . . . I love my kids and I love myself today and I've learned that through therapy. . . . One of the tools of therapy for me was music therapy.

When we started coming to music therapy . . . we didn't have . . . a family day, a family night. And coming to music therapy gave us a family day. . . . It was something we did together and they enjoyed it and it was also constructive for them, for their well-being. . . . That day, [it] was understood that no matter what [happened] . . . this [music therapy] was something that we did together.

ALFONSO. I kind of figured that . . . I got to be careful what I do [around Carlos] 'cause I see that he looks up to me. So, I . . . see that, like, when I'm around him I got to act in a certain way so that he'll know how to act with other people. . . . I saw that . . . when I first came here; I was interested in the saxophone and then Carlos wanted to go to the saxophone. And I didn't want to go to the saxophone no more, so I went to the drums. Then I stuck with the drums and now Carlos went to the drums and now he sticks with the drums. . . . [Having Carlos in the group] made me, like . . . prouder to carry myself better so that he could carry himself better.

Individual Music Therapy

ALFONSO. My lessons with Rick were really something 'cause . . . you can ask anybody . . . I've got, like, a bad temper. Like when I come here, sometimes I'm mad, but I could just beat on the drums and I feel better sometimes. . . . Rick, he's, like, a good teacher 'cause . . . I come and listen and [I'll] be mad, and he'll say, "Get on the drums and tell me what's wrong." And as I'm banging on the drums, I talk to him. And, like, it's a good way to . . . express your feelings. . . . Sometimes you get real mad and you just want to hit something. . . . I think the drums are real good.

CARLOS. I like the . . . private lessons best 'cause in the group . . . there's a whole bunch of people and stuff and you can't really do the stuff that you want to do. Like, somebody's hogging the drums and stuff. So . . . I like the private lessons. I think . . . we should have private lessons in the group. . . . I wanted to play the . . . saxophone when I first came here, but then, like, in my school people started really talking 'bout the drums more and stuff. And I felt, like, left out, like [I was] the only person who wanted to play the saxophone. So then I moved to the drums. Then when I started playing the drums, I was, like, "I don't really want to do this.". . . [I kept] on so that I can be, like, cool and stuff. So then, when I started playing . . . it started being fun. So I kept on playing.

Music Therapy Group

TAI. Being in the group with [the other group members] and singing with them and writing songs especially, I got to see their perspective of life and what they wanted and how they felt at the time. . . . Our friendship has gotten like cousins or sisters. . . . I may not like this one, I may not understand this one, but through the group I got to understand them and like them better.

ALFONSO. In the group, like, there are some kids . . . that you see . . . on the street, and you think, "I don't want to mess with him 'cause he's a thug" or "I don't like the way he looks; he looks like he's real bad or strung out." But sometimes you get, like, real nice kids; [you] just need like to give them a closer look and stuff.

CARLOS. It's not easy to sit there and not play the drums. It's not easy to sit there and listen . . . for a long time while somebody's talking 'cause you get bored. And so I start . . . to do other things. When I hit the drums, I get screamed at [*laughter*]. So I don't try to hit the drums. But it's hard. But I get really excited about playing the drums.

ALFONSO. When people don't listen, they go on their own way and make just a whole bunch of noise.

Thoughts on Therapy and Music Therapy

TAI. I learned from therapy as well that there are certain things about people that you are not going to like. And it's not your job to change people. . . . It's up to you to decide whether or not . . . you could deal with what you don't like for [the sake of] the good things. . . . If I like something about you . . . is it worth my dealing with the bad thing? . . . I don't know if this is for every family or if this is for everybody, but in my family, we identify with music a lot. . . . I'm not one for therapy. I hate therapy. I mean, I hate therapy. I hate it. But I don't look at this as therapy. I look at this as a way of expressing myself. And it's a good opportunity 'cause . . . it's music and you get to talk to people at the same time. . . . When I first started, I didn't even realize . . . I was talking to my therapist [in individual lessons] about my stuff. And so afterwards I thought about it. So I think it's a sneaky way to get therapy in. [*Laughs.*] But it's good; it's effective . . . especially with this generation.

ALFONSO. Before I came to the [music school], I liked a lot of hard-core rap and stuff. But now I . . . spread it out and I like the different stuff, like Alanis Morissette and stuff . . . [that] I didn't picture myself, like, a year ago listening to.

TRACY. Over the summer when [my kids] weren't in music therapy, I saw that they weren't together as much: you know, like, together . . . being cooperative with each other or together with how they wanted to go about expressing how they felt about something. . . . I realized that . . . because we had the break over the summer time. . . . Coming to the music therapy had helped [us], you know . . . to deal with feelings and to . . . be more centered. And I'm glad we're back.

My relationship with Tai . . . has a lot more components than with the boys. . . . The therapy, music therapy, I felt, helped us work through a lot of our disagreements, a lot of feelings that we had. You know, I was able to understand her better . . . and I like that.

I remember one particular time . . . when we were expected to move into an apartment together—when they were in foster care. . . . I made the phone call and the lady said that she wasn't able to move me in and we weren't going to be together for Thanksgiving. . . . We were all hurt. . . . The boys were really hurt. . . . They started crying and stuff like that, and I was really angry. . . . I wanted to go out and use drugs. . . . And I went to therapy, I went to music therapy, and I talked about it and . . . I was able to, like, recommit myself to my recovery, you know, and to, like, get . . . a good grounding [and] . . . realize what my priorities were. . . . Right then and there, I was really hurt. . . . I was powerless and I didn't like the powerlessness of it.

I didn't do a lot of . . . music exploring in my music therapy sessions because at the time there was so much going on for me. . . . Basically I used my therapist for, like, talking about my feelings. . . . I always ran from [my problems], and this time, I didn't. . . . I needed the music therapy as, like, an extension of everything else. . . . And because everyone [at the music school] knows the family, it was like it was okay to talk about . . . my kids and have someone tell me it was okay to feel the way I felt. . . . It gave me a new perspective [on] how I could see my children. . . . It helped . . . the relationship, and I hope this year that we learn to communicate better and that we learn to understand our needs as a family and our needs as family members, as individuals.

TAI. Like I said before, I hate therapy. [*Laughs.*] I really do. My mother always tries to get me and my brothers to go to therapy. . . . I would not go. When they would have family therapy, [it was] minus Tai. I was not there; I would never go. And some of the reasons I wasn't there were because every time . . . [I went], I never liked it. . . . My mother would always get a therapist from wherever she would go because she goes to regular therapy. . . . Well, she would get someone from there so the person already knew her stuff. . . . It just seemed like everyone was against us, me and my brothers; [they would ask us] why are we stressin' my mother out. . . . I didn't like that.

With the [music school], it was like everybody was neutral there. We had people we could talk to who were neutral. . . . Even if someone didn't . . . teach me my group or individual [session], I still had a relationship with them there from seeing them every week or just talking to them or whatever. And I still was able to talk to someone, you know, and say, "Well, you know, this is going on." And everyone wasn't always, like, [asking me], "Why are you stressin' out your mother?" Some people were, like, [saying], "Oh, I see your mother is stressin' you out." You know, it was, like, a different thing. It was neutral. . . . I felt like . . . everything wasn't my fault.

I . . . think that music is a good way to kind of, like, hide. . . . It's more like just express yourself, you know, through music or whatever. . . . It sneaks up on you, you know, 'cause you're [asked], "How did you feel singing that song?" And I'm, like, [saying], "Ewww" or "I thought blah blah blah last week." And it just comes out. It's a real comfortable thing . . . just like friends talking.

PLAYING MUSIC IN THE GROUP

Mary, Eric Miller, and Lynn Miller

ERIC AND LYNN'S INTRODUCTION

Mary (not her real name) is a resident, or "friend," as they are called, at Goal House, a halfway house in a beautiful rural setting. A nondenominational facility, Goal House emphasizes friends' strengths through participation—often through the arts—in a supportive community. Mary, 38, has been living at Goal House for 4 years. She has a history of psychotic episodes, suicide attempts, depression, and institutionalized treatment since the age of 20. She has been one of the most creative, expressive participants in the music therapy group. This chapter presents her written responses to questions we provided.

Music therapy group participants use percussion instruments, strings, piano, and voice in improvisations on individual or group themes. Through playing and discussion, they learn about their roles and relationships in the group and in the larger community.

MARY'S ACCOUNT

Music therapy has been a great way to encourage me to take risks. Looking back, one of the most destructive things I did to myself was chickening out when I had a challenge. It was mostly out of embarrassment because other people were watching. I'm learning to risk my pride. Eric (the therapist) has given me some basics about improvising on the piano while he plays guitar, usually while other people are singing or playing instruments. I'm finally creative! I'm not trying to be funny. I always bemoaned the fact that I've always been imitative but not creative. And I can do this! Of course sometimes it's great, sometimes it's so bad it hurts. In retrospect, I can see that I don't do as well when I stop listening to the rest of the group. The give-and-take, cooperation, conversation, and helping ourselves out make all the difference. When I'm in with others, I don't care about being judged.

It was an effort to attend the first three or so sessions of music therapy, like anything new, but it got real good real fast, and so far, it hasn't been going back again. We (the music therapy group) have really come up with some beautiful, spontaneous pieces of music singing. We all wished afterwards we had been recording them.

It's just good to see I can do something with my feelings, something I won't regret or get flack for and sometimes something actually creative. I've gone around in joy telling people that I can finally create. I'm hoping to get better and better.

Sometimes I come into the group and one or more persons and I are not getting along. It's very hard not to be on good terms again by the end of the group. This music therapy should also be applied to international relations.

One thing in my life that held me back was risk. It seemed as though I chickened out more than other people. I always had trouble opening up—it's pride, wanting to be alone, and wanting to be separate. It goes back to the food issue. I started to take risks in music therapy. Music therapy is great because I can do it with a synthesizer. I couldn't take the risk to get up and dance in front of people, but I can through music.

Eric says that if you don't get upset, you can quickly correct, make something good out of it. The whole thing about being self-conscious is being in front of an audience. But I think sometimes I feel like saying, "Let go, let go," but I still can't; I still go on caring so much about how I'm judged. Well, he says it's a skill you learn, to just accept the present and go on. An analogy of music to life, of course! Just a little like what we were saying earlier: people say you never get married until you totally give up on men. But I've heard that part too much for that ever to work for me. Sometimes I really care about whether I get married or not even though I don't want sex and I don't think I'd be a good mother. I just feel left out.

I remember singing "Be Not Afraid" when I was the only one in the church and Father was at the altar. Oh well.

I came up to the group from biofeedback therapy and Ellen (a group member) was at the synthesizer. I really felt the blow! Especially with the smile she gets on her face when she knows she has had that effect on me. It is like when several different meetings happen and she sits where I always used to sit with a big grin, almost challenging me to say something. In fact, I'm still angry about that. Generally she's always out to hurt because she feels so miserable; that's all she has. Aren't we all like that, but we just hide it somehow? When this happened with the synthesizer in music therapy, after we finished one song, Lynn (the therapist) asked for reactions and I said how it hurt that Ellen was playing the synthesizer. I did not talk about what she was doing, but I guess I said I was jealous. I was intent on getting some growth and affirmation out of this situation, knowing that's why God lets things happen that upset us. Ellen was not angry when I said how I was jealous. And I said sincerely that she played well. She was very grateful for that and then graciously offered me the keyboard back.

Earlier in my life, what I would have done in that situation is say, "No, thank you," kind of closing off a little because of my pride. But here I said, "Yes, thanks," and it hurt a little. The whole thing is about relationships—like we were saying earlier—about together or apart. So much I do is just to avoid "together." We have "together" growing up and it hurts so much that we learn to blank it out by the time we're adults. But that hurts even more.

Since Eric has shown me a little how to improvise, it's clear that I'm only good at all when listening to the rest of the group. It's true and such a clear analogy to all of life. If we're there, there's a part there for each of us to play, precisely for us and necessary for the whole. Even competing can be seen as good if we see that our competing helps us each to go on further; it almost helps. We all learn eventually that standing up and competing with another person is often the best way to make them feel comfortable. I think when people are apologetic, it often hides resentment and it's manipulative. I did it for years and complained that other women were being bitchy when I hadn't done anything to them.

But closeness, it's awful—to get as close as we were as adolescents, remembering feeling the flesh, the sweat, the tears, the skin of my sisters, and the horrible way we fought. I feel no warmth or emotion now from touching anyone's flesh. My flesh is dead. Ellen brings that back too much. I held her once while she sobbed. It was awful; it almost made me sick.

If I could take the pain and fear and hate and need inside me and change it into beautiful melodies; oh, God, it would be wonderful. I believe I can someday, no matter how little evidence or promise of it there is now.

My big block is fear now, although it's pretty clear that the fear is unfounded! I would have never believed I could be comfortable in the life I'm in now, doing the things I do, looking the way I do. It would have sounded horrible, like a life of hell, but I feel better than ever before in my whole life! So things that sound scary to me now probably aren't anything to be really afraid of. What keeps me from moving on in trust? Well, while improvising in music, I guess one thing is I'm afraid to take initiative; rather, I'd say I have that prob-

lem in life and should look to my music to see a way out of it. It's
being afraid to make a mistake. We're back to fear, to just trying
something with the distinct possibility of failing. The opinions and
judgments of others, like Eric and I were talking about, they hurt so
much growing up.

I should get the emphasis off myself for a minute and see what's
going on with the others, but I feel treated unfairly by them. Also I
have to be real with what I'm going through. Does that mean not cen-
soring my thoughts? That feeling of going on and on in a keyboard
solo, knowing it is awful, wondering if you should just give up—
reminds me of sex I used to have. I feel like everybody there in the
room feels the same way and is aware of your every emotion and
thought played out in your terrible music. I've definitely found that
that is not true, at least not always. What other people think ties
most of us in knots, I think—ties us up more than almost anything
else. Does anyone get past it totally? Would I want to get past it
totally? What else blocks the music? Not being honest with myself,
expectations, taking myself too seriously? I'm too blocked on blocks.

I don't know too much about self-esteem. Is it valuing yourself,
not being conceited? People always used to say to me, "Well, you can't
love other people unless you love yourself first!" and I always
assumed that they meant that I had to change somehow, to love myself and that I couldn't love myself the way I was. But I don't think
they meant that, not all of them. We have to love ourselves with our
faults. I think I always took that the wrong way, like an insult. In
music, I know that any effort, anything I play is okay, even with all
the mistakes. I stop feeling like I have to measure up to anything.
Other people's musical mistakes in the group don't make me like
those people less. And if I did, that shouldn't have an effect on their
self-esteem.

The truth is I have been really, really embarrassed in music
therapy pretty much in the way I feared; the fears were coming true
more than in real life. After the embarrassment passes, though, it
hurts, and I remember it hurting for a while afterwards; I remember
feeling pretty sure people were gloating and smirking at my failure
and embarrassment. But I would never have chosen for that not to
happen. Probably I knew right away it was furthering my growth.

Eric just asked me, "Were there times while playing when you
just forgot the embarrassment and really got into your playing?"
Sure, it was the best. It was so sweet to feel and create a short little
melody. I haven't brought—well, I have brought this into life a little.
It's the greatest, even just the fact that I'm being braver than I ever
was. I need to do that a lot more in life, though. I know that the point
it brings you to can be so fulfilling.

Narrative 12

JAZZY THE WONDER SQUIRREL

Jazzy, Leslie L. Hunter,
and Donna W. Polen

LESLIE AND DONNA'S
INTRODUCTION

Jazzy, who calls himself Jazzy the Wonder Squirrel, is a 19-year-old who began music therapy in 1993 at a center-based alternative school for learning disabled and emotionally disturbed students run by a county cooperative. Leslie worked with him in individual as well as group sessions, in which he improvised on the piano, keyboard, and synthesizer. By the time Jazzy was recommended for placement back at his home district, he was composing complete song phrases and songs and was becoming a master of the synthesizer. Donna began work with him during the 1995–96 school year. We interviewed Jazzy jointly and have transcribed the interview here.

THE INTERVIEW

*Do you remember any of your playing back in the alternative program days? How would you describe your playing?**

Sometimes I feel it wasn't as bad as I made it out to be and other times I feel just the opposite—[a perfect description of] my life. I had a lot of anger. I don't have very much self-esteem and never have. I have a lot more than I've ever had. Now I'm able to put on a façade, but sometimes it's kind of fun, so it's not that hard to put on anymore. Sometimes I would get really pissed off; I'd skip a class and say, "Mrs. Hunter, mind if I hop on the piano?" "Do you have permission?" "Yeah, I've got permission." Of course she knew I was lying to her, but I needed to play. Sometimes I was really angry or really depressed. If I couldn't get to the piano because there was a class, I'd just do my little bass tapes stuff on the keyboard. . . . Now I'm able to

---

* Throughout, Leslie's and Donna's questions are italicized and in separate paragraphs from Jazzy's comments.

take ideas or my feelings [and put them in my music]. I always had my feelings. . . . I think everybody puts their feelings at times in their music, meaning to and not meaning to. I believe a lot of people think that you accidentally put your feelings in your music. I don't think that's always true. I really don't.

Over time, did the actual playing help clarify things?

I would go in there and I'd play. I don't know if it's because you get wrapped up in it or what it is, but I wouldn't necessarily feel better, but if I didn't feel as pissed off or as hurt as I was, then I just completely forgot about it for a few hours. I'm willing to bet anything that it was just because I got wrapped up in it, 'cause that's how I am. When I get wrapped up in something, nothing else really matters.

Don't you find that your attention can be really focused for very long periods of time when you're involved in the music?

Yes, when I'm interested in something or when I'm actually accomplishing something, I don't like to leave what I'm doing, because once I stop, chances are I'm not going to go back to it, and if I do, it will be a quick rush job. For me, it's more tedious than hard. Getting the ideas and staying with one idea at a time is a challenge.

What emotional release do you get out of playing piano with someone else?

I love playing along with people. My music therapist is just as creative as I am and she doesn't even realize it. I don't think she does. She always makes me start. She knows it's a little task thing for me. [She] always lets me figure out what to start off with and she adds on unless I say, "Why don't you start us off today?" I always find a really slick way to get out of working. I usually stay on the right side [of the piano]. I like to do the bass line, but if I do the bass line, it's the same thing over and over. . . . When we do a duet, I actually do have fun. Sometimes it's hard to figure things out and not feel stupid and laugh at yourself, but even if I'm not really getting much accomplished, it's fun just to be able to jam. My friend, R, has one of those incredible, nice-sounding wooden flutes. [It has] great sound, man. I'd play the piano and he'd flute back and forth and he'd play the flute like this one [Ms. Polen] plays the piano. I mean, she's like you [Ms. Hunter]. You guys are great pianists. [*Jazzy makes swooshing sounds.*] She can do everything I'd be able to do with five hands in just one of hers. I love to jam.

How has your keyboard and piano improvisation changed over the years?

While I was still at the alternative program, I would just play solos. I would sit in the soundproof room at the keyboard and pound away at the keys and it sounded kind of like a bass tape. It was very generic and cheesy sounding. I've gone from that kind of cheesy techno to trance techno, which is an intense form of relaxation techno music. Now I've gone straight to industrial, which is heavy metal and techno mixed; my basic style now is mainly industrial and if it's not an industrial song, then it's mainly trance. I'm also doing some jungle techno as well. . . . I have a thing for black keys—I'm in love with black keys. I have actually been able to move away from the black keys and go down to the white keys. And now I'm kind of getting back into mixing them both, which is what I should have been doing all the time anyway. It takes practice, but I'll get it. I play what sounds good. That's why I want to learn some key signatures so I can learn what goes with what and get more ideas. I've been able to get off the black keys and intermix the two. I've also been able to kind of be very free or loose with my hands while playing. . . . I really have no use for it [my left hand] except basic things, but it gets me by. Even though I'm still not very loose with my left hand, I have sometimes been able to go all out. . . . [Sometimes] it almost sounds like I know what I'm doing when it comes to fingering and stuff like that.

What has music therapy meant to you?

I've gotten a lot out of music therapy 'cause for one, Ms. Polen's been a great friend to me and she's taught me quite a bit I didn't know. She's got me looking at things differently from how I used to.

Perhaps you didn't have a real awareness of what it [the music] was doing; you just knew you needed it. And now the awareness has sort of caught up with the effect of it and you know what it can do for you. . . . That's all come along and you hear it in the development of your music.

I never even realized what it was until a few months ago when I was talking to you [Ms. Polen]. I love my girlfriend, N; she's great, but at the same time, she's 17 years old now and we're going through problems. Every relationship has problems. That's fine; I understand that. I go to visit her and I get ignored a lot and it took me a long time to realize this. I always knew it—I didn't realize it. Just like with the music. . . . I said to N that part of the reason why I get so mad, sometimes even jealous of the fact that the phone sometimes seems to be more important . . . is [*emphasizes*] I need to be nurtured. I didn't have it much as a kid. I always knew that, but I didn't realize that until I was talking to N. Just like she likes to be cuddled, I need that kind of cuddling; I need that nurturing. I guess sometimes I can get that out of the music. I can relate that to the music. When I start to get somewhere and I have to stop—I hate that. I think that with the music, when I start to get somewhere, I don't have to stop. In a way, that is kind of like a substitute.

When we first started working together, the music was just driven—constant eighth notes in a fast, loud 4/4 meter. There was no variation of tempo, dynamics, or meter.

[When I started working on my CD], I think that was where I got what you guys were saying: the da-da-da-da pounding rhythm. I started expanding and sort of learning more. . . . A lot of my stuff is very full and very busy, but at the same time, it doesn't have that constant same beat. A lot of my stuff is starting to be like jungle.

That's because there are so many more levels. How did that happen for you? How did you go from one style to another?

It came from my inspiring bands and they are all 100 percent different from each other. Led Zeppelin is one of my inspirers. There's another group called Enigma. One of my main inspirations is Trent Reznor of Nine Inch Nails. He inspires me in a lot of ways. I like his music. He does his music very similar to the way I do mine. I mean, his is a lot more complex than what I do. He has people come in with him and help him. [He's] kind of like my singer; my singer would stay after school with me every day and whenever I needed him, he was there. . . . I read an article and Trent stated that he was going to switch from industrial, "since it isn't a happening thing," to hip-hop just to anger his fans. If I have the chance to get in the music business, if I can get anywhere in the field, I almost guarantee that I could take over from where he is. If I had the equipment he has, I would probably do better stuff than what he does. I hate to say this about someone who inspires me, but these are my beliefs. I'm starting to discover more about myself. I'm starting to have a little more faith and confidence. . . . My fourth inspirer is Orbital. They are probably the best band you'll ever hear in terms of trance. The music blows your mind; all their music is this way. If I had $100 and I hadn't heard them in 20 years and their latest CD cost $100, I'd go out and get it, because they have never let me down. I don't think they have one song I don't like. They have songs I can't listen to all the time because their style is slowly built up, but it builds up correctly and spontaneously and it keeps my attention—and I have a short attention span.

Mental Labyrinth
Quickly turn,
And see what you can.
Time is running out,
Time has ran you down,
And your life
Has ran you all around.
Time has stopped,
And left you feeling down.

Slowly halt,
And watch the clock's hand,
Spinning all around . . . around . . . around . . . around.
Time made your frown.
Too busy for a life,
Time ran you down.
Time has stopped
And left you with a frown.

The clock has stopped ticking.
Your heart has stopped kicking you.
The world has been placed.

In your mind,
In your mind.
Trapped in time,
Time and space.

Space—
What a
Beautiful place.
Lost.
Lost in your mind.
I can't find an exit.
Where is the sign?
Where do you keep it?
Way, way down, or
In front of my face?

Trapped,
In my mind,
Without you,
What could I find?

When you were getting ready to leave the alternative program for the high school, you had a huge amount of anxiety. You said: "How am I going to fit in? No one's going to like me."

Everyone loves me; I have too many friends now. Everyone wants to hang out with me and I don't have enough time. I hang out with the understanding crowd, the ones that everyone picks on. I feel mostly comfortable with them 'cause they're understanding people and very accepting people and they don't look like everyone else does. I have a few jock friends and a few preppy friends, but for the most part, I tend to stick with the punk and the freak crowd. They're the best kids I'll ever know. . . . Kids look up to me; I even have fans! . . . I just think I'm very lucky I go to the high school. I think I'm very lucky to have teachers who care about me. I think that's another thing I learned. That's something I gained at the alternative. I didn't care about anything but being a wise guy until I got tired of seeing everyone else do it. I got close with Mrs. Hunter [and other teachers]. I started understanding that teachers are people, too. And actually I get along better with teachers now. I guess you could look at me and say, "He's a teacher's pet," but I'm not like that. If someone's cool to me, I'm cool to them. Most teachers aren't jerks. Starting last year, Mr. B [one of the high school music teachers] asked me to record a couple of kids. Then I started recording all the concerts at the high school: orchestra, band, choir, jazz ensemble. When I first got to do that, in a way, I felt that I was, in a sense, a teacher. I told my music teacher that it felt really great to do that. To record those kids made me feel like Mr. B or like a music therapist. When I recorded those two kids, I gave them a little drumbeat to help them out 'cause they needed to keep a tempo. One of those kids is now my singer. I told Mr. B that I really appreciated having the chance to set up the recording because I was able to give a part of myself and show that I do know something. I felt like an authority figure; I felt like I was doing something good for someone else. Whether it was something small or not, to them, it meant a great deal. I was doing something responsible and I have never really been responsible before. Now the kids at school know that they can come to me if they need something recorded or if they want to work on a tune. I was so psyched—I loved it! Mr. B realized how important all of this was for me and he asked me if I'd be willing to show a few high school students some of the basics of music technology: how to turn the keyboard on, what computer program to use, and how to record. So I started teaching my own class at the high

school. Mr. B and I interact with each other about the music soft-
ware; we kind of converse about it. . . . It feels good when people ask
me to do things for them 'cause they feel like they can count on me.

*What are you going to tell the kids that you see at psychiatric
center next week?*

What I think I'm going there for is basically because I was in
a similar situation. I was in this mind-set that I'll never be any
better and I never have been: I'll never get out of the alternative
school, I'll never get out of the "being alone syndrome," and I'll
never get out of this or that. Basically all I needed and basically
all anyone ever needs to get anywhere in this world is . . . a goal
and you need something you love to do. You need something you
enjoy. Otherwise you're not going to be doing anything. . . . And I
believe for me that goal—one [goal]—was having a girlfriend.
That was a big thing for me. It always has been, because, like I
said, of the nurturing thing. . . . I mean, I feel with the music I
can't be let down; can't be let down any more than I can let myself
down. So that's something that I can almost count on for me. [It's]
my goal or my hobby. I think it's very important for people to have
a hobby. That's what got me to where I am: having a hobby, having a goal, having the need to be better than I am, having the
need to make people happy, having the need to basically show off.
I show off all the time. It doesn't mean I'm doing it in the bragging
way. . . . I guess that's about the closest I do to being kind of
bragging when I do show my stuff. I love to show what I'm doing. I
hide things in my music; that's my main part, that's my problem. I
hide things in there and I want people to hear them. . . . I hide a
lot of things in my music. Ask Ms. Polen. You can listen to it.
That's why I like [the group] Orbital so much. You gotta think
about what you're listening to. I have never, ever been able to
hear everything they've ever done on any song. I honestly believe
this. I don't think I heard every part 'cause they hide things in
their music. It's almost like in the seventies when they did the
backward stuff. It's a similar idea; it's also conscious, but they
hide tubular bells over here to the left [so] you don't even know
they're there until you really, really separate the music and listen
for it. The only problem I have with that is now I tend to separate
a lot of stuff, making it sound completely different—sometimes
better, sometimes worse than it really does sound.

*When we were talking about going to [the] psychiatric center a
while ago, you said that maybe this [going to the center] isn't such
a good idea. I said, "Okay—why?"*

My concerns were [this]. When I was at the alternative, if some-body came in back then exactly like me with the computer and the keyboard and all this other stuff, it would have been cool. I would have loved it; I would have loved everything he or she had to say. And then I would have been really pissed off and really angry 'cause I wouldn't have had the funds for it. But I was wondering—and my concerns were—"Gee, if these kids are a little bit worse off than I used to be and I couldn't handle it, how is this going to affect them?" Ms. Polen opened my mind to think of things I never thought of. I was afraid I'd hurt these kids more than I'd help them. That was my main concern. I had mentioned it to her. I said, "I don't really know if it's a great idea." Plus, my computer likes to shut off and it won't even work for me. I think I figured it out, though. Ms. Polen said, "That's a good concern you have, but was it [the music hardware and software] just handed to you?" And I said, "Oh yeah." It wasn't just handed to me. She said something like, "You earned it; you saved hard and you struggled to get all this stuff." I said that, yeah, I struggled to get the stuff and to continue on with it and that was a really good point. I would never have thought of that. And it actually felt good 'cause it reminded me [that] lately I've been starting to actually realize things about myself. I've done this, this, this, this, and this. . . . [I didn't real-ize] until I actually had to consider how to put it on paper and do a résumé. Now I have a separate résumé for just my volunteer and music stuff. . . . [It contains] making the CD, teaching, talking to the kids at the psychiatric center, doing this chapter, the leadership pro-gram, and the portfolio CD program. I started thinking more and more about what I have done. I think, "Yeah, that's pretty cool; I made a CD." I think that's nice, I got a CD. But until I actually had to think about everything I've done, it wasn't that impressive to me. It still wouldn't be all that impressive to me. The one nice thing that N [girlfriend] always says to me is "I don't know anyone else who's ever made a CD before." And that's a true statement. When they build up like they do, that's when I start feeling actually I'm not that bad a kid. I actually have been doing some special things.

Stiph
You were aware of the way I feel about you;
You were the one who put loving in my life.
The stars in your eyes reveal the secrets to your lies,
And every time I turn around, I feel your sweet demise.

Hey, hey, everyone is hating you;
Hey, hey, they're all looking down upon you.
Hey, hey, everyone is hating you;
Hey, hey, they're all looking down upon you,
Upon you.

You are my secret,
My secret world.
You were my sacred,
My sacred girl.

Every time I look in the mirror,
It's you, you, you I see.
Every time I see you, it's clearer
You're not for me.

Hey, hey, everyone is hating you;
Hey, hey, I want to break you.
Hey, hey, I wonder what is eating you;
Hey, hey, I wonder who is touching you.

You are my secret,
My secret world.
You were my sacred,
My sacred girl.

POSTSCRIPT

If it was just the CD and maybe two other things, I wouldn't
be like this, but now I realize I've done so much more. I mean, for
cryin' out loud, I'm going to the Concord Hotel to play a song off
my CD that I'm not too proud of, but a lot of other people are. I'm
proud to be going to the Concord. I'm one of five people who were
picked by the statewide school music association to perform at a
special electronic music composition session. I'm going to play at
the Concord in front of a lot of people and I'm finally getting recognition for recording the concerts at the high school. And one
more thing: I love the group of kids I spoke with at the psychiatric
center. They are just a wonderful bunch of kids. I'm looking forward to my next speech with them.

SINGING MY WAY THROUGH IT: FACING THE CANCER, THE DARKNESS, AND THE FEAR

Maria Logis and Alan Turry

ALAN'S INTRODUCTION

Maria came into music therapy with a willingness to open herself to new experiences. It was clear that she loved music, and as she playfully explored the instruments and her voice, she began to allow herself to express her feelings through creative interactive musicmaking. Despite tremendous upheaval in her life, she seemed determined to gain from the crisis, to glean something meaningful from it. Often at her most painful moments of despair and hopelessness, Maria would begin to create a melody or the potential for a melody and words from deep feelings. I admired her integrity as she entered into the unknown.

We have used the writing of this narrative as part of our ongoing therapy. For Maria, the act of participating in this writing project is one more way of overcoming the lifelong feeling of being silenced. Maria has written her account from her journals and tapes of the sessions, and I have added my experience of the music. Maria has always been open about her experience in therapy and is proud to use her real name.

MARIA'S EXPERIENCE

Crisis

I was diagnosed with non-Hodgkin's lymphoma in the fall of 1994. I was in shock. I could feel nothing; silence and paralysis took over. In the midst of all my anguish, I turned to God for help, and the help that came was not at all what I would have imagined. I found music and, in it, a balm that made it possible for me to resist the crushing silence that enveloped me when I learned that I was sick.

As I look back now, I know that the experience forced me to decide whether I was going to fight for my life or not. The diagnosis shook me deeply and somehow made it possible for me to break out of my habitual thinking patterns. I began to search for and was open to new experiences.

Finding Music

The thought that came to me was that I should sing. My musical training was limited to piano lessons that my mother forced me to take—that I hated—and some singing lessons as an adult. Some 10 years before my diagnosis, I went to a music and t'ai chi workshop. All 80 participants got to sing and improvise. I had a ball. People there encouraged me to sing. I started private singing lessons and enrolled at a music school for theory and duet singing. I was very excited and had a great time! I had never dreamed I could sing. Soon I joined a gospel choir. It was all quite wonderful! My friends were excited for me. Slowly, the lessons got tougher. I wasn't good enough; I didn't practice enough; I lacked discipline; I couldn't read music; it was taking too much of my time. I dropped the choir and then I dropped the classes, hoping to salvage the singing lessons. But after 2 years of singing lessons, I gave up, totally frustrated and defeated. It was absolutely clear that I could not keep up with even the most minimal standards. I kicked myself for ever thinking I could sing.

So the recurrence of the thought that I should sing seemed pretty ridiculous, yet I pursued it. I got names from friends. On some days, I had appointments for tests (to pinpoint the diagnosis), and on others, I went to see singing teachers. I really had no idea what I was doing. I just was putting one foot in front of the other. My dentist gave me a name that turned out to be a colleague of Alan's, and since she lived too far away, she referred me to him. The first time we met, we made lots of sounds, and I found myself laughing for the first time in the weeks since the diagnosis. I decided to come back. What began in November of 1994 and continues to this day is a process that has completely transformed my life.

My struggle to accept my diagnosis and my great fear of treatment came up as soon as I started to sing. We created music together in which I expressed my terror of treatment and my deep distrust of the doctors. The words just kept coming. I surely had a lot of feelings about the doctors and chemotherapy. Alan treated my music and words like they were important; he kept me going by improvising on the piano. So I kept singing and more and more words and feelings came out:

> She didn't want to go ahead with the treatment.
> She told herself it wasn't what she wanted to do.
> She didn't trust the doctors.
> She didn't want to get sick.
> She didn't want to follow their advice.
> She said . . . *No, I'd rather not do it!!!*
> But all the logic said,
> You have to go for this treatment.
> Oh . . . *No! No! No! No! No! No! No!*
> Oh yeah, you've got to go for this treatment.

I sang about myself in the third person, trying to get some distance on the situation. It was deeply satisfying to sing *"No."* I didn't dare say those words to the doctors. Then there is another voice, the one that tells me that I must go for the treatment. It is the voice of all the doctors and my own logical thinking side. The logical me starts to yell at the frightened me, and in fact the volume in the following section is quite high and scary to listen to.

> Tell the truth.
> What is it?
> Stop this stuff.
> Tell the truth, tell the truth.
> Ugh . . . ugh . . . ugh.

Alan had told me it was okay to make any sounds at all, so from the yelling, I started groaning, and then all these sounds led me to a deep lyrical lament.

> They tell me I'm sick.
> They tell me I'm sick.
> They tell me I'm sick.
> And I have to learn to believe it.
> I have to stop saying it isn't true.
> How can I believe it?

How can I believe it?
How can I believe it?
They tell me I'm sick.

THEY TELL ME I'M SICK

Figure A

When I would speak to my friends about my illness and my concerns, I was logical, organized—and even if I was upset, I had a plan. It was when I sang that I felt my fear and anguish. The words that came out of my mouth both surprised me and didn't surprise me because they were about my "truth." I had not expressed that level of feeling to anyone, yet I knew the feelings well. Alan's improvising made it possible for me to get the feelings out into the open in sound and to create melodies in the process. He communicated a deep acceptance of my words and music. I was amazed but did not have time to reflect on that for several months.

Alan suggested that I might want to tape our sessions; this sounded like a good idea, so I started to bring a tape with me to each session.*

I thought it might be helpful for Maria to listen to these improvisations and suggested she could make a tape of our sessions. In this way, she could have something to hold on to—I hoped a way of

---

* Throughout Maria's narrative, Alan's comments are italicized.

*expressing, identifying, and containing feelings that threaten her emo-
tional stability. I hoped she would gain some sense of control over
what was happening to her. Maria asked me how she would feel listening to the tape. I told her I didn't know, but after she began to talk
about it, I encouraged her to listen not as a music critic but as a person searching for her truth and to express herself honestly. She spoke
of how hard it was for her not to be judgmental. She continued singing and started listening to the tapes outside of our sessions. She listened to one session and said it was intense and sad. It helped her
deal with her ambivalence about picking a doctor and having courage. She began to share the tapes with other people. This led our therapy in a novel direction.*

A Breather

In January 1995, I went for a second CT [computed tomography]
scan in advance of chemotherapy and, much to my surprise, learned
that the lymph nodes had shrunk. One doctor, a world-class lymphoma expert, insisted I start the treatment immediately because the
lymph nodes may "wax and wane, but your lymphoma is in the bone
marrow, and if you wait till you have symptoms, it will be too late for
the chemotherapy to be effective." I got a second opinion, and that
doctor felt that I could start treatment right away, but [because of]
the shrinkage of the lymph nodes, he saw no harm in waiting for a
month or two. He emphasized that lymphoma can't be cured and
[that] at some point in the near future (as soon as the lymphoma
became more active), I would need treatment. The third opinion I got
was like the second. I struggled in rejecting the first doctor's solution
because of her highly regarded expertise and the fact that neither the
second nor the third doctors thought her course of action was off the
mark. They were simply willing to wait and she was adamant about
the need to start immediate treatment. I could not decide which doctor to pick.

So pick a doctor you can trust.
Pick a doctor you can trust,
And trust your judgment; you'll pick the right one.
You've certainly done a lot of research

I breathed a sigh of relief once I decided to wait; it felt like a stay
of execution. I was full of gratitude for each day.

Singing for My Friends

While working with Alan, I also met Janet Savage, a wonderful singer and coach, and started to work with her, too. She listened to some of the tapes from the sessions with Alan and said, "These are songs." I was really astonished when she suggested that I perform these "songs" for a gathering of my friends. I had already begun sharing the tapes with my close friends; they would stare at the floor, unable to make eye contact, since the intensity was sometimes too much to bear, yet they genuinely thanked me for sharing this music, so I prayed about Janet's suggestion and discussed it with Alan, and soon we were planning a celebration of 1 year without chemotherapy, a celebration in song.

Maria selected musical motifs she found meaningful. She began to memorize the words and melodies, creating songs. We had not thought of them as songs before this point. It seemed to be a way of containing them in an aesthetic way that would reach others. This was not something we set out to do, but it became a part of the therapy process.

It took a while to get used to calling some of these improvisations "songs." What did that make me, I asked myself again and again, a musician, a singer? No, it was not possible for me to call myself a singer or a musician. I wasn't disciplined, I lacked training, yet I moved ahead, trusting Janet. It is hard for me to describe how fantastic the process that we then entered into was. Janet coached me, helping me to put a program together, to sequence the songs, and, together with Alan, we began to rehearse. It was like dying and going to heaven. It was absolutely unbelievable. Rehearsing was fun; I felt so important. I let my fantasy go wild. For the hours that we were rehearsing, I was a singer. It meant so much to me that these improvisations [that] came from my guts and my heart could have value to someone besides [me] and Alan.

When I called to invite my friends, they were flabbergasted. Here I was dealing with a life-threatening illness, yet I was inviting them to a concert of original music at my house.

When Maria first introduced the idea of a concert, I was unsure. I wanted to support the natural direction that our therapy was taking.

We discussed the idea together. Would it contribute to the therapy process? The event itself fueled the therapy process as Maria focused on the event in the next session. She wondered what her mother, with whom she struggled throughout her life, would think of her involvement in music.

DO I DARE IMAGINE

Figure B

Preparing for the concert was an exhilarating experience. I practiced the songs and rented a piano for the concert, thinking that I might eventually decide to buy one (this in the face of the terrible experience I had playing piano as a kid). Singing the songs for my friends was one of the happiest days of my life, and I have had very few days in my life that I could describe as happy. When I look at the photographs, I see myself smiling in joyous exuberance. I was celebrating a year without chemotherapy. It was like flying. I felt so alive. I was "singing my way through" the anguish of this illness.

The freedom of the music therapy process was exhilarating. I could not get over the fact that I could not make any mistakes in improvisation. I sang not only about being sick but about my lifelong sadness and despair.

Pain and Darkness

As I sang, what started to come out was the despair and the sadness and silence of my life. The lyrics poured out of me. I was going beyond my cancer to my lifelong depression, my own oppression. Somehow I was able to give it sound and to express my feelings in a way that I had never done all my life. What I discovered in music therapy was that I had "no voice." I would not have used that term before, but it came out of the music. Images of silence, oppression, and darkness abound in the improvisations. I was overwhelmed, full of tears, and wondered why all this was coming up in me after so many years of psychotherapy.

After many years of psychotherapy, I had come to understand that much of my sadness went all the way back to a toxic relationship with my mother. I was to have no individuality or identity. I was to be an object perfectly in tune with my mother's desires. But it didn't work out that way. Instead I was fat, ugly, sad, and stupid. My mother got frustrated. I just went through the motions. I was compliant, but I started to eat compulsively, was depressed, had no opinions, and was convinced that I would not or could not live to be 25 years old. However, I always acted as if everything was fine. It was a requirement that I never questioned. So I never learned how to know what I was really thinking or feeling. I sang about my pain and about having "no voice."

> Woman, why are you weeping?
> Woman, why are you weeping?
> Woman, why are you weeping?
> They've taken away my voice.
> They've taken away my song
> And I can't find it anymore.

WOMAN, WHY ARE YOU WEEPING?

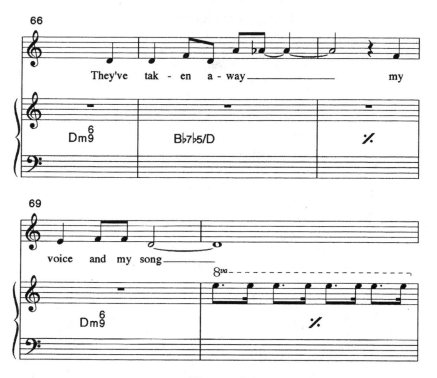

Figure C

The image of pain that came up for me again and again was a dark place with two people in it, the oppressor and the oppressed. In some songs it is a dark cave and I sing:

> She was silent.
> She asked for nothing.
> She wanted nothing.
> In the face of destruction, she was silent.

In another song, it's a dark cellar:

> Struggling to keep quiet,
> Struggling to keep silent.
> What's the sound inside the child?
> Choking, choking on her tears.
> Choking on her tears,
> Suffocating,
> Choking on her tears.

In another, it's the Everglades, with the silent alligator ready to "mangle" the child if she steps out of line. I looked up the definition of *mangle,* since that was the word I used in the improvisation. It said: "mangle: to disfigure or mutilate by cutting, bruising, crushing, to mar, ruin, spoil."

And in many songs, I sing about a dark castle. Bartók's opera *Bluebeard's Castle* inspired this image. In his opera, there are only two characters, the oppressor and the oppressed. The walls of the castle are covered with tears and there are seven locked doors. The terror of the castle is behind them: moaning, a torture chamber, a garden of flowers covered with blood, brilliant jewels tainted with blood, a lake of tears, and, finally, dead women. The music made it possible for me to explore these images in a very deep way. By singing, I found out how much power these images had for me and I began to see that it might be possible to journey out of this darkness (see "Rats in the Cellar" lyrics—"why do you go back to the cellar?"). I was trying to give up my deep attachment to the oppression.

The process of singing about the oppression is the very process that is freeing me from it. Because of the music, the images came easily, and the images, combined with the music, illuminate the dark and hidden aspects of my pain and anguish.

Trusting God

When I was diagnosed with cancer, the old issues came to the fore: Was I worthy to live? Was I willing to lift a finger to help myself? Something miraculous was happening as Alan and I worked: melodies and words poured out of me.

Do I really want to be alive?
Do I really want to get through this or not?
Maybe I would rather not make it.
I kinda just want to slide,
Slide down and give it all up.

I was grateful that when this illness hit me I had a relationship with God that I could turn to. I found myself praying in song. Alan and I were improvising vocally, an a cappella duet, which then led me into a time of intense prayer. The words of Mary's prayer (the *Magnificat*) in Luke's gospel filled my being. Alan played the melody that I was singing and enhanced it, making it more beautiful. When he sang with me, we just took off. Then I came back to my solo and my tears and my fear.

My soul magnifies the Lord, my God
And my spirit rejoices in God my savior.

I prayed for courage and for the strength to tell the truth about my illness and my sadness.

Through God's grace, I found music and, in it, a balm that made it possible for me to resist the crushing silence that enveloped me once I learned that I was sick. As I look back now, I know that the experience forced me to decide if I was going to fight for my life or not. The diagnosis shook me deeply and somehow made it possible for me to break out of my habitual thinking patterns. I began to search for and was open to new experiences. I turned my life over to the power of God and found music.

"Rats in the Cellar"

I was singing about being invisible; it was something I longed for when I found myself with people. I never knew what to say; my mother had done her job well. The melody that accompanies the words *I want to disappear* is incongruous with the words—it's a kind of piano bar music that seems to have no importance.

I don't want to be seen; I don't want to be heard.
I just want to disappear, I want to disappear,
I want to disappear, I want to disappear
So you can't see me, so you can't know me,
So you can't hassle me.
I want to disappear.
Then I don't have to worry what you think.
Then I don't have to handle what you say.
Then I don't have to be bothered.
Then I don't have to give a damn.
I'm going to disappear, I'm going to disappear,
And you won't find me, you can't hassle me,
Criticize me, bother me, no, no.
I'm just going to disappear, I'm just going to disappear.

Yet as I sing, I am filled with despair. This then leads to me imagining an invisible world with invisible people.

I go to the invisible world.
I go to the invisible world—
It gets too hard in the real world—
The invisible world.
I sleep, I sleep, I sleep.
I don't do a thing but sleep,
Go through the motions.
I sleep, I sleep, I sleep, I sleep.
I hate to remember my life.
I sleep, I sleep, I sleep.

The music changes to a softer dynamic, is rubato with alternating minor and major chords based on the Dorian mode with some delicate dissonances. There is more of a sense of fragility in the music, as the chords are in inversion and not in the bass end of the piano.

I have finally said what I feel when I sing "I hate to remember my life." It took going through the anger about food, the desire to disappear, and the invisible world to get to the deep despair. At this point I started looking for an instrument and I found the guiro. The scratching sound was fearsome. A scream started to come up in me. The sounds I made imitated the shrieking/screaming guiro and I was filled with the image of rats. I wanted to scream.

Ka . . . gruks . . . kruks.
Rats in the cellar . . . rats in the cellar,
Rats in the cellar.
Ugh . . . rats in the cellar, eating my bones, ooh.
Rats in the cellar, eating my bones, ooh.
Rats in the cellar, eating my bones.
Rats in the cellar, eating my bones.
Rats in the cellar, eating my bones.
Rats in the cellar, rats in the cellar,
Rats in the cellar, eating my bones, ooh.

The music builds to dissonant clusters as Maria alternates between singing a line and vocalizing long tones on "ooh." Maria's voice has changed here. It sounds more rooted in her body, in her lower register, and supported strongly with her breath. The music has an ambiguous tonal center; it alternates between a Phrygian and Locrian mode. Maria herself is helping to shift the tonal center, widening her vocal range.

I was overwhelmed with sadness, and the next melody knocks me out as I listen to it now. It is a poignant moment when I ask myself to give up the return to the painful and oppressive cellar. It is a heartfelt plea for sanity and I ask, with the utmost care and gentleness, "Why?" It is so clear to me that another alternative exists, yet I persist in repeating the same old destructive patterns.

Suddenly Maria sings a very clear melody as she asks her question, "Why, I'm asking you why?" The time for the dissonant clusters is over. Now she needs harmonies that would help her to explore this melody. As she sings about the turquoise waters and sailing south, I encourage her with flowing arpeggiated chords. Her voice and lyrics are full of a very deep sadness.

As Alan played, I could see and feel the turquoise waters, the warm sun. He played music that was exactly in tune with me, and I felt my sadness more intensely. My song continued.

RATS IN THE CELLAR

Figure D

I should ask you why; I am asking you why.
Why do you go back to the cellar?
Why do you go back to the cellar?
Why don't you stay on the ship sailing south?
Why don't you stay on the ship sailing south?
Why? . . . Oh why do you go back to the cellar?
Why, tell me why, tell me why
You go back to the cellar.
Why, oh why?
Stay on board; we're sailing south.
Stay on board; we're sailing south.
See the dolphins, see the dolphins
Jumping, leading the way, jumping.
See the dolphins, see the water; we're sailing south,
Sailing south.
Oh, woman,
Stay on board, stay on board.
It takes courage to stay on board.
Stay on board; we're sailing south.
Blue skies! Turquoise waters.
Would she rejoice?
Would she rejoice for me?
We're sailing south.
It takes courage to stay on board.

The music that Alan played with my turquoise water lyrics was refreshing and delightful. Again I asked myself, "Would she rejoice for me," referring to my mother and to the improvisation in another session where the turquoise waters originated. The theme of courage came up again—I had been singing about courage from the very first session. The music gives me courage, so I continue to explore the images and themes again and again, trying to learn, to change, to gain the courage to go on.

"I Don't Know How
You Love Me Through It All"

This music is about the deep struggle to accept myself and to believe that I am worthy of love. In the session, I start out talking to God, wondering how he can continue to love me despite the fact that I continually go backwards, repeating the same destructive behaviors again and again.

> I don't know how you love me through it all.
> I don't know how you love me through the stubbornness.
> I don't know how you love through the selfishness,
> The insensitivity.

> I don't know how you love me through the self-will,
> Through all the times I ignore you.
> I don't know how you love me through it all. .

The melody haunts me and I long to repeat it. Alan is playing strong chords and they keep me going. The tears start to overwhelm me when I decide to try to sing God's voice responding to me. The tears choke me, but I keep on singing, as Alan echoes my melody and words to give me the courage to go on.

> Oh my child, oh my child, oh my child,
> Oh my child, oh my child, oh my child,
> Oh my child, you are precious in my sight.
> Oh my child, you are precious in my sight, in my sight.
> All the hairs of your head are numbered in my sight.
> Oh my child, you are precious in my sight.

When I sing God's words for a second verse, I am far stronger vocally. Alan continues to sing with me, giving me the strength to go on. I end up belting out God's words to me: "Believe you are precious." This leads me to a prayer where I ask God to give me perspective and vision.

> To see myself through the eyes of God,
> To see myself through the eyes of my father,
> Not to see myself through the eyes of my mother,
> To see myself through the eyes of God,
> To see myself through the eyes of God,
> To see myself through the eyes of God,
> This is my prayer,
> Oh . . . God . . . my God . . . most high.

Intellectually, I can say that God loves me, therefore I am worthy of love, but as I sang about it, I believed it; it was real to me and that's why I was overwhelmed with tears. No longer was this a concept about God's love; it was the real thing. My loneliness started to have less power over me.

What followed next [was] a dark piano duet that led slowly to a mood change. I started to fool around vocally and on the piano, the dark mood lifted, there was lots of laughter, and pretty soon, I was singing.

> Maybe we should fool around a little.
> The piano has the giggles.
> We've got the giggles, we've got the giggles.
> We've got the giggles, we've got the tears,
> And everything in between.

This led us to a lyrical piece full of gratitude and joy. Alan was a little surprised when I said, "Who's better than us?" He laughed and repeated my question, not quite sure what I meant, so I went on to explain and he echoed my melody and words for a very touching closing.

> Who's better than us?
> Who's having more fun than we are?
> We have the tears, we have the giggles,
> And everything in between.
> We have the music.
> We have the music.
> We have the music.
> It goes to our souls.
> Our souls can sing.
> My soul can sing!
> My soul can sing!

The closing soared to a spiritual high.

MARIA'S SUMMARY

Creating a Notebook

Over time, I started to listen to the tapes of our sessions and wrote out all the words. I eventually created a notebook of lyrics from these tapes and many months later found someone who was able to transcribe the taped music onto music paper. I was deeply moved the first time I saw one of these "songs" on paper. All of this required a great deal of time and resources. By expending this effort on my own behalf, I was making an important statement to myself that I was worth something.

Sharing the Songs

A few months after the concert in my home, I had one at my church for a larger group of friends. Their support and love was deeply satisfying. In the spring of 1996, Alan arranged for me to share the music with students and faculty at a local university. Each experience of sharing the music publicly has helped me to claim my "voice."

I was amazed at the process. Dwelling within the embrace of music has helped me to create images about the many painful issues in my life, and the whole process of singing about silence is a way of defeating it. As I sing, I claim my voice.

Why Music?

What I know now that I could never have seen initially is how perfect this solution is for me. I asked God for help; he knew that my lifelong anguish was about silence and oppression, so he showed me a way that I could deal with all that pain. What could make you feel better in the face of crushing pain and silence? Utterance.

So he led me to music. Why music? Because it reaches me so deeply. The music made it possible for me to go deeply into my hunger, my fear, my anguish. It helped me to stay present and true to myself. There are few "ahas!" in music therapy, few insights. Instead there is the deep experience of exploring, touching, smelling, and feeling the pain. It's not a process of understanding the pain but rather a journey deep into the underworld and I have come back changed. Improvising creates an environment of greater focus and attention. If I can remain present, I make all kinds of discoveries. It's interesting, exciting, and it's full of surprises. I can be deeply authentic and that has made all the difference in my life.

Making Music

I am trying to understand the process by which all this music is created. I meet with Alan; everything is externally okay in my life; the cancer is in a partial remission; work is okay. We start making sounds, and ideas, words, and feelings come up out of me. Where do they come from, I wonder. How can I understand this? Pain and anguish pour out. Silliness and fun abound. I weep. The critic yells at me. Alan listens intently. He plays such beautiful music. I am touched deeply. A story unfolds over several sessions as words from one session come up again and again. For example, "Rats in the Cellar" eventually leads to the image of broken pieces all over the floor; they are the broken pieces of my life. The music allows me to discover my deeper reality. Alan and I build on each other's music, and at the end, the music brings me to a compassionate place of sanity.

A Radical Change

By creating all this music, something is changing radically in me. Sometimes I dare to call myself a singer, a musician. And this has tremendous implications for my life. It is [I] who always thought of herself as having nothing to say and always acted as if everything was fine, who was just getting by each day. I have lived with so much sadness and depression, and all those years of therapy and all the king's horses and all the king's men couldn't do anything about the broken pieces. But the music is God's great healing vehicle. I sing about the "song coming down on golden wings." I have faced the critic again and again in each session. She keeps telling me to shut up, that I'm boring, that no one wants to listen.

What has this music-making created in my life? I described myself as a changed person. I have struggled for some time with a label for what I am doing. Am I a musician? The answer is *no*. Am I a singer? The answer is no. Why? In my mind and in most people's view, a singer is someone who falls into one of two categories: professional and amateur. I clearly do not fit the category of a professional singer. But the word *amateur* has an air of condescension about it. It implies a hobby or extracurricular activity, a pleasant way to spend time as in a distraction or amusement. *Amateur* does not communicate the commitment, passion, and relevance that music now has in my life.

> I found my life at last,
> Leaving the darkness behind.

Music sustains me. I am deeply involved in listening to music, making music, and trying to learn more about singing as well as about music theory. But I don't meet even the most minimal requirements of a professional singer, songwriter, or musician. So I struggle mightily with these labels and my music is full of lyrics about the struggle. I wonder how long I will be allowed to continue to do what I'm doing. I fear that it will soon be over, there will no longer be any music.

> It can't last.
> It's almost over,
> And you'll be plunged into the darkness,
> Making believe that all is okay.
>
> You are a fool not to think that the glass is running out of water.
> You know the score; you know what's coming.
> It was temporary, temporary,
> Passing, passing, passing, passing, passing, passing with time.
> You know what's coming; you can't stop it.

At the end of the above session, I was so worn out I could barely walk home. Despite the doubts and fears, I am a person whose life has changed radically and dramatically through music.

In my case, improvising in music therapy was the magic carpet. I met a gifted therapist, teacher, and guide who does not operate within limited narrow definitions of music. He has allowed me to express myself in music, to develop a musical vocabulary. The word *support* in this context is completely inadequate, since it does not describe how the music he plays and his intense listening allow my flower to grow.

I am a gardenia.
I've got the blues because no one knows that I'm a gardenia.
I've got my gardenia covered up good.

I am a gardenia, I am a gardenia, I am a gardenia.
I will let you see me.

Cancer Update

As of this writing, the summer of 1998, I have not had to go for chemotherapy. When I see the oncologist, he reminds me that my lymphoma can start to grow at any time. This "partial regression, remission" might end tomorrow or it might last for years. I am convinced that the only way for me to deal with this situation is to trust God completely, and God has given me this wonderful gift of music to get me through the fear and anguish.

MANY STORIES, MANY SONGS

Diane Austin

INTRODUCTION

I have gathered words from more than eight of my clients. Three of them have agreed to be interviewed (Linda), written poems (Mebane), or written prose (Joseph). In one section, five or more clients are anonymously represented in quotes gathered in my journal over many years of practice as a music therapist. At the end of the narrative, I present a poem I wrote using one person's words. In my music psychotherapy sessions, clients and I use improvised playing and singing and we talk about the feelings and meanings, both conscious and unconscious, that emerge in the playing.

The people speaking in these pages may—as many of my clients do—have histories of physical or sexual abuse, have histories of substance abuse or eating disorders, or be adult children of alcoholic or emotionally disturbed parents. Many are writers, actors, musicians, artists, and therapists. I will introduce each client before I present his or her word.

INTERVIEW WITH LINDA

I include my questions (italicized) and the answers of Linda (not her real name), a 28-year-old music therapy student. I have shortened our interview.

Can you talk about your experience as a client in music therapy? What has it been like for you?
Where do I begin? Well, there's something about coming here and going to the music. I know that parts of myself I contact in the session are not parts of myself I could explain or talk about or intellectualize. . . . Sometimes I can't even put a description on the feeling I'm having. There are no words to say what it feels like.

When I go to the piano, I can play my experience. I don't have to put words on it, and when I'm through playing, I feel more heard than if I had said it.

You do?

Yeah. I feel as if somebody is really hearing what's going on with me when I'm playing my feelings. . . . And after the session, it feels like another brick has been lifted off my shoulder or chest. I feel lighter when I feel like someone's really understood, really heard what's going on.

How is it that you feel heard?

Well, it's very safe. It's more comfortable for me to have someone playing with me because it's scary to get in touch with very deep feelings. It helps to have the encouragement of someone else continuing on even if I stop. Sometimes all I could do was to let the tears come out of me, and when you continued, it was like the bottom didn't fall out even though I felt like my bottom was falling out.

I guess I feel when I come here that if I cry, there is a container to cry into. If we're having a conversation, I don't have to stop crying. I can have the conversation in the music. I can cry and the music can still be going on. The music doesn't have to stop.

Have you experienced other feelings in the music?

Well, it feels more acceptable to yell and to scream while toning [singing]. When I'm drumming and toning, it's like permission to express angrier feelings.

I've had images sometimes when we played and sang, images of my mother when I was very young. She was an alcoholic and yelled and hollered a lot. She'd say things like "Stop crying or I'll give you something to cry about." A theme for me throughout therapy has been self-expression. I shut off my expression a lot. My mother couldn't handle feelings, so she made me stop experiencing and expressing myself. . . . In my family, you shut down; all of us kids did the same thing. We closed off. . . . So many times when some feelings came up here [in therapy], [they] wound up in my throat. I think 90 percent of the time when something happened, where I'd feel it would be in my throat, as a lump in my throat that I couldn't swallow.

Do you remember what helped you at those moments?

The singing and toning helped me to release feelings: fear and pain, crying. . . .You know, I was never allowed to scream. I was never allowed to raise my voice. I was always shut up. . . . I always thought my voice had a certain range, a certain limited range, and I always thought that for whatever reasons, I didn't have certain notes in my range. Then I started to experience a range that I actually did have, but I couldn't express it because the expression of it resembled my mother's high-pitched screaming voice and I didn't want to have that as part of myself. As soon as I got to that register, my throat would just shut off. I would stop the sound. I couldn't get any volume in that range. The more I used that part of my voice when we were toning, the more available to me it became and I had control of it. I found a part of my voice that I didn't think I had and that was related to finding a part of myself that I was finally allowed to have.

What part of yourself are you referring to?

The part of me that was never allowed to be angry or upset or scream or cry. . . . Screaming to me was always taboo because of the amount my mother screamed: screaming to the point of not coming back. So the fact that I could sing in that high part of my voice and go to other parts of my voice and go back to that high part of my voice was a major realization for me that this is a part of me that I have control over now, and it doesn't mean that I'm going to lose control like my mother if I use that part of my voice.

That's true. . . .What else do you recall when you think back over our work together?

[It was] the time I was feeling angry at my boyfriend, and you and I were singing together. I had the image of my mother standing there holding a knife in her hand and hollering at me. I was standing in front of her and I was a child, scared. I think I cut off from my emotions because the fear was too great for me to be able to be present to it; so I would watch her, but I wouldn't hear anything she was saying. It was like I was standing behind a big wall of glass, watching everything but not hearing or participating in it. . . . I shut down and stopped singing and you took over for what I might have been saying if I was a child feeling what was going on in the present moment.

Do you remember what that was like for you?

Yeah, it allowed me to go back to that time and to be in that position. It was like reliving it but it was a safe way to relive it and feel it and not be cut off from it. Doing it with you, with the music, was a safe way to go back and to actually stay present with my mother.

I just had a phenomenal experience this last time I went home. I think that part of my therapy transferred into functioning in a healthier way with my mother. She got angry about something and started to scream and hop up and down on the floor and I didn't have to cut off my feelings. I wasn't 3 years old anymore. I could just get up and walk out of the room if I wanted to. I wasn't scared anymore, so instead of shutting off and ignoring her, I waited for her to have her tantrum and then I said: "I want you to know how I experienced what just happened to you. . . . I want you to know that I love you and I wouldn't hurt you on purpose and your anger is very upsetting for me. It makes me want to leave because of the way that you used to get upset when we were very small." And I said, "I want you to know that if you want to avoid this kind of upset in the future, the best thing for you to be able to do with me is for you to be able to see what you need and try to ask for it."

That's great!

And she just looked at me and she said, "Okay, that's fair enough!" I was just sitting there in her living room saying, "I think I've got this; I think I've got this down." I got off my chest the fact that it bothered me; I didn't run away from it. I was able to stay present and not have to go behind the glass wall. I think what happened when I grew up is that when she would have a screaming temper tantrum, I would go back behind that glass wall like I was still 3 years old. When you and I worked through this together and you [took the role of] me behind the glass wall and you sang what I wanted to say, I realized that it never occurred to me to say something. It never occurred to me that I could say something. It never occurred to me that there was a person behind that wall that had rights; there was a person that has the right to get up and walk out of the room, that has the right to say, "Excuse me, but what you just did was not acceptable!"

You've come a long way. It's exciting!

Yes, it is!

Is there anything else you want to talk about before we end the interview?

Well, I think a real theme for me this whole year has been integration. . . . There was that session when I came in and we started improvising vocally on the two chords and the melody reminded me of "Somewhere Out There." So you started playing the song, but I couldn't remember the words, so you told me to make them up. And I did and the song turned into "Somewhere In There." [*Laughs*]

[Laughs.] *I remember.*

It's not somewhere out there; it's somewhere in there. It's like one part of myself would find the other part of myself to make a whole. I've always looked outside of myself for what was missing—to another person or thing—to make me whole, when it's really me that I've been looking for.

MEBANE'S POEMS

Mebane is a 32-year-old singer, songwriter, and novelist. He has chosen to use his real name in presenting these poems.

Mebane
It was an accident.
I shattered the mirror
That held me complete as one.

I considered the thought
Seven-Years-Of-Bad-Luck
To be my only superstition.

But it struck me as strange
When I knelt to pick up
The pieces there on the floor.

That each little piece
Should reveal the whole me
Reflected in miniature.

Confession of the Panic Box
It came back to me again—that old fear.
I thought I'd done with naming it for the year.
You remember. "Give it a name," you said
Last October when I was up in bed
All night and frittering around all day.
"Name the fear," you said. "It will go away."
So I took to it, and after a while

I must have had a hundred fears on file.
I thought they'd work like the legend of a map.
The panic I'd scribbled on some odd scrap
Would make it all clear and I wouldn't be
Puzzling over what Fate would do to me.
But sometimes it seemed this business of a name
That wore off each day, seemed itself to blame.
I must tell you how I've felt. Sometimes the phone
Rings when you're out and I'm here alone.
And I just let it ring. Two days ago—
It's ridiculous, even I think so—
But I feared you'd find the file, my panic file.
I went poking around the house a while,
Thinking, I don't know what. It happened there,
Crouched behind the sofa, out of nowhere,
I saw the naming was only half of it.
If I could just tell you a little bit,
That little bit of the fear might go away,
Just by showing you the things I couldn't say.

JOSEPH'S EXPERIENCE

Joseph (not his real name), a 32-year-old drama therapist, agreed to write this short description of his experience of music therapy.

I can talk circles around myself. Give me a topic and I can discuss it effortlessly off the top of my head. I am a smooth operator and sometimes even fool myself. But music therapy helped me find a way around verbal defenses. While there was time to talk and reflect, this was not the center of the experience. The center was the music.

After Diane and I had introductory conversations that usually led to feelings about a particular issue, she would ask me to "play it." Whereas talking often reflects what I think about an issue, music captured my feelings. I could not hide from my feelings when I played the chimes or the xylophone or the drums. In a sense, the music led me, not the other way around. The music took me where I needed to go.

One example of this occurred toward the end of my time in therapy. I brought in a picture of a tree that I had drawn and was surprised how much feeling it evoked. Diane began to play chords on the piano and I just allowed sounds and broken syllables to emerge. Gradually, phrases developed, like crawling toward the tree; looking for light; remembering the wind; where is this hole leading me; where am I now; I feel dirt in my fingers; crawling, pulling myself forward; I'm going deeper down; searching for the roots of a tree that would somehow lead me to the light. These images had great psychological and spiritual significance for me. They seemed to represent the basis of my work in therapy: delving deeper into the pain and obscurity in the search for new life.

At first it was not easy to sing in therapy. Although I loved music, I feared my voice and the tunes that might emerge. I was afraid it would make me too vulnerable and unprotected. I was afraid of being crushed. But I sang, and the little child that emerged was not crushed. He was held by the piano chords and Diane's voice and the safety of the room. The child felt free.

Having a background in theater, I am able to see the link between music and drama. In a sense, different instruments and styles of playing represent different roles. And very often in life, roles choose us. The difficult part is trusting these roles and letting them expand. Likewise, in music, it is an act of trust to play improvisationally and allow not only the pure ring of the chime but also the deafening "clack!" of the wood block. Each sound corresponds to a part of ourselves and each one deserves to be heard.

DIANE'S POEM

This poem is an empathic reflection of what I feel the three clients, Linda, Mebane, and Joseph, may have experienced in sessions.

It's safe here.
I can curl up in the chords,
Wrap myself in sound,
And travel through time.
Travel to the deepest part of myself,

To the place where the forgotten songs are still playing.
And if I listen—really listen—
I can hear a child's voice singing.
Her tones are fragile poems
Whispered in my ear.
And if I listen—really listen—
I can hear glass shattering,
The sound of a heart breaking free.
I never knew the music could be so beautiful.

VOICES ON VOICE

These quotes are taken from various journal notes of clients talking about singing. I have created three composite characters out of the combined experiences of five clients in a narrative form called a collage.

VOICE ONE. I'm afraid of coming here and falling apart. Another voice, another me, comes out here, especially when I sing, and I'm not sure I want it to.

VOICE TWO. I didn't want to sing. This took me by surprise because my voice is my main instrument and here it was not available. I just kept playing the piano. I concentrated on staying present. That's a major issue for me. Then I stopped and listened for a moment. My voice emerged from deep within me and went to meet you. That's how it felt.

VOICE THREE. Initially, I was feeling sad. As my voice became more assertive and forceful, my feeling changed to more of an angry feeling. I started to sing about finding a new job, making a new start, and having a new life. When I finished singing, I felt really good.

VOICE ONE. I'm afraid of making mistakes. I still have a voice in me that wants a perfect song with a lot of insight and musical freedom. How can I live up to that?

VOICE TWO. The strange thing is that I couldn't really hear what you were singing. I could only feel the changing vibrations, very subtly, as you went from one tone to another: from the lower register and a big deep vibration to a higher register with a clear, sharp vibration. I played with those moving vibrations. I had to listen with my whole self rather than just my ears. I waited for the music in me to move rather than making it happen.

VOICE THREE. This is perhaps the place I would rather be more than anywhere else on earth. It's like walking between the worlds. It's an altered state that I didn't try to induce. I'm in the middle of sounds and open to receiving them.

VOICE ONE. When I come here and sing, I often feel the split in myself. There's an older more developed part and a more feeling part. The feeling part feels more like a baby.

VOICE TWO. I felt connected to you. I felt energized and "bigger" than myself, like my energy was coming out in all directions through my voice. I felt like I was expanding the amount of space I was inhabiting.

VOICE THREE. I felt so relieved to actually sing what I had been feeling.

VOICE ONE. My voice comes from a very deep hidden place. I'm afraid to bring it out into the world more completely. I'm afraid of my stronger emotions coming out—my pain and anger.

VOICE TWO. When you sing with me, I feel like you're reaching inside me, past all the things I can do for people, past how I look and how smart I am—to just me. This feels very new, to be contacted in this way.

VOICE THREE. Afterward, it took some time to fully return to a verbal state. I didn't want to return. I knew I could and would, but I would rather have stayed there for another hour or so. This world of music is where I find inspiration and healing.

VOICE ONE. The music had a magic and a power that was very healing. The resistance I had felt about singing was still standing in front of me but now it was only a dwarf, where earlier it had been a giant!

VOICE TWO. I closed my eyes and felt the sound. Then I started humming. You hummed with me and I felt more secure. I began to sing: "I don't want to cry. I want sunshine." You sang these words with me. I liked the mirroring. But when you harmonized with me, I felt like you took care of me, sort of like a mother. Your low tone and the piano and the harmonizing made me feel safe and secure. I wanted to keep singing forever.

VOICE THREE. I felt love in these sounds. It's hard to put into words. The only thing I know for certain is that this work connects me to my soul and it heals. Of this, I have no doubt whatsoever.

DIANE'S POEM

I wrote this poem using words of one of my clients.

Holding

"I feel like a little girl learning how to walk," she said.
"So vulnerable—what if I slip?"
Her tears fell on the keys and she skipped a beat.
"Please don't stop singing," she said.
"Your singing makes me cry."
So I sang and I sang and I sang till the storm passed over.
"Why is it so powerful?" she asked.
"It's such a simple thing.
Why does it feel so sad to hear someone sing 'Welcome'?"

Narrative 15

RACHEL DESCRIBES LEARNING ABOUT HER PHYSIOLOGICAL RESPONSE

Eric Miller

INTRODUCTION

Rachel, a middle-aged female psychoanalyst, came to me for biofeedback therapy. She suffered from Raynaud's disease, a condition marked by poor blood circulation to the extremities, usually fingers and toes, which may turn white and become numb with cold or emotional stress. Rachel hoped that she might learn to promote relaxation and increase circulation through biofeedback; she was especially interested in the possibility of using music as an agent for change.

I am a music therapist as well as a biofeedback therapist. Rachel and I explored various aural stimuli, such as her favorite music and environmental sounds, to see what might produce the most significant change in her body (finger) temperature. In 10 sessions with Rachel, I used a biofeedback machine with electrical hookups that monitored her body's reaction to various stimuli I presented to her (on her suggestion). Among the physical functions monitored were the temperature of her fingertip and her heart rate. Her physiological changes in response to the stimuli were displayed on a screen and heard simultaneously as audio tones that varied in pitch up and down as her physiology changed (the feedback).

Rachel has written responses to my questions about her experience of the therapy. I have included a few graphs that summarize her physiological changes.

RACHEL'S RESPONSES

*What brought you into treatment?**
I was alarmed by the increase in Raynaud's over the last few years. It was at its worst around October 1996.

What was your initial attitude upon entering therapy utilizing music and biofeedback to treat your Raynaud's?

---

* Eric's questions are italicized; his comments about findings are indented.

I had the idea that it worked for this condition but of course wasn't sure it would work for me, since I have had an antagonistic relationship with machines and computers [Figure A].

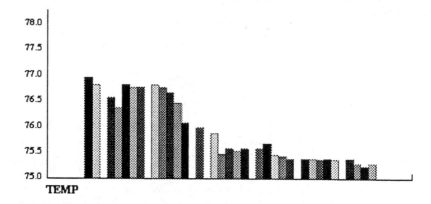

Figure A. In her initial session, Rachel shows a decrease in temperature measured by a thermistor on her fingertip. This is due to vasoconstriction (stress produces a tightening of arteries) at the first stress period, in this case induced by her thoughts of something stressful in her life. She is unable to make significant recovery during the subsequent relaxation periods. There is a 1-minute average per vertical bar on the graph, or approximately 40 minutes represented by the entire graph.

What is your relationship with music?
Music is very important to me. In my youth, I played violin in the Scranton Philharmonic; I have sung in various choirs and now I drum and tone [vocalize].
What do you recall about your body's physiological response to various musical pieces [in these sessions]?
I was surprised they didn't have more effect. I wonder, however, if some of that had to do with the use of my ordinarily calming music in—as I recall—our second or third session [Figure B]. The place (the old building) and the computer screen especially were anxiety producing. I think I was still looking at the screen a bit then. I also wonder whether the music (I have played the Pachelbel on my violin) accessed a different part of my mind than the sounds [such as fish tank and heartbeat used later]. Also I think that assessing the effect of any particular stimulus always seemed to make my hands colder.

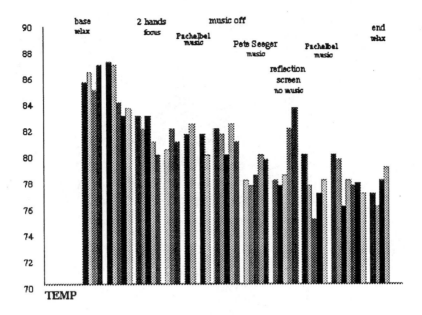

Figure B. Rachel shows little warming during Pete Seeger, more warming when presented with the visual graphics screen called the reflection screen, and the only slight warming with the Pachelbel pieces. She tends to cool between periods, possibly because of cognitive processing, or mental analysis.

Describe your response to removal of the visual feedback.
The visual screen was associated with tests and somehow with a feeling of shame. It was much better to remove it.

> Without the visual screen, Rachel was relying on tonal information for feedback. It began to be apparent that most music Rachel chose stimulated an analytical response, which often impedes hand warming. We changed direction to see if sounds with a different emotional content would be more effective.

What did you like about the treatment?
It was a big learning experience about the effects of thoughts and associations on my body temperature. For example, when I first listened to the fish water, I thought of that fish tank [in the studio], which was dirty and poorly cared for. That disturbed me—I really like fish and have feelings about the care they get—so I listened to the tank water and thought of my own fish [Figure C]. That worked.

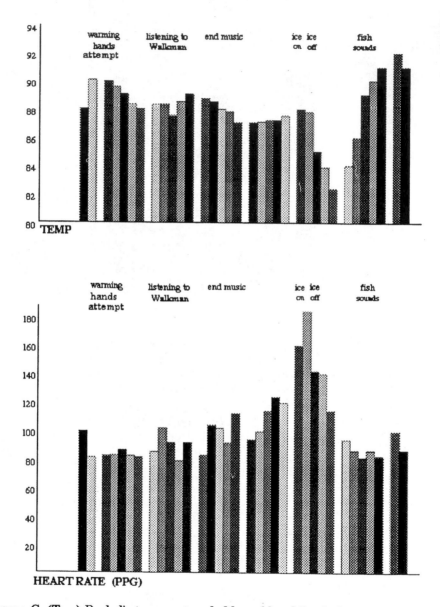

Figure C. (Top) Rachel's temperature holds stable while she listens to music on her Walkman, although it decreases during the warming attempt, no music, and the ice test. Rachel warms beyond her initial temperature with fish sounds at the end. **(Bottom)** Rachel's heart rate (ppg = picopicograms) during the same 42-minute period as in top graph. Her anxiety as measured by her heart rate increases in anticipation of the ice test and decreases with fish sounds.

What do you recall about your body's physiological response to sounds and rhythms, such as the fish tank and your heartbeat?

As for the sounds, they were all nature sounds and connected with images: coal stove, fish, and heartbeat [Figure D]. [Listening to my] heartbeat seemed the most powerful, and since it is simple and accessible, I have used that many times since.

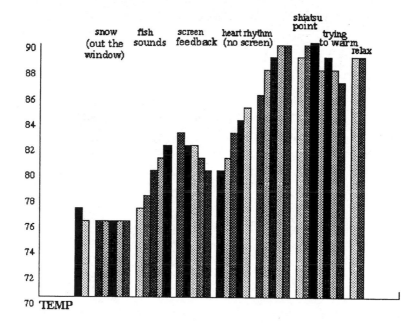

Figure D. Rachel shows increases in temperature with fish sounds and the focus on her heart rhythm. She cools with visual screen feedback (looking at the feedback screen) and "trying" to warm. The overall increase went from 76 to 90 degrees in this 45-minute period.

Although it wasn't good for me to watch the screen, I liked having the data to look at afterward. I liked the hard evidence of the effect of my thoughts and mind on my body temperature. I think when I focused on sounds, I was also going into a meditative state; my eyes often were closed. I meditate more now.

Do you still use any skill or knowledge from these sessions?

The focus on breathing and heartbeat.

Please describe the frequency and intensity of both your symptoms for Raynaud's and headaches over the past year since treatment finished.

After the sessions, my Raynaud's didn't go away, but I felt less panicky about it because of having a tool and knowledge about the effect of my mind over my fingers.

Are there any other comments you would like to make?

Basically, I think the sounds worked when they facilitated my going into a meditative state. Since I am a musician, there may be something in the way I listen to music that I know very well that interferes with that.

Musicians, because of their heightened music discrimination abilities, tend to listen to music with a more analytical process than do nonmusicians. The process of learning to increase temperature demands a letting go of rational, analytical thinking.

A TAPE FROM LILLY

Madelaine Ventre

INTRODUCTION

Lilly is a survivor of childhood abuse. In Guided Imagery and Music, she produced imagery and healing from her subconscious while listening to carefully selected classical music in an internally focused state. Sharing with me her images as she experienced them, she faced her fears, her anger, and her grief and discovered her strength and beauty. I feel privileged to have shared this part of her life's journey. As we approached our final session, Lilly asked if she could plan it. That day she arrived with an audiotape. It began with her recorded voice saying, "Hello, Mady; it's Lilly. I just thought I'd make you a tape, kind of a collection of different songs or readings [and] just things I wanted to share with you."

Lilly said much about herself, her therapeutic process, and our relationship. Her words—the words she chose in the poems, readings, and songs on her tape—show her generosity of spirit, sense of humor, and strength.

LILLY'S TAPE

The following are excerpts of the first poem, "The Child in Me." Lilly commented, "I really like this. It says a lot and I feel it certainly was a bit of my own journey." Ellipses are used where portions of the poem were omitted.†*

> Had I heard a voice? a child's voice? . . .
> A plaintive echo over and over again. . . .
> Nothing could have prepared me for what I discovered.

---

* Source unknown.
† Throughout the rest of this section, Madelaine's comments are italicized.

I found myself a small, thin child of five. . . .
I told the child of my life
Of the risks taken and not taken,
Of my constant battle with the enemy shyness.
I relived again the pathways life had taken
With their accompanying brambles, weeds, and thorns
As well as the more pleasant happenings.
The child in turn asked me many questions,
Until satiated with the knowledge of my own growth and plateaus
She reached out and took my hand. . . .
Gradually I felt her body relax.
The world seemed in complete harmony. . . .
I knew that never again would I ever part with this small child.
I would carry her in my heart with love and acceptance.
For this child and I are one. . . .
I again reentered the stream of daily living
Feeling much richer and much closer to wholeness.

In another poem entitled "No Gentle Way," Lilly found a voice
for how she experienced her growth as a woman.*

You're splitting now, woman seed.
Crack, wrench, bulge, break.
Not stepped on or crushed,
Nor pried open in force.
But splitting wide,
The seed from within is bursting itself.
There is no gentle way to break.
There is no gentle way to break.
So split little seed.
Birth sprout your pain.
And wait in the darkness of your needing.
You're splitting now, woman seed.
Be split and enjoy.
Crack wide, let pain out.
Crack wide, let love in.
You will not sprout until you split.

---

* Source unknown.

You will not birth until you die, die freely.
There is no gentle way to break.
I am breaking and I am glad.

Lilly continued with this reading and then commented in her own words:

I walk to the edge of all the light that I have and I take that step into the darkness of the unknown. I must believe that one of two things will happen. There will be something solid for me to stand on or I will be taught how to fly.*

I've made it this far. I'll do fine. It'll be hard but it'll be okay, I'm sure. More than okay, I bet.

Lilly had much to say about our therapeutic relationship and what it meant to her. She begins with the poem "You Gave Me Love" (Jordan and Cloninger, 1979).

You gave me time when no one gave me the time of day.
You looked inside while the rest of the world looked away.
You smiled at me when there were just frowns ev'rywhere.
You gave me love when nobody gave me a prayer. . . .
You touched my heart,
You touched my soul,
And helped me start all over again.
You gave me laughter after I cried all my tears.
You heard my dreams while the rest of the world closed its ears.
I looked in your eyes and I found the tenderness there.
You gave me love when nobody gave me a prayer.

I think of all the hard times we went through together. You're the only one who dared deal with my anger up front. . . . I'm sorry for the times I might have frustrated you [and] was so needy, not really able to consider you more. You'll probably be all over me for that, but I do apologize. As someone who has shared my story with you and someone who has certainly been helped to a new and better life, I'd just like to thank you. Thank you for the mat, the warm fuzzy blan-

---

* Source unknown.

kets, and having a bathroom nearby. Thank you for everything you've done, everything you've been for me. I really am in awe of the whole process. I never expected all the depth of what we touched.

Then Lilly quoted part of a song (Norbet, 1972):

> I want to say something to all of you
> Who have become a part
> Of the fabric of my life.
>
> The color and texture
> Which you have brought into my being
> Have become a song,
> And I want to sing it forever.
>
> There is an energy in us
> Which makes things happen
> When the paths of other persons
> Touch ours
> And we have to be there
> And let it happen.
>
> When the time
> Of our particular sunset comes
> Our thing, our accomplishment
> Won't really matter a great deal.
>
> But the clarity and care
> With which we have loved others
> Will speak with vitality
> Of the great gift of life
> We have been for each other.

I do believe friends are friends forever in some cases, I guess, in cases where it is a matter of love and not dependency.

I remember thinking one time that in your office where it all took place, this is holy ground for me. And that very spot of the land will be transformed one day. I'd like to extend an invitation that in the future—in whatever form the future will take and when the earth is transformed, when we're transformed—that I'd like to get together with you in that spot and have a cup of tea. That would be great.

In closing, Lilly read a poem called "The Journey Has Ended."*

The journey has ended.
The journey has begun.
Each person travels the path closest to our heart.
Sometimes the trail is easy to follow
Sometimes hard to follow.
As the trail markers become harder to understand
Some give up the journey to settle down.
Those that continue the journey
Discover that the trail ends where it began
And begins again where it ended,
In the heart.

---

* Source unknown.

MUSIC OF THE SPHERES

Colin Lee

COLIN'S INTRODUCTION

Charles referred himself to music therapy. We had a total of 50 sessions spanning 2 years. When Charles came to see me for an initial discussion, he was depressed and ill. Just over a year earlier, it was found that he had human immunodeficiency virus. He had recently lost his job and was having to consider relinquishing both his car and property because of financial constraints. Charles stressed that he did not think of the potential of our work as life-extending, but rather he hoped music therapy might offer him, through musical expression, a richer quality of life. Our first 20 sessions thus focused on exploring improvisation as a creative yet clinical tool.

It was an important dynamic for many people I worked alongside that they share their experiences in the hope that their battles might help others in the future. Charles was fervent in expressing his views on music therapy at every opportunity. Charles's introduction below comes from a letter written in support of our work together after the first year of sessions. His words introduce our work better than I can.

CHARLES'S INTRODUCTION

In the beginning, I did not know what to expect or realize how music therapy could help someone get better from their illnesses. After a few sessions, however, once the trust between us had been established, I started to understand the importance of searching within ourselves. Having the facility to express through music, without the constraints of technical or learned ability, enabled me to express my feelings in a totally new way. Listening to tapes from sessions gave me insight into the way I was feeling and the way I interacted with people, depending on the environment I was exposed to during the week. This additional facility has helped to establish a balance, with the result that I feel more able to tackle any diseases and difficulties that come my way (Lee, 1996).

CHARLES'S MUSIC

I* present Charles's comments as he listened to the tape of a long improvisational piano duet we did together during session 21. The two excerpts of our music and his concise verbal interpretations give an essence of his experience of our work in music. Session 21 included three improvisations, the excerpts here coming from the second. Each improvisation had its own distinct character, expressing in music the many sides of Charles's growth and personality. Session 21 was a stage in our work when the improvisations were held solely on the piano (four hands)—Charles would take the bass and pedal. He showed two distinct sides to his musical expression during this improvisation: a constant rhythmic pounding [Figure A] and a calm melodic gentleness [Figure B]. As therapist, I attempted to give color and context to Charles's musical language. I did not try to affect or change the tempo of his music—I sat close by and gave support. Charles's simple verbal testimony portrayed the strength of his understanding of Music #1:

This is my bass heartbeat. It is giving the giant within me a voice. It is getting faster and giving more energy. I feel the iron within my soul.

In contrast, his slower, lighter playing (Music #2) came near the end of the improvisation. His developing C-minor melodic line flowered in a way that could be seen as a harvest of his previous musical venting. Charles was clear in his assessment:

---

* Colin's descriptions, interspersed throughout Charles's comments, are indented.

Figure A. Music #1.

Figure B. Music #2.

I felt that this section is where I had been trying to get to throughout the whole improvisation. When this slower music began, at first I thought it was wrong and should have been a separate piece. But then I realized that I had something different to say that was connected to the first part. I was able to express the pain that I was feeling directly through this simple melody.

Charles was always resolutely honest in his demeanor;
he never evaded difficult issues and constantly explored
the boundaries of his own communication. He said:

Music is at once a part of me. Music helps me to explore my fears for the future. Words are a part of our everyday life, but music speaks to me of heaven.

Narrative 18

PEG'S CENTURY OF MUSIC

Sally A. Hough

INTRODUCTION

"I can't move right now, but I'll come to St. Rita's to live when your rooms get a little bigger," Peg explained over the telephone.

"Tomorrow the staff is looking forward to welcoming you to St. Rita's Nursing Home," the social worker replied, smiling to herself as she thought that the bedrooms would still be the same size as today.

With that conversation, Margaret Mary McGovern arrived at St. Rita's Nursing Home with her beautiful wardrobe, lovely hats, comfortable chair, and a dresser adorned with over 20 framed photos of family, grandchildren, and great-great-grandchildren. A tall, thin woman with white hair, Peg carried herself elegantly. She made room 9A her new home.

Peg is 92 years old this year and for 6 years has lived in the nursing home where I supervise music therapists. I have known her (she has chosen to use her real name) all that time, seen her in music groups, and interviewed her for this narrative. Peg has many music experiences in the nursing home, from participation in a tone chime choir to sessions in which familiar music is re-created to stimulate physical movement, instrument playing, singing, and conversation. In addition to presenting Peg's words transcribed from our interviews, I have constructed monologues (in italics) from the words I've heard her say many times.

PEG

I'm so lucky to be here. I am able to go to Mass and Rosary every day. The sisters are so loving to me. Oh, how I love it here. They are so good to me. Now where should I hang these?

Would you be so kind as to help me hang this crucifix? Yes, right above my bed. That is where it goes, next to those two pictures. That is John.

There we are in the garden, both of our arms around each other's shoulders. How I miss him. There's that wonderful big smile of his.

You know, he didn't live long. I could never marry after he died. This is Mom and Dad seated in the middle, surrounded by all eight of us children. My father was full-blooded Irish and my mother was German. My parents were born singing and dancing together. Yes, hang it there, right where I can always see it.

There were eight Downey children. John was the oldest, played the piano, and had a beautiful voice. Rose was the eldest girl and played the piano with Brian, who played the violin. Then there [were] Joseph, Anthony, Mary, myself, and Ellen. Ellen played the piano before she went to school. She was mimicking Rose. Music was just like eating to her. You have to do it every day. As sisters, we were very close. We went to St. Aloysius Boarding School together.

"It Might As Well Be Spring"—what a lovely song. "Playing the piano is easy," she would tell me. Music is just like eating. You have to do it every day.

Ellen played everything on the piano since she was a tiny child. She could make the piano roar. I would say to her, "Ellen, play the piano for me." I just missed the piano, hearing it. Nothing could break the family structure. We were very close. We had a happy life.

Peg moved into St. Rita's and instantly made her new home her happiness, attending Mass and Rosary every day. Peg flows through her days, from the hymns of Mass to the various music therapy groups.*

---

* Sally's comments, interspersed among Peg's words and soliloquies, are indented.

What would life be like without music? Why, it would be terrible. When you hear a good piece of music, it stops you dead still. God is there. It changes you. [*Pause*] It changes you. Music is what keeps people going in life. That's what I feel.

What is so special about music? Well, rhythm, melody, lyrics; [*Pause*] no, no, it is the music, the sound of the piano. My little son would say to me, "God is good to usses, right, Mommy?" and I would say, "What would we do without him?"

Music comes from God. Anybody that lacks music lacks the best part of life. Music gives you an outlook and an outlet. Music is a God-given gift. [*Pause*] You know, God gave my daughter to me for only a short while. She was a gift.

I wonder if she knows how much sunshine she [one of the music therapists] brings to St. Rita's with her music. What is her name? It must be Wednesday, 10:30 A.M. We will sing. We will play instruments. We will laugh. No matter what, we will have joy.

When I see you, my whole life lights up and we have a wonderful day. You don't know what you do to this place! Oh, I'll be there right away.

Peg receives tone chime number eight. She cannot see the numbers on the chalkboard, but she musically anticipates her cue to play her tone chime, never missing a beat. Sitting erect on the edge of her chair, face aglow, she leans toward the music therapist, using all the strength in her hand to produce the musical ringing. The group ends and she is tired, exclaiming, "Music really keeps us hopping around here! Thank you. Thank you."

Oh my, the "Tennessee Waltz." Now when is the last time I heard that? Oh yes, these are the hoops. Both hands up, around in a circle, two, three. Both hands down, around in a circle, two, three. There is my roommate, poor soul.

Honey, everyone has waltzed at some point in his or her life!

It's the Vienna waltz. Peg tries to imitate the therapist's movements with two hoops, colorful in the air, but her eyesight is too poor to see the details. No matter. She laughs and successfully twirls one hoop on her arm, so fast, before it launches up into the air across the room. The group laughs and tells her that they will buy her a Hula Hoop for her waist. The musical strains of the Viennese waltz fade away.

Ah, John, my father, my brother, my husband, my sons. How I love them all.

Both my daddy and husband would sing this to me. [Daddy owned the] John M. Downey Carpet Cleaning Company. Did you know the company in Columbus? He married Rose M. Paulus. My father and mother were so much in love. They taught us real love. There is something about family. You wonder what you'd do without them.

You can have only one real love in life. [*Pause*] John McGovern, he would start singing that song to me. He didn't have a good singing voice. He would sing it to me, especially when he had been bad. [*She lovingly smiles.*]

Johnny thinks I love his brother Bill more. It's just not so. A mother can't love one more than another. Love's not like that. How I love them both.

"Peg O' My Heart" plays on Peg's tape recorder in her room and she lights up in recognition, smiling and exclaiming, "Well!" She sings the lyrics, waving her coffee cup in rhythm, side to side in the air, in tempo between sips.

Peg o' my heart, I love you; don't let us part. What month is it? May. The days seem to jumble together as I lie in bed. I am so weak. I don't feel like eating, but Sister says I must at least drink—ah, my coffee, nice and black. Oh, I am so weak. Johnny, Bill, I love you.

Peg has been in bed for weeks. Her son Bill, from Chicago, arrives knowing that each day may be her last. Her heart is failing and she sleeps so much. Her son Johnny visits and the two brothers sit by her bed, waiting. A music therapist enters. Bill requests "Danny Boy." A strained moment passes, then the sound of two voices singing softly is heard: "Oh, Danny boy, I love you so." Peg stirs and turns her head.

Music, love, and communication—it's a feeling. Oh, how my father loved my mother. He worshipped her. "I Want A Girl Just Like the Girl That Married Dear Old Dad." What music does for a family is wonderful! We had the happiest family. The music always came after the meals: communication. We would all sing together. Dad would listen to all his four girls. We were a happy bunch. Music was in our home from the moment we got up, from morning until night. Is it night now? Is that you, Bill and Johnny?

Is that you, Bill and Johnny? What are you doing here? Please sing to me some more.

Bill, John, do you remember the neighbors? The neighbors wanted to get away from all of the piano playing, telling me that they had seen a new house that we could move into [*Pause*] way down the block.

My brother played the violin. We had a piano. With eight children, I was number seven. Everyone couldn't wait to get home each day because our home was filled with music, singing, dancing, and fooling around. When Ellen started playing the piano and we heard the music from down the street, we would come running home. Music was alive in our house all of my life. My brother Johnny woke up singing every day when my sister Rose played the piano. What a group we had in the family.

What would we do without music?!

Yes, I remember, John. Whenever you would come home from work, you would say, "Don't tell me who called. Let me get my bearing first by playing the piano." How he loved to play the piano.

My husband John McGovern was a labor and wage examiner for the Pennsylvania Railroad. We would sing on the trains. That song takes me back to the good old railroad days. We sang on the trains with the grandchildren. We would take them to New York.

We would go the theater in the morning or afternoon because it was cheaper. I had the best grandchildren. They were all good. I could take them on the railroad free. I had a break all around. We were a lucky family.

Yes, we moved because the Pennsylvania Railroad told us to move. It is good for children to move. They liked the changes, seeing new things.

We would take the train into Chicago to go to the five-and-dime store to buy the latest piece of sheet music or record. We'd be so sad if the store did not carry the music. "I think I'll just go home," we would say. "I think I'll just go home."

How did I meet my husband? Well, we met walking downtown at the music counter. Music was the base of our lives. Before we married, we hid the fact that we were both in love with music. Happiness, they can't take that away from me. We had so much happiness in our family. We had a big family. I think that makes a difference.

No one can take happiness away from me. No one can take music away from me.

Oh, I tell you, I had a great life. You get lonesome sometimes. You put on music and it takes away anything that's got you whacked at that time.

"Do you have any chest pains, Peg? Good-bye. I'll see you next week."

"God knows I hope so. I'm tired. We'll get together once in a while soon to sing."

I was the only one who did not play an instrument. I was the housekeeper. I was important. I was needed, so they could practice the piano and sing. That was what I did. I was the singer. I was the only one who didn't play an instrument. "Mom, listen to this one," they would say. I was the listener. We would dance and sing. I never touched the piano. I never had any talent. I was important. I was the singer.

Narrative 19

REVIEW OF GUIDED IMAGERY AND MUSIC SESSIONS: WILLIAM'S STORY

William and Alison Short

ALISON'S INTRODUCTION

Two years ago, William, a midlife businessperson, experienced the beginnings of change in his relationship with his wife during his time with me in music therapy. Their relationship is reflected in his imagery and in subsequent discussion during sessions of Guided Imagery and Music (GIM). In a typical GIM session, we first talked about the issues he wanted to work on, then I helped him into a relaxed state and put on selected classical music, after getting his input about what music he felt he needed. As William experienced imagery in this altered state, he and I maintained an active dialogue. I took verbatim notes of his imagery and of my remarks, as well as of the discussion that we had after the music and imagery.

Recently, we met again to discuss and review the imagery and the postimagery discussion from the sessions to write this chapter together (2 years later). I audiotaped and transcribed our recent meeting and incorporated William's statements from that review into this narrative. We reviewed all the drafts of the narrative.

In the GIM sessions, William's relationship to his wife was often discussed but infrequently experienced in his imagery. In the sessions, there were only four instances when William directly imaged his wife during the music. We have chosen to present these particular instances (which occur in sessions 2, 3, 5, and 22) in the first part of the narrative. For each session, we have included my description of the music, William's reporting of his imagery during the music, plus my questions and comments, my summary of the discussion following the music, and William's comments about that session from our recent review. In the last section, William talks about his experience of the therapy and of the therapy review in words transcribed from the tape of our recent meeting.

REVIEW OF THE SESSIONS

Session 2

This was William's first session with music; the initial meeting had been a short informational meeting. In this first experience of a GIM session, William imaged his wife as he first knew her. This imagery occurred near the end of the music programme; the selection was Turina's *La Oracion del Torero*. The latter part of this music features stringed instruments in high registers, with long notes and a slow, upward-rising figure combined with a slow rate of harmonic change and piquant tonal harmonies. It ends with an extended chord in upper registers, potentially conveying an ethereal quality.

> THE IMAGERY. There are a few paddocks and trees, a bit of a rise, a few cows. I am with Sharon when I first knew her. There is a creek running through the paddock, so fragile and so substantial at the same time. *(Is there something you would like to share with her?)** I didn't know she was going to have to go through so much pain. *(Is there something she would like to say to you?)* She would like to say, "Help me." [*End of music*] *(Is there anything else that you would like to say to her?)* That I will help her. *(Is there anything she wants to say back?)* I don't think so.

> DISCUSSION. In the discussion following this music part of the original session, William commented that his wife appeared "as she was when I first knew her 26 years ago." I asked how it felt, and he said, "It feels good and sad. Perhaps we both started out starry-eyed. Perhaps if we saw what [was] ahead, perhaps we wouldn't have [*hesitates*]."

---

*Throughout William's narrative, Alison's words during the music are in italics and within parentheses; Alison's comments in the DISCUSSION sections are indented.

Session 3

In the next session, William also had imagery that included his wife; it happened near the end of the last selection of music, Vaughan Williams's *Fantasia on Greensleeves.* This orchestral arrangement of a popular English folk tune features broad sweeping melodic lines in the strings with a supportive bass line and potentially conveys a sense of spaciousness.

THE IMAGERY. I am just lying on the grass near the valley. [*End of music*] I think I am lying in the grass with Sharon. (*Do you need more time, music?*) No, I don't think so.

DISCUSSION. Since the bulk of the session dealt with family and bereavement, this is also what dominated the discussion afterward.

In our recent meeting, William said about that session:

Even that session there, where I might not have said much, I can almost feel what it was like at the end of that—because that was one of the first times that I had approached that point [and] because it was very early in the number of sessions I did. Well, it's a relaxation, and what I remember is the discovery that because of my openness to music, I could come here and just be really open with the music.

Session 5

William's wife appears near the end of the music programme. The music was the end of Wagner's *Lohengrin,* Prelude to Act 1. Since William's imagery sequence had not reached a natural close, additional music was then put on to extend the programme—Elgar's *Enigma Variations,* number 8. The end of the Wagner selection features largely strings and is of an upward rising and ethereal nature, with the final chord disappearing from the bottom up so that one is left with a single upper note. The Elgar is orchestral but has mostly strings in the beginning. It is slow, with long legato notes creating a thoughtful, reflective character with an uplifting sense of movement, and climaxing with full orchestra before dying away.

THE IMAGERY. My mind starts to wander. What is the lump that comes between me and Sharon? *(What could the lump be like?)* A stone, a rock. *(What is the stone like?)* It's just stuck there. She's got a stick, a lever. It's grey like granite [*end of Wagner, beginning of Elgar*]; the music's trying to tell me it's soapstone—soft—that you can work easily. *(Would you like to try?)* Yes. Yes, I would. *(Can you find a tool to work it with?)* Yes, I've got a little rock chisel. *(Can you try working the stone?)* I don't want to break it up to nothing—just take a bit off the sides. *(Can you do that?)* Yes, I have a mallet to take ridges off the sides; I can work a shape. *(Can you do that?)* Like a quarter of an orange. You can carve it out. *(What's Sharon doing?)* I think she's just looking at the moment. I think she likes the shape. The texture's got scratch marks from the teeth, but it looks good. *(How does it feel to do that?)* It feels good; I like it. I'm capable of doing that. *(You're capable of doing that. [Pause] Is there anything else you would like to do with the rock?)* Put it with some trees, grass, sand. *(Is Sharon still there?)* No, I don't know where she is. *(Do you have a sense of where she is?)* No. *(How do you feel about that?)* I think she's around somewhere. [*End of music—silence; the imagery continues.*] *(Is there something you would like to say to her?)* I think she doesn't trust me. I think she thinks she'll get hurt. *(Is there anything else you would like to say to her?)* Not right now.

DISCUSSION. William commented in the discussion after the music that he was surprised that the rock or stone could be soft. In the discussion before the music, William had stated feelings of being "out of control." He was now reminded of this in light of his subsequent statement during the music: "I am capable of doing that." William's comments and nonverbal cues, such as facial expression and voice tone, also indicated to me that he felt much more peaceful and focused.

William comments, in our recent meeting, about that session:

Oh, that's interesting isn't it? I mean, I'm just putting this together and thinking about where I was and what was happening then. I remember a lot of this coming up, and it seems really strange to be looking at it now. And I was doing therapy that was interesting because it was using music that's significant for me.

It's something [soapstone] my wife has used a bit, and we have some lumps of it at home; we don't do it now. You put your hands on it and it feels like you could almost rub it away; it is soft, easy to work. If I see something like that and I say it's like gran-ite, then that's saying that it's hard. But if I see it and I say that's like soapstone, it's something I can start to work with. Hmmm.

[*Reading*] "Can you find a tool to work with? Yes, I've got a rock chisel." Now then, I'm starting to do something to it. The rea-son that I was impressed with myself talking about actually doing something is that one of the major things that I've noticed about myself [is] [*hesitates*] I've found particularly in the last couple of years that it makes a big difference to me that I actually do some-thing—act, rather than just talk. Even if I might even think it's the wrong thing, it's better for me to do something, rather than adopt the mode that I've spent most of my life: "I'll hang back and let it all sort of happen." And it's significant that it is here [in the transcript from the session], and I mean I'm actually doing some-thing! And I can remember what that felt like, too.

Session 22

There was now a long series of sessions in which William did not report imagery of his wife. In session 22, 8 months after the previous example, imagery of his wife again occurred for William during GIM therapy. The music was by Gounod, *St. Cecilia Mass,* Offertoire and Sanctus. This music came as a respite after the deeply extending *Adagio for Strings* by Barber. The two selections by Gounod are potentially sacred and nurturing in character. The Offertoire begins with strings playing gentle supportive melodic lines and predictable harmonies, later joined by the rest of the orchestra. The Sanctus starts with a very definite chord, followed by repetitive notes in the strings, and then the solo male voice enters, to be later joined by the choir. The climax of this piece of music follows an extended choral buildup of layer upon layer of voices on the dominant seventh chord, finally resolving to the tonic with a recapitulation of the main theme.

THE IMAGERY. I am just looking in a car. Sharon is with me; she is pointing to something in the car. I don't know what it is. *(Would you like to take a closer look?)* No. I think it is just something [*hesitates*]. *(Is there something you would like to say to Sharon?)* There's a lot, about "I'm sorry" [*pauses*]. There's something she wants. *(Can you ask her what that is?)* I think she wants me to look inside myself because I forget me. *(Is there something you would like to say to her about that?)* I recognize that there's pain involved, but I also recognize that I've got a lot of years of "past." And I'm looking for change, for it not to be another year like the last 26. *(Is there something you would like to ask her?)* To work with me; I know it's painful. *(And does she respond to that?)* She's a bit guarded. I think that she really wants to, but she's been disappointed. *(Is there anything else that you need to say to each other?)* Probably a lot. [*Climax of the Sanctus; William's voice is louder and stronger.*] That we need to acknowledge each other as individuals. *(Can she hear you say that?)* I think that she hears, but she needs to protect herself because she's been hurt. *(Is there anything that you would like to give her?)* Not now.

DISCUSSION. In the discussion after the music, I asked William how it felt to be talking to his wife in the imagery and at such depth. Was it strange? His reply was "Yes, but good!" The imagery seemed to indicate a fundamental shift: that William embraced a desire for change in the relationship.

On reviewing that session, William comments:

[I'm] going through it and it's almost building up in me the possibility of change because of the looking at change in the imagery. I mean I'm not changing my relationship by saying these things in relationship to the music, but something's happening inside me, and it's almost something [*pauses*]—I have a sense that I was that stuck.

There was the talking therapy that I had had a few years before, but then at the time that I came to see you, I was in couples therapy. So there was talking there, and change started to happen there, but I was not free enough, and I know I wasn't free. But I was detecting that I needed to, you know—there was a message coming through to me—that I needed to move.

WILLIAM'S STATEMENTS
DURING OUR REVIEW

About Relaxation

Oh, I had done relaxation exercises, but it's a different sort of thing, a different depth of relaxation, particularly with the connection with music. [As a] matter of fact, I can remember many years ago going to a very good GP [general practitioner], and he was trying to teach me progressive relaxation, and I tried to do what he said. I was in a situation where it was noisy and I was anxious about everything, and it just didn't work for me. He didn't put music on. And I am certain that even then if he had . . . said, "Oh, I'll just play a bit of music," then that [might] have been enough for me to start to understand what he was on about and relax!

Well, it's a relaxation, and what I remember is the discovery that because of my openness to music, I could come here and just be really open with the music.

About the Music

I think that music for me has another sort of motherly connotation, especially classical music. I have to say that, thinking about my early childhood. I have images of being small, of my mother always having the radio on classical music. I was from a large family, and, see, when everyone else was there, of course the radio would be on something else—and noise and stuff like that. But there were these times when there was classical music with my mother and if it was popular sort of classical music, she'd be singing along to it. Do you know what I mean? So there's that sort of comfortableness with music that I had. And so I could stay with these images, perhaps, a lot easier than I would have had [I not had that experience].

I don't know where the music goes to, but it certainly gets inside of me! It kicks around things. But I would deliberately not [analyse the music], not even think in terms of who was the composer or what style of music is it or even those general things. I would just say, it's just music, it's part of coming here. And I think that was probably the most effective session, when I was basically . . . relaxing. I know [in] some of them, I didn't like the part where you started talking because [*joint laughter*] . . . I was "down there," and maybe in one sense . . . I had not been able to relax like that before.

Yes, I am sensitive to loud, rich music; in some sense, it can be overwhelming. Now, in a normal environment I would switch off from it, block it[s] getting through, but here [in the therapy], I was open. So I wanted to keep myself open and so I would need to go through and say "It's a bit loud" at times. I like dynamic music; I just love it, but I've got to be careful. I've got to think a bit more about it because the other thing that that triggers for me again is my father, because there had to be quiet in the household for him.

About Music
and Energy States

And the other night, I was doing some energy-flow healing work. You also relax a bit with it; it's contemplative. And I was playing some [New Age] music and I knew the music. It started very quietly, and then the piano comes in with just this one note like that [*indicates with a jab of a single pointed finger*]—a real attack! And what it did [to me was that] I had a real burst in my head as a reaction to it. It was really loud, and I got a visual thing with it, which I normally don't. It was like an explosion. So, I've still got the sensitivity! [*Laughter*]

About the Imagery Process

I was also thinking, "Where does it come from?" Because after a while, I was getting images. I seemed to get more images when I was in a GIM session than I would in my dreams, and that surprised me. I wouldn't have thought I could get images like that! Where is that coming from? It's somewhere in there because it just feels right.

About the Therapy

The more I did here, the freer I got with what I would say without putting a heavy filter on, [like] saying it doesn't make sense and it's illogical and that sort of stuff. So I would try to get the words flowing freely.

One of the things that strikes me now, as I think about it, is that I have had talking therapies and I achieved so much [indicates small amount with hands], but it wasn't—it has never been—a real natural way of my communication. I know I have had to work at it, and coming to music therapy, that was something I trusted and that was what I think triggered the freedom. I was relaxed then.

What I found is that the more I have done, the more I can see that I need to do. And also I can no longer escape from it; I can't "cop out."

About Reviewing the Transcripts

The focus [in my therapy experiences] has always been on "family of origin" and then secondarily [on] how it would affect my relationship or whatever else is happening. But this [material under discussion], this is directly on my relationship. It's interesting the way and where it comes in, how it works.

It's a little bit spooky. I'm reading words that I said, and I read them [and] wonder why they are familiar. It's not like something that I've only just said. It's interesting: the words themselves have an effect on me—rather than just words—because I said them at a certain time and in a certain way, with a certain meaning. I know that I've said them; that's what I'm just coming to grips with. It does stir up the feelings for me, seeing it down in black and white, because it has the power to take me back there.

Part III

Client Experiences
Are Written About by Parents

In these narratives, parents write about the music
therapy experiences of their children or adolescents.
The parents are speaking for children who are unable
or unavailable to write themselves. Their narratives
present broad stories of the children's lives and lifelong experiences with music.

Narrative 20

SHARING SESSIONS WITH JOHN

Anna Jones
and Amelia Oldfield

AMELIA'S INTRODUCTION

When I first heard about this book, I immediately thought of Anna and John. The progress that 3-year-old John had made had been exciting and interesting. I also felt that his mother, Anna, and I were working well together in these sessions in which the three of us participated together in movement and music games and playful improvisations. I was a little unsure about how Anna would feel about writing a chapter and also wondered whether she would have enough time to do this while looking after three young children. Her response was enthusiastic and positive, however.

We are both pleased with the narrative. I am very moved by what Anna wrote and Anna has gained satisfaction from the process of writing about her little boy.

ANNA'S ACCOUNT

John is the second of our three children. Our eldest, Thomas, is 20 months older than John and our daughter, Maria, is 17 months younger. John was born on a very windy day, and as we waited in the delivery room, workmen were planting trees in the hospital car park. On my frequent visits to the hospital with John, I see the trees and they always remind me of his birth.

John's birth is not a good memory for me. The midwife we had was very busy and made me feel as if I was making her life difficult because John took such a long time arriving. When he appeared, he looked like a white ghost and I immediately worried about a small mark on his lip. This quickly disappeared, but unlike my other two children's births, which I remember with great pleasure, John's birth seemed to be surrounded by anxiety.

John was a very different baby from Thomas, who had slept through the night very quickly. John seemed to cry continuously, especially between 5 P.M. and midnight. He would scream and go stiff when we tried to comfort him and seemed to resist being cuddled.

I remember one evening, holding him on my lap at 11 P.M. and thinking, "I've had enough. I can't take any more nights of your crying." Just then, a friend rang, saying she had lost the 29-week baby she was carrying. I cried as i held on to John and thought, "You just keep on crying. You're here, you're mine, and nothing else matters. We can cope with anything as long as you're here."

The one thing that seemed to calm John down at this stage was the theme tune from the *Postman Pat* television programme. This was particularly useful on long car journeys, when my husband and I would spend hours singing the tune to him again and again. We would have done almost anything to stop him crying.

It was when my daughter Maria arrived that I started suspecting there might be something seriously wrong with John. When John was born, my older son, Thomas, was very aware of the new baby. I remember him saying "Mummy" and "John" and helping me by fetching things I needed. When Maria was born, John seemed completely unaware of her existence; he didn't say any words or show any interest in either the new baby or his elder brother Thomas. I tried to convince myself that John was 3 months younger than Thomas had been when John arrived but the seed of doubt was sown. I was worried about John from then on.

Unfortunately, although I did voice my concern to various health professionals, it wasn't until 10 months later that John was seen by a clinical psychologist at the child development centre situated at the same hospital where I had delivered my children. After a 2-hour session with John, my husband, and myself, she told us that she thought that John was on the autistic spectrum. I began to cry. This was not what I wanted to hear. Deep down, I wasn't surprised. I had known all along that there was something very wrong, but it was still a shock to have my fears confirmed. She gave us a leaflet and a book to read on autism and told us to come back a week later when we might have more questions after we had had time for the news to sink in.

After the children had gone to bed that evening, my husband and I sat up all night talking about what this might mean for John and for us as a family. We cried as we discussed what we were reading in the literature we had been given. The next morning when I went to see John, I somehow expected him to have two heads or to have changed in some way. But there he was, jumping up and down in his cot in his usual way. I knew then that we would manage, no matter what the future had in store for us.

A few months later, John saw a specialist doctor, who confirmed the diagnosis of autism and also told us that John had severe learning difficulties. As soon as we knew for certain what John's problems were, we determined to do everything we could to help him as much as possible. I was pleased we were given a diagnosis so soon—when John was only 2½ years old—because it meant that we were able to get him the help he needed from an early age.

When I heard that there was a music therapist working at the child development centre, I immediately thought that John might benefit from some work in this area. Our house always has music of some sort coming from one room or another and we like most kinds of music. Even as a small baby, John would calm down when he heard Johann Strauss's "Blue Danube" waltz. He would get excited when he heard Tchaikovsky's *1812 Overture* and seemed to try to sing along to Robson and Geromme's *Unchained Melody*. I enquired about music therapy sessions from John's speech therapist and she referred us to music therapist Amelia Oldfield.

Amelia agreed to do two individual music therapy assessment sessions to see whether he would benefit from more regular work in this area. In our very first session, I was very worried that Amelia would think that John was uninterested and unresponsive to music and also too naughty. He screamed whenever she offered him anything and refused to sit down on the mat when this was suggested. However, Amelia explained that music therapy was a way to help children with difficulties and that they weren't expected to be good or perform well in these sessions. She said she could see that John enjoyed different sounds by the way he looked up when something in the improvised music she was making changed and by his obvious (though very fleeting) moments of delight when the music started.

In our next session, Amelia asked me whether I thought that John would mind coming into the room on his own, without me. I wasn't sure about this, but I suggested we try it. It was terrible! John very quickly screamed his head off and I had to go into the room to comfort him. However, far from being put off, Amelia saw

John's need for me to be there as a positive sign. She explained to me that many other young autistic children she had worked with had no apparent strong bond with either of their parents and that she had to work through music to create an initial link between herself and the child. Since John clearly wanted me to be in the room with him, Amelia suggested that we should continue with the three of us in the room together.

After the first two assessment sessions, Amelia told me that she thought that John was very responsive to music and sound and that music therapy might well be a way to help him. She wanted to know which areas I felt John particularly needed help with. Speech and communication was my first thought, but we also agreed that he could use help with concentration and with learning to accept adult direction without kicking up an enormous fuss. Amelia then suggested that we work together for a term of weekly half-hour sessions using improvised music and sound exchanges to focus on these areas. After this term, we reviewed his progress and the sessions have continued for almost a year now, with regular reviews of John's progress.

Although we were both [eager] for John to start using words, Amelia did not actively encourage the use of words. Instead she would pick up on John's many vocal sounds, imitate them, answer them, and weave them into the musical improvisations. She also would often sing or chant commentaries to go with what John was doing at the time: "John is playing the drum" or "John and Mummy are having a cuddle."

Three weeks later, while John and I were traveling home in the car after a music therapy session, John started saying "Muma," repeating the word *Mummy* I had just said to him in the same way that we had been repeating vocal sounds to one another in the music therapy session we had just had. I remember the feeling of sheer joy and total disbelief. My son had said a word, something I thought might never happen. I cried as I repeated the word *Mummy* over and over, the first word he had ever said. I was convinced from that moment that music therapy had given my son the pathway to speech.

As the sessions went on, I remember thinking that it was a good thing that John hadn't wanted to stay in the room without me. It was a delight to be able to see John, who usually took no notice of anyone or anything for any length of time, become totally engrossed in making sounds and music. His enthusiasm and pleasure were so intense that it was impossible not to feel happy myself, especially when he started to share his enjoyment with me, bringing me instruments to look at or rushing up to me to give me an excited hug. He wanted me to show some reaction to the noises and sounds he was making, which I tried to do by making slow movements when he played softly and rapid ones when he was banging wildly. Gradually he has let Amelia come into his little world, permitting her to take turns to play the instruments and allowing her to run around the room excitedly with him, playing percussion instruments placed all over the room. He will now even give her an occasional hug.

The structure of the sessions is very informal; the room is laid out for John. Amelia sits on the mat on the floor with her guitar and sings the same "Hello" song every week, encouraging John to strum the guitar strings to mark the beginning of the session. During the first 4 months, Amelia alternated between encouraging John to do something with us, such as playing the xylophone on the mat or running around playing large percussion instruments, and allowing John to do whatever he wanted while she accompanyed his movements and actions by singing or playing other instruments. Initially this approach worked quite well, since John found it almost impossible to concentrate for any length of time and he needed "time off" after each attempt to communicate with him. The clear structure of the sessions reassured John, allowing him to have great fun, but also the structure allowed Amelia to introduce a whole range of different instruments and ideas which John might not have discovered if there had been no direction from us. Although he didn't care for suggestions being made to him, the novelty of the instruments and his excitement about the music-making helped divert him from his indignation at being directed.

Gradually, however, he became more and more resistant to any suggestions being made and would fight and struggle fiercely when I tried to hold him on my lap for even 1 minute. After a couple of very stressful sessions, Amelia decided to stop being directive in any way if John started resisting or fighting our suggestions.

Three or four sessions later, a very interesting thing started to develop. John had clearly become used to the "on/off" approach, and when we stopped providing this structure, he found his own way to have time out and then rejoin us. When he felt he had had enough of interacting with us, he would disappear into a little playhouse behind some screens in a corner of the room. After a few minutes, he would return, quite happy to sit and play with us on the carpet with the instruments for a few minutes before disappearing again. Each time he retreated behind the screen, he would say "bye-bye" and then greet us again excitedly as he reappeared. Amelia would leave silences while John was "invisible" but respond to any small vocal sounds he made. Gradually, John came to anticipate and enjoy these "blind" vocal exchanges, usually bursting into fits of laughter before reemerging with loud hellos. At home, John invariably repeated these games, hiding behind the furniture and rushing out yelling "See ya" at the top of his voice.

As sessions progressed, John spent less and less time behind the screen. Occasionally when we felt that he was beginning to be frustrated or upset, Amelia or I suggested to John that he might like some "time out" by saying "bye-bye" and pointing to the screen. Sometimes this worked very well and allowed John to retreat for a minute or two without getting too distressed.

John continues to enjoy very much his music therapy sessions. We still have some weeks when he is not as responsive as others, but he seems happier now because he fully understands the structure of the sessions and feels he has some control over the situation. He will often choose instruments for us to play or indicate to Amelia that he wants to play the piano with her. He loves peekaboo games and likes to pretend to go to sleep to quiet music and be woken up by a sudden noise. All his games are incredibly intense and engaging, and it is impossible not to be completely engrossed in his interactions.

He has also just started making full use of dynamics. At the moment, he particularly likes the bass xylophone, which he initially didn't like, preferring just to take the note bars off and on. Now, however, he uses it to make very loud noises, then actually crouches in on himself to play the softest notes you could imagine, only to bash again a few minutes later. I am full of amazement when I watch him doing this. He seems to be really feeling the music and understanding what the instrument is doing.

It is quite remarkable how much progress John has made over the past year. From no words, he is now using three- or four-word sentences. In fact, at times he is such a chatterbox I wish he would be quiet! He still gets very upset when he can't get his own way, but he gets over these upsets more quickly and can be more easily diverted than previously. Toward the middle of the year, he started being more aware of his brother and sister. I believe his sister's learning to talk has helped him with his language, as he likes to copy her and in this way join in with a lot of the things that she does. Maria thinks the world of him and although they sometimes cause havoc together, it is lovely to see the strong bond between them. They are always cuddling each other and love to hold hands when walking outside.

I recently had to bring 2½-year-old Maria with me to John's music therapy session, as my child-care arrangements fell through at the last minute. John was very caring, wanting her to join in and have turns on all the instruments, shouting "Maria's turn, Maria play." I felt a little frustrated, though, as I wanted this to be a time specially for John and I felt torn between helping both of them. Amelia agreed that although it was nice to see John's positive relationship with his younger sister, it was better to devote the sessions entirely to John, especially as after the novelty of the situation wore off, Maria was determined to play the noisiest instruments all the time.

I continue to enjoy the music therapy sessions with John very much. I feel as though I am sharing something with him that he really enjoys, and that he very much wants me to be there with him. I like laughing with John and Amelia in the sessions and enjoy making a bit of a fool of myself, joining in with the music and the games. If blowing a horn or pretending to go to sleep helps John, then why not make the most if it.

SINGING A SPECIAL SONG

Christina Rago and Julie Hibben

JULIE'S INTRODUCTION

I am grateful to Christina, Franny's mother, for writing about Franny's life with music. Christina has always been perceptive about the value of Franny's music and a strong advocate for her needs. Franny and I worked together (in sessions they called music lessons) for 3½ years, from third grade until sixth. Franny, who has developmental delays and mild cerebral palsy, used her sessions to sing and record familiar songs and to role play. Franny is now 15. Christina has chosen to use their real names.

CHRISTINA TELLS OF
FRANNY'S MUSIC

Music and Franny have been together from the beginning. Before she had language, she loved to sing and be sung to. She loved to rock and be held and watched my lips carefully as they moved. She'd copy my movements and I'd move her fingers and hands in fingerplay or in rhythms.

Her sister, Maria, was learning Suzuki violin, and "Twinkle, Twinkle, Little Star" was played often in our house. Maria's Suzuki teacher encouraged us to rub or tap the children in the same bow movement as the song to reinforce the rhythm of the music. I used this technique with Franny as well, to practice songs and integrate the music into her mind and body.

Franny's disabilities are traced to agenesis of the corpus collosum (the nerve bundle that connects the right and left hemispheres of the brain never formed) and mild cerebral palsy. She also has overall developmental delay. She walks now in her own style, which can be viewed as awkward at times, but it gets her where she needs to go, and she has made enormous progress. She is 15 years old, and her condition was diagnosed when she was 9 months old. The prognosis at that time was that she would not walk, but she has gone from a walker to a wheelchair, to a walker again, then crutches, and finally, at 7 years old, she was able to walk without help. Music, in the meantime, was a rhythmic link to the perambulations and movements of the outside world. She learned sign language before she was able to vocalize speech. She began to talk in kindergarten and now speaks quite intelligibly. She still receives language and speech therapy.

Throughout Franny's life, music has served as a way to order aspects of her life. For example, we would sing together: "Clean up, clean up, everybody clean up" or "Hungry, hungry, I am hungry." Music was a soothing influence during her morning wake-up period and for her evening lullaby. Music remains a form of socialization in group chorus at school and when she sings hymns at church. Music deepens feelings of comfort and security at home and with her family and friends. This summer, she attended an overnight camp deep in the northern woods for a week. While [she was] there, I know, music and her repertoire of many songs made it easy for her to make friends quickly and share experiences.

In preschool, Franny sang a number of her songs during circle time. The songs were familiar and were a way of being together as a group, of enjoying friendships, of combining song with sign language, and of demonstrating a sense of community. As the songs were introduced into our household, the familiar world of home became integrated into the new patterns and structures of the preschool.

In third grade, Franny began private lessons with Julie Hibben. The work she did with Ms. Hibben supported and supplemented the public school's music program. The songs from the public school were the springboard for improvisation and were expanded in the sessions. The public school music teacher had said that she felt ill equipped to deal with Franny and that Franny's classroom aide needed to bear the responsibility for her music instruction. In one of my arguments for the public school to continue support for Franny's outside instruction—when she was in fifth grade—I explained how her one-on-one instruction was crucial to the success of her "integration plan." This individualized program allowed Franny to work in depth and without pressure so that she could take part more fully in all aspects, including performance, of the public school program.

Music is Franny's most integral subject—it is as critical and reinforcing as language. It *is* another language for her. Since Franny doesn't participate in the school foreign language program, she should at least have music. Franny remembers the music she hears and responds to it vocally. Music helps her memory, her language, and her counting skills. The music program reinforces and supports everything the special-education teachers are working on as outlined in the individualized education program (IEP) and the goals we periodically set for her to meet in her daily life. Franny needs reinforcement to learn to use her voice appropriately—with the right amount of loudness, intensity, and expression. Music does this and more for Franny.

The sessions with Ms. Hibben included singing the songs she was learning in her music class at school, listening to the sound of her own voice in recordings where she heard herself through speakers while using a microphone, making new recordings, and doing imaginative play. Ms. Hibben gave Franny the freedom during these sessions to make choices and order their "play." I saw a tremendous release in Franny's face after her sessions. She would enter the room appearing tight and walk out unburdened. Ms. Hibben used the sessions to help Franny explore her feelings in the course of their play together. The play would include setting up the space (a trip, restaurant, a party, putting a baby to bed) and getting dressed (using scarves). "Several weeks ago," Ms. Hibben wrote in her first report, "Franny said we were not going to play doctor anymore, perhaps a sign that she is letting go of some of those fears." I know that the operations Franny experienced in first and second grades to enable her to walk had a terrible downside. The trauma of the experience was healed through music.

Franny used tapes from her public school music class and learned the songs for that class with Ms. Hibben. This process built her confidence about singing. She was no longer too shy to take part in the music class with the other kids. Franny's interactive playing on pianos and drums was uninhibited and she used expressive gestures. Using language with the playing helped Franny organize herself: "My turn, your turn." She would often initiate words or sing to herself while playing.

The structure of the sessions with Ms. Hibben was very much a participatory construct. Ms. Hibben used a typed list of things they did together during the lesson, and Franny chose the order of things. Being in charge was a critical part of Franny's learning. Sessions always began with a long duo-piano improvisation. Franny was always reluctant to try something new, so Ms. Hibben was careful about what to introduce. For example, early in their work together, Franny would ask to hold the mike but would make no sound. After about 2 to 3 weeks, she began to sing into the mike and record her songs. She always enjoyed pretend play: "You be the wolf and I'll be the gramma," she'd say, and the play would evolve into acting out going to the doctor and having Ms. Hibben's (not Franny's!) foot examined for new foot braces. They would listen to a tape of songs prepared for Franny to learn by her public school music teacher and Franny would sit down with the printed version and sing them.

By the fifth grade, Franny had made considerable progress. At home at this time, she was singing Ella Fitzgerald songs and liked sophisticated melodies and words. The rhythms and syncopation of the music from the thirties and forties intrigued her. During Franny's sessions with Ms. Hibben in fifth and sixth grades, she began to experience herself as an artist. Because of her music skills, she began to have a sense of competence and control. She used about 15 songs regularly, exploring her own ideas and practicing skills. The songs she used linked her to her social milieu and her family. She created a series of miniperformances during their sessions.

Franny was developing her innate sense of musical idioms. Ms. Hibben wrote that she would repeat the last phrase of a song to signify the ending or she would add a two-beat cadence on the piano at the end of her song. She would also alternate phrases with Ms. Hibben, spontaneously making up words to a familiar tune. They created many variations in a call–response style. Franny filled a 90-minute tape with her recordings.

Franny could now sing many songs from memory (multiple verses) and stand confidently in front of the mike and read song sheets. Her finger work on the keyboard was in synchrony with the rhythm of the words of her song. Ms. Hibben wrote, "She is never at a loss for an appropriate song; when I sing 'Hush Little Baby' to put her to sleep, she will sing 'All the Pretty Little Horses' and 'Consider Yourself' to put me to sleep!" One of Franny's favorite songs was "So Long, Farewell." She did this with hand movements and performed it at school.

Music has a special emotional charge for Franny. She uses music to induce moods, to relax, and to self-entertain. Her repertoire of songs continues to expand, and these songs are friends or emotional contexts and have meanings associated with the words. She likes to end a song with a bang on the piano; by doing this, she feels and shares the tension and release. Ms. Hibben feels that the songs Franny sings and the music she hears represent emotional peaks and valleys and provide her with a broader spectrum of emotion than she normally experiences.

Franny's responses to music are spontaneous. By that, I mean that in all other aspects of her life, she has to think hard. Her movements need to be thought through because of her cerebral palsy. Walking is something she must do with great concentration, as she makes sure that her voluntary movements are made with precision. She doesn't want to step too high or too far; she needs to coordinate where she goes with what she sees. Eating, playing with toys, and talking all require motor planning and forethought. Music reaches her ears and she responds with delight, enthusiasm, and direct participation.

Music was used in the early grades as a way to formalize or structure transitions through the use of a "hello song" and a "goodbye song," and at home, we used lullabies for nap time and a song for washing up: "Now it's time to wash your hands, wash your hands, wash your hands; now it's time to wash your hands so early in the morning." By contrast, her present program in a new school consists of "ensemble" playing. She learns songs with eight other special-needs students who use a guitar, a harmonica, drums, an electric piano with sound effects, a small harp called a music maker, and a voice amplified by a mike. They sing a range of simple songs—from Native American to Irish folk songs—characterized by a simple melody and repeated phrases. Franny enjoys being with others and sharing the joy of music.

Music is a key part of Franny's preparation for enjoyment of an independent life. She likes to sit at the piano and play an accompaniment to her own voice. She sings songs we have collected in a three-ring binder over the years from her music classes. She likes to return to old favorites and add to her repertoire. She enjoys singing along with tapes at home in her room and she listens to music from the radio on the AM station, like any teenager. At 15, she likes to read aloud to herself and is learning to modulate her voice. She is learning to recognize within herself the range of her vocal abilities and is trying to carry tunes on pitch and maintain her breath control throughout a song.

There seem to be great possibilities open to Franny as she grows with music in her surroundings. Music has opened different avenues for expression and understanding. It will always be a part of her life.

Narrative 22

THREE STORIES
ABOUT SUZUKI PIANO EDUCATION

Laura, Catherine I. Shaffer,
Victoria Haskins, and Mary Ann Froehlich

> Where love is deep, much can be accomplished.
> —Shinichi Suzuki

MARY ANN'S INTRODUCTION

To the learning-disabled children I work with, I am their music teacher and they are my students. I integrate the Suzuki music education process with my private music therapy practice. I do not use the terms *therapist* or *client* because those terms suggest the world of disability and treatment—an abnormal world. These children long to be normal and have already suffered from labels and repeated visits to doctors, therapists, and specialists. The Suzuki method focuses on ability and success through immersion in a joyful musical environment. Suzuki parents participate in periodic group classes and become the home teachers of their children; this helps them build a music community with other families. Students and their families learn to support one another in a spirit of cooperation, not competition.

Expression in written or verbal form is difficult for my students. Music is the way they communicate. For this reason, I have asked parents to share their observations. Three parents have written their stories: Laura writes about 10-year-old Sarah, who is at the beginning of the music learning process; Catherine speaks about Ryan, her adolescent son, who is in the middle of the learning process; and Victoria speaks about her son, Jake, who is now in college. Catherine and Victoria use their real names.

LAURA SPEAKS ABOUT SARAH

I choose to be anonymous because my daughter's limitations are not commonly known. Sarah is an intelligent 10-year-old girl with perceptual motor difficulties. She experienced a severe allergic reaction to a virus when she was 2 years old. Her immune system attacked her myelin sheath, creating a condition called cerebral ataxia.

Sarah loves literature, but the actual decoding of the words is difficult for her. She enjoys making music, but reading music is a barrier to achievement. Because she is bright, Sarah is fully aware of her limitations. This causes her frustration and gives her a sense of failure. Because she loves music and dance, we began music lessons and ballet classes. We have observed a marked improvement in Sarah's motor skills. Her small-motor coordination is improving slowly.

As a credentialed teacher, I homeschool Sarah to protect her from the labeling that special classes would bring. In addition to helping Sarah's motor skills, music-making has been a bridge to connect her to activities she enjoys and has given her a normal childhood. Music invites her to risk being in new situations, such as group classes or recitals, instead of simply observing life as a fearful outsider.

Sarah works hard to learn to play the piano. She has auditory strengths, so the Suzuki method's emphasis on auditory training is effective for her. The encouraging environment and creative approach in the Suzuki method ensure that Sarah will experience success (success building upon success) instead of more failure. She enjoys being able to make music.

CATHERINE SPEAKS ABOUT RYAN

My son, Ryan, was born 12 to 14 weeks premature. Weighing 2 pounds 11 ounces, Ryan remained in the intensive care unit of Children's Hospital for his first 6 months of life. He was on a respirator for 5 months, causing speech delays as well as fluency problems that remain problems even today. Ryan also had a severe intercranial bleed following his birth, causing problems later in life with reading comprehension.

Following his release from the hospital, Ryan had motor and speech delays. He entered a regular kindergarten class but was put in a special-education class in first through third grade. Ryan is now 14 years old. He is mainstreamed with the help of district therapists in the local high school. Ryan is extremely shy but well liked by his peers and highly motivated to strive to do his best.

Ryan has always had a good ear for music. We noticed that he played pieces on the piano by ear and we wanted to give him music lessons. The benefits of that music training for Ryan have been numerous. The primary benefit is the increase in Ryan's self-esteem. Ryan does not like to talk in front of people, but he does not hesitate to play the piano for them. In making music, Ryan is able to focus on a musical task, master it, and enjoy a great sense of accomplishment. He takes pride in his music-making efforts.

Music is one way that Ryan can express himself and deal with the emotional upsets of adolescence. It is difficult for any adolescent to verbalize feelings but especially difficult for those with speech problems. This method of coping was critical this past year when Ryan's beloved grandfather (my dad) suddenly died. This was a very difficult time for our family. Ryan coped with his loss by trying to support his grandmother in her grief. I helped him select a favorite piece of music that his grandmother played when she was young. The piece was challenging, yet Ryan worked hard to master it. Though Ryan was still grieving for his late grandfather, he would play this piece to release all his pent-up emotions. The more he played, the more he was healed. He performed "Rustic Dance" for his grandmother. The smile on his face and the sense of pride in his accomplishment truly were a reflection of Ryan's healing. He felt good about bringing a moment of happiness to his grandmother during this painful time. The kiss and hug they shared after his performance at the recital are ones he will always treasure. Soon after, the health of Ryan's grandmother began to deteriorate. Six months later, she lay dying. While she was spending her final days in the intensive care unit, Ryan went to his teacher's house to prepare a tape of his grandmother's favorite songs that he often played. Although he could not visit her, he could touch her through his music. Ryan seemed to cope with his grief by focusing on this project. The tape was played at his grandmother's bedside. Ryan's music reached places in all of us where words failed.

VICTORIA SPEAKS ABOUT JAKE

Thunderous applause rang out as the last joyous chords of Handel's *Messiah* echoed through the college auditorium. I stood silently at my son's last performance at the community college, tears streaming down my face. These tears were not a response to the glorious music, but rather tears of gratitude to God and the ministry of music. My son, Jake, would soon enter Washburn University in Kansas as a music major with a voice scholarship. As he took another bow before the standing ovation, Jake exchanged glances of satisfaction with his friends in the choir. Looking at the stage, I saw the man my son had become, yet I could not help but remember the frustrated little boy who had struggled and failed in school. My husband and I had feared that Jake might go down the well-traveled path of rebellion, anger, and juvenile delinquency in response to that failure. Two very special people helped avert Jake from this possible fate, a music therapist and an Orthodox priest, rather an unlikely pair. It is that mixture of music and faith that defines Jake today.

As I look back at Jake's school career, certain events stand out and I am still amazed at his resiliency. When Jake was almost 5 and ready to enter kindergarten, he just did not seem as ready as his older sister had been for school. He didn't like to cut or draw and he seldom tried to write, so we decided to keep him out of school for one more year. In one attempt to help Jake get ready for school, we enrolled him in a summer preschool program in which the children did crafts and paper and pencil tasks. Each day when I arrived to pick Jake up from preschool, I would scan the little tables and chairs filled with children intently cutting, pasting, and coloring, in hopes of finding him. Each day, I would have to retrieve Jake from the sandbox outside, where he sat with a few other boys in reckless abandon, pouring sand into buckets and digging holes. That year, we bought a sandbox for our home, and his medium proved to be water and sand, not scissors and paper. I felt frustrated because everything I had read stated that small-motor coordination was important for school success. So out came the bucket of Legos, the containers of clay, the pots of paint, and various other craft materials for Jake to explore in hopes of developing his small-motor coordination, but he just was not successful at these tasks.

My concern over his inability to use scissors and his lack of interest in writing may seem out of proportion, yet it proved to be at the root of his problems that developed later in school. Although it is not uncommon for little boys to prefer the outdoors to writing, Jake's case proved to be more severe and it took several years to diagnose. When we finally did put him in kindergarten, he received a "needs improvement" for his writing grade; his teacher suggested that he just needed to try harder and to apply himself. To make matters worse, he was having difficulty learning to read and his teacher recommended he be held back. We debated the pros and cons of retention and sought advice from other professionals. Since Jake was tall for his age and was very bright verbally, we decided not to retain him in kindergarten.

After a carefree summer marked by the greatest achievement in a little boy's life, riding a two-wheeler without training wheels, Jake was ready to start first grade. He happily bounded out the front door with his new red Spiderman lunch box grasped firmly in his hand; however, the boy I picked up at school that afternoon had an entirely different countenance. Jake's expression looked sullen as he slowly walked to the car, opened the door, and slumped down in the seat. Hoping that he was just tired, I asked how the day had gone. In exasperation he cried, "My teacher wanted me to spell *orange* and *yellow* and I don't know how! I just can't!" I tried to comfort Jake by telling him that his teacher was probably just trying to see what everyone knew so she could help them learn. He would not be comforted, because in his mind, he had failed. Taking the bull by the horns, I taught Jake to spell *orange* and *yellow* as we drove home and promised that together we would work on all of his spelling and reading. This small incident is still so vivid in my memory because it was indicative of Jake's intelligence and his perception of what he should be able to achieve and what others thought of him.

Jake continued to struggle. He would sit at the kitchen table, hunched over his homework, with his pencil gripped at the very tip and positioned in that strange twisted manner left-handers use to get t.. 'r letters to slant like right-handers'. Homework that should have taken 30 minutes would take Jake an hour or longer. His slowness was obvious to his teachers, his classmates, and himself. The sense of failure and frustration built up within him. By the third grade, we began to lose him to this frustration. This gentle child was now pushing and shoving his classmates and falling further and further behind in his schoolwork.

As parents, we found it very difficult to see our child struggle and fail, especially when the icons of society seem to be academic success, athletic prowess, and physical beauty. At times, we felt as if we were failing. I loved Jake so dearly and yet I realize I had begun to focus on his failure at school rather than who he was as a person. My silent prayer that day was that God would reveal to me Jake's positive qualities and help me to encourage him. Then, mustering all the courage I had, I asked two close friends if they saw anything in the way we were raising our son that could be causing his difficulties. We were willing to make any changes in order to help Jake succeed. They encouraged us to look into the possibility that he had learning disabilities. At about the same time, his teacher told us how she was puzzled by the fact that he could conceptualize with the GATE (gifted and talented) kids in the class, but he could not get his work finished. Orally, Jake could confidently answer the questions; however, if you asked him to write his thoughts down on paper, it would be a slow and laborious task filled with misspellings and eraser marks. This was a clear indicator that something was wrong. At this point, we asked if Jake could be tested by the school psychologist for learning disabilities.

The tests were inconclusive and the only solution the psychologist offered was that I not let the teachers make me feel guilty for his problems in class. When we appealed to the principal, she suggested a special day class to remediate his work. We left the meeting feeling abandoned by our school and its professionals and caught in a maze. Here was a boy who was creative, intelligent, and not succeeding at school, yet no one could help him. My husband and I refused to abandon our son to this system. We asked ourselves, "What adult would go to the same job for four years and daily fail at that job?" Yet was this not exactly what we were allowing to happen to Jake?

Our solution seemed clear; we would homeschool. Back in 1987, homeschooling was not a common occurrence, but encouraged by close family friends who had already chosen that route, we decided to take both of our children out of public school and teach them at home. We also decided to find out what lay behind Jake's learning problems and have him tested privately.

That summer, we applied for an interdistrict transfer and enrolled in a pilot home study program that would supply books and a mentor teacher. The teacher assigned to Jake was a godsend. She had been teaching in the district for over 25 years, understood learning disabilities, and had overcome dyslexia herself. She felt it was crucial to rebuild Jake's self-concept and rekindle his love for learning. Part of the plan was to find an activity in which he would succeed. I had met a music therapist in our community who taught piano; she came highly recommended. I contacted her, and after a brief interview in which I explained his learning problems and school career, she accepted Jake as a student. Little did we know how life-changing that would be for Jake and our whole family.

Jake began his piano lessons with the Suzuki method that involved parent as well as student participation. This method allowed for immediate success. Jake had an excellent ear and learned the rhythms quickly. The therapist wisely stayed away from any music reading, allowing Jake to experience success and revel in the sheer joy of making music. Each week he practiced diligently and eagerly looked forward to his lesson. Soon he started creating his own little compositions and proudly shared them with his piano teacher. She responded to them with joy and enthusiasm. Her home became a safe haven, a place of accomplishment and achievement. During the lessons, his teacher skillfully corrected any mistakes without ever saying no. Jake had heard those words enough in the last 4 years to last a lifetime. Music was healing those deep wounds and his attitude was starting to change. His grandmother, commenting on how happy he seemed lately, stated, "We're starting to get our little boy back again." These words were so true. Jake was blossoming under the tutelage of this skilled music therapist.

The success Jake was experiencing with his music lessons transferred to his academics. He willingly read and worked on his assignments with a new determined attitude.

One of the main concerns about homeschooling is a lack of socialization with other children as well as with adults. The music lessons allowed him to build relationships with an adult (the music therapist) and with other music students. As part of the music curriculum, Jake attended group meetings with other music students and their siblings. These meetings explored such things as different types of musical instruments, composers, musical periods, and the various types of music from those periods.

At one meeting, Jake and his sister, Amanda, did a presentation on aleatoric music and the composers John Cage and Charles Ives. Jake gave an oral report and had great fun composing a piece by throwing a penny on the piano keys to select the notes in the composition. To illustrate the haphazard manner in which this music is often composed, Amanda had each student take an instrument from the therapist's music basket and then instructed them to play any note or rhythm they wanted when Jake pointed to them. This impromptu aleatoric piece ended with a chaotic chorus of all the students playing their own note and rhythm at the same time. These group lessons helped Jake and Amanda to form lasting memories and friendships.

Jake also participated in piano recitals with members of his group. He was excited to be able to perform and have his family and friends come hear him. Jake begged us to buy him a new sport coat for the event. His first recital was held in the safe and intimate surroundings of his music therapist's home. That evening, the soft glow of the living room seemed particularly inviting.

Jake took his place at the grand piano. He sat erect and impecca-
bly dressed. Jake carefully arched his fingers in the proper position and began his song, remembering to include the dynamics
and expression he had diligently practiced. When he finished,
there was spontaneous applause and Jake stood and bowed, revel-
ing in the well-deserved praise.

These recitals were beneficial for all the music students; however, they were especially beneficial for Jake, helping him build
self-respect, diligence, and confidence. Each recital was preceded
by weeks of hard work on the dynamics and emotion needed to
interpret and properly execute the piece. These performances
instilled the qualities needed for good musicianship, as well as a
sense of belonging to a special group of talented people. Music and
the special skills of the music therapist helped to heal and restore
Jake's self-esteem and love of learning. The ministry of music,
truly a gift from God, gave us our gentle, loving boy back and he
regained the ability to try things at which he might fail.

At this point in Jake's instruction, the music therapist began
to teach him how to read music. She started by giving him a large-
print book that would eliminate any visual confusion and later
moved on to smaller print, motivating him with Christmas carols.
The last big step was to read the regular-print Suzuki book itself.
The ability to read music proved to be a valuable skill later in
high school and college, when he was often the only percussionist
in the orchestra who read music.

Seeing Jake succeed gave us the courage to pursue the diagnosis of what appeared to be a learning disability. We endured
another maze of testing with different specialists that finally
confirmed that Jake was slow in reading, yet high in comprehension and math. His small-motor coordination test showed that he
had neurological problems. Jake was diagnosed with finger
agnosia, a rare neurological disorder in which the signals from the
brain that instruct the fingers are interrupted.

Finally we had a reason for Jake's limitations, not an excuse.
Yet his finger agnosia did not prove an obstacle in playing the piano. Through music, Jake had learned to work hard and compen-
sate for his disability.

Jake's experience with learning disabilities and music therapy affected our whole family. Our daughter, Amanda, had been
treated for 3 years at a children's hospital for a grave illness and
as a result had decided she wanted to work with children in a
hospital setting. After observing the benefit of music therapy
firsthand in Jake's life and witnessing how music helped to

change his attitude toward learning, she realized she could help children by using music. Amanda went on to a university and received a degree in music therapy. My husband discovered he had disabilities similar to Jake's. He said it was as if someone wiped the steam from a mirror and he could clearly see himself and see why he struggled with certain things.

After advocating for Jake and learning about different disabilities, I went to work for our school district as a special-education instructional assistant. Following 5 years in that position, I went back to college to receive my bachelor's degree. This spring, I graduated and was accepted into a graduate program in occupational therapy. I know what it is like to face problems that seem insurmountable and I've learned that with help, those problems can be conquered. Jake's experience taught me about resiliency of spirit, willingness to change, and the importance of never giving up. I believe those valuable lessons can be applied to anything I pursue.

Music continued to be Jake's greatest strength through high school. He expanded his music horizons by taking up the drums and then going on to play the bells, marimba, xylophone, and timpani in the school band. Though always painfully shy, Jake joined a local children's theater group and played lead roles in the musicals. We hadn't realized that Jake's voice was one of his strongest assets. He was reaching his potential.

Today Jake is a voice performance major in college. His true love is choir. He hopes to become a music educator and someday an Orthodox priest and church musician. He has excelled in his courses, using a computer instead of pen and paper to complete his assignments.

This struggling little boy who was labeled as a failure by so many teachers has one of the lead roles this fall in Haydn's operetta, *La Canterina*. Music unlocked the door to a rewarding life. It is this gift that Jake wants to share with God and others.

Part IV

Client Experiences
Are Inferred by
Therapists Through
Multiple Means

In these narratives, the experiences of clients who do not have meaningful language or whose words are not available are presented by their therapists. (One narrative is written by a supervisor.) The writers use more than one means or source to suggest the experience of their client(s): observation and description of behavior; testimony of spokespersons, such as cotherapists, observers, or parents; the client's music; the therapist's journals; and imaginative representations in soliloquy form of the client's thoughts and feelings inferred from long experience with the client and from a synthesis of the above sources. By these multiple means, the writers attempt to go beyond description of the client's behavior to suggest what the client's experience of music therapy might have been. In two narratives, joint writers combined their analyses to present the experience of their clients.

ROSE

Michele Forinash and Sally McKnight

MICHELE AND SALLY'S INTRODUCTION

This is a study of Rose, a 90-year-old Jewish immigrant who is blind and has chronic schizophrenia and Alzheimer's dementia. Rose's severe and long-standing mental illness, lack of ability to speak English, and dementia (apparent in attempts at communication in her native Polish) make the gathering of her history difficult, if not impossible. It is thought that she escaped persecution in Europe during World War II. Some sources mention the death of a husband in the war and the death of an infant daughter during the period of the war in which Rose and the daughter lived in the woods. The documentation suggests that after her arrival in the States and the dissolution of her brief second marriage, Rose lived for a number of years as a street person. A lawyer, who had passed Rose daily on the street, became interested and concerned about her—enough so to become her legal guardian. As Rose was then in her sixties, the guardian had her placed in a nursing home. Despite her severe disabilities, Rose has actively participated in music therapy sessions while a resident at the nursing home. We have worked with Rose for 5 years (Michele first and then Sally), adapting familiar songs to enhance communication.

How do we begin to describe Rose's experience of music therapy? It is impossible to ever fully know such a client's experience, but it is imperative that we attempt to understand as much as possible about her, since she is unable to report her experience or actively share in the decision-making processes involved in her treatment. We realize the difficulty and immensity of the task of articulating Rose's experience, yet we hope that through the approach of "constructing a narrative" (Ely et al., 1991, p. 153) we may be accurately representing what might be an aspect of her experience. Although this is not a formal qualitative study, we have adopted guidelines for creating our narrative on Rose's behalf from Garner (Ely et al., 1991) and Aigen (1997). In this case, a construct narrative is a soliloquy that we have made on Rose's behalf. It is based on repeated observation of Rose's unique responses and behaviors both in and out of music therapy sessions and contains statements that are central to the way that she appears in the world (Ely et al.).

To create the construct narrative for Rose, Michele conducted four videotaped music therapy sessions (25 to 35 minutes long) with Rose during a 3-week period. These sessions were very representative of the wide range of Rose's responses and participation in music therapy during the 5-year period we worked with her. We present sessions 1 and 3, as they best represent Rose's typical responses in music therapy sessions. We independently analyzed the videotape using phenomenological methodology (Forinash, 1992). From each analysis, a narrative of Rose's experience was generated. These narratives were compared and brought together to form a portrait of her experience in and of music therapy. We include actual transcriptions from the videotaped sessions, interspersed with the construct narratives or soliloquies we have constructed on Rose's behalf (in italics).

ROSE IN THE NURSING-HOME ENVIRONMENT

Rose is a somewhat self-contained geriatric resident. She is frequently found sitting in her wheelchair outside her room. Monica, Rose's nurse's aide, is attuned to her appreciation of music, so there is often a radio nearby tuned to a classical station. Sometimes Rose just sits quietly, her blind eyes staring straight ahead, whereas at other times, Rose seems agitated. The staff and guardian are always trying to find the appropriate balance of medication that will calm her anxiety without making her lethargic. This is not an easy balance to achieve. When Rose is agitated, her hands beat perseveratively on the tray table attached to her chair. Patricia, the recreation therapy staff member on the unit, created a pat mat for Rose's tray table, to stop the bruising of her hands during her periods of incessant patting and to give her a sense of texture as she pats. When engaged in the patting, Rose averages a rapid 178 pats per minute. Sometimes she pats on the soft mat; sometimes she reaches to the extremities of the tray table where the mat doesn't cover, so that when she pats on the hard surface, it resounds with a thud. Sometimes she reaches all the way to pat the empty space that surrounds her chair. The patting is broken up by a motion of smoothing what she has patted, as if she is patting down and then smoothing linens to put away. Rose will also voice an occasional "oy," make hand-washing motions, and then take a momentary break from her patting.

Rose is often a passive participant in recreation therapy groups; she doesn't initiate any contact with the outside world. She seems either unable or unwilling to make connections to herself or others. We have wondered if she is simply confused in a large group setting with so much stimulation or perhaps her psychosis and dementia have left her with such a poorly developed sense of self that she no longer sees herself as a separate being capable of acting on and interacting with the world around her.

Rose seems very self-possessed, self-sufficient, and independent.

I don't need anything from you. My patting is important and keeps me busy.

Yet she seems controlled by and possessed by her compulsive behaviors.

If I stop this patting, something terrible will happen. This is what keeps me going. I must keep going. If I stop, I won't exist.

ROSE IN MUSIC THERAPY

In session 1 (as in sessions 2 and 4), Rose displays much of her typical perservative behavior, the incessant patting of the tray table. She is still and engaged for approximately 5 minutes. In session 3, however, she is quiet and engaged for 20 of the 25 minutes in the session. We present only the portions of the sessions in which Rose was engaged.

Session 1

Rose sits in her elaborate wheelchair. Her white hair is neatly tied in a bun and she is dressed in a flowered housedress. She sits and pats her tray table.

[Pat, pat, pat, pat, pat, pat.] *I have work to do. I must build up my work. I must keep busy. This work is familiar and I feel safe here, busy like this. I know what I need to do.* [Pat, pat, pat, pat, pat, pat.] *If I stop, the noise in my head gets too loud. Keeping busy helps stop the noise.* [Pat, pat, pat, pat.] *I hear something.* [Pause] *Is someone talking? Is someone talking to me?* [Pause] *Is she talking to me?* [Pause] *She is talking to me.*

Michele (the therapist) touches Rose's hand. She immediately sits back and stops patting. Michele holds her hand and says slowly, "Good morning, Rose. Good morning. Good morning." Rose replies "Good morning?" Michele repeats, "Good morning. It is time for music." Rose withdraws her hand and continues her patting.

Michele, sitting close at her side, begins to sing a verse of "You Are My Sunshine" (Davis and Mitchell, 1940) alternating using words with singing on "la." She pauses at the cadence of the verse, waiting for Rose to join. Rose continues to pat. Michele sings it a second time, again pausing to create a space for Rose to join. Rose sings "la" in pitch on the final note of the song.

I hear her singing. I am so busy. I must finish my work. I hear her singing. It isn't that I really want to sing with her now; it is that I can't help but sing with her.

There is a pause in which Rose continues to pat. Michele begins to strum the guitar and hum *"Bei Mir Bist Du Schoen"* (Jacobs and Secunda, 1937). Rose is immediately still and listens for 6 seconds. Michele continues singing on "la" and pausing at the end of phrases to create space. Rose does not sing but continues to pat.

There is that music again. Do I know this music? Oh yes, I know this music. I need to keep up with my work. It is important to keep up and not stop. Go all the way to the edge. I don't want to miss a section.

Michele continues with the song but begins to reflect Rose's patting tempo in the tempo of her strum. Rose immediately stops patting and sits back, breathing deeply for 15 seconds. When she does resume her patting, it is slower and has accents that reflect the phrasing in the music. Rose and Michele play together in this way for nearly a minute. As the song draws to a close, Rose slows her patting and stops just shy of the final cadence of the song. She rests for a few moments and then resumes patting.

Oy, finally some help. She is helping me do my work. I need someone to help me with this. At least now I can take a short break. It is so much easier to work together. I am tired. [Pause] *Back to work.*

Michele begins to sing *"Tumbalalaika"* (public domain). Rose is still, appearing to listen. Then her patting resumes. At the chorus, Michele, singing on "la," verbally invites Rose to sing. Rose begins to sing and does so in tempo and on pitch. She sings intermittently as Michele completes four repetitions of the song. In the middle, Michele praises, in both English and broken Yiddish, Rose's beautiful singing voice. Rose continues to sing consistently throughout the final repetition of the song.

The music is so familiar. I know this music. It is my favorite. It is so beautiful. I love to sing it. What is she saying? She hears my singing. [Pause] *She thinks my singing is beautiful! I love to sing this. She can hear me, ya!*

The song ends and Michele again praises Rose's singing and strokes her arm. Rose continues to pat. Michele rests her arm on the tray table; Rose inadvertently pats Michele's hand. Rose realizes she is touching someone and again becomes quiet. Michele, leaving her hand under Rose's, places her other hand on top of Rose's and gently pats and strokes Rose's hand. Rose is quiet for nearly 40 seconds.

That was beautiful music, but I must go back to work now. What's this? What am I touching? She is so close. She is touching me. That feels nice; she is helping me again. [Long pause] *But I have to keep going.*

Session 3

In this session, Rose exhibits no patting behavior. She does occasionally stroke her pat mat, and at times, her hands, held out in front of her, shake quite strongly. Michele finishes singing a hello.

Rose's hands are initially clasped together in front of her. As Michele begins singing, Rose sings with her and her hands, still clasped, begin to shake. Rose completes several music phrases by singing "la" on pitch and in tempo, then continues by adding several notes leading up to the ends of musical phrases in subsequent song repetitions.

Sometimes it is hard to keep still. But today I am resting. When I am still, I can hear the music better. My hands don't want to stay still sometimes. I hear the music. It feels good to listen and to sing.

As the song ends, Michele reaches out to stroke Rose's shoulder and says, "Your singing is so beautiful! Yeah?" Rose replies, "Yeah!" Michele continues by asking, "What shall we sing next? How about *'Die Greene Koseene'* [Brizant and Schwartz, 1922]?" Rose replies, "Ya, *'Die Greene Koseene,'* " and chuckles.

It feels good to sing. She hears me and she likes my singing. I am not alone in this. I hear the music. I feel it, too. It makes me want to move. I like "Die Greene Koseene." I want to sing that!

Later in the session, Michele says, "Shall we do *'Oif'n Pripetshik'* [Warshavsky, n.d.]?" Rose is quiet and Michele asks a second time. Rose chuckles and says, *"Oif'n Pripetshik."* She sings throughout this song on "la" in long, expressive phrases. She needs little encouragement to continue. She seems very engaged and connected to the music. She has extended moments of musical connection that last for as long as 34 seconds. Her voice is full and expressive. At times, she carries the melody while Michele accompanies on the guitar. Her eyes are uncharacteristically closed and she appears very involved in the music.

There is not so much noise in my head today. I can really hear the music. She waits for me and I join her singing. It is very beautiful. I feel so peaceful right now. It feels good to sing. I want to sing more. I will sing more. The music calls me in. I feel very warm now.

At the end of this song, Rose seems tired and rests her head on her arm for a moment. Michele asks if she is getting tired, and Rose responds, "Yes." Michele then sings a Yiddish lullaby while Rose listens.

It feels good to listen. I can hear her singing. She is singing to me. I can feel the music. I am tired, so very tired.

In the following and final session, Rose returned to her patting behavior, had few musical responses and had no sustained responses. It seemed that in the final taped session, Rose needed to get "back to work" and didn't have time to engage in the music. Although we are not sure of Rose's cognitive abilities, she had been told this would be the last session. We have wondered whether her lack of engagement was due to the fact that it was the last session with Michele.

DISCUSSION

In our viewing of the videotape, we noticed several things. Rose turns toward Michele and the music throughout the sessions, and the music appears to allow her to rest at times from her labors. When she is working, her patting is often rhythmically synchronized to the music and reflects the musical phrasing as well. She seems to respond to the accents, dynamics, strum patterns, and articulations of the music by the quality of and patterns of her patting. At times it seems that her hands are almost "dancing" to the music.

There is a level at which Rose seems very aware. It is not exactly a conscious awareness, but rather that she seems very aware of and sensitive to her environment and the atmosphere of her surroundings. There were many times when she seemed to respond to the mood and emotional expressions of Michele. One example of this was when Michele, who was genuinely moved by Rose's singing, praises her beautiful voice. Rose seems to understand the nature of the interaction and she giggles, as one often does after receiving a compliment.

In her work with Rose in previous music therapy groups, Sally recalled that even when Rose was not responding by singing, it was evident that she was aware of the music and would respond to changes in the sound. Sally remembers that when she played her flute in a session for the first time, after having sung songs to keyboard or autoharp accompaniment, Rose would literally "sit up and take notice" and would stop her patting behavior when focusing on the music.

We hope that we have been able to convey on some level Rose's experience of music therapy. We would like to dedicate this study to Rose and the caring staff who see the beauty in this rare flower.

Narrative 24

THE SPECIAL PLACE OF MUSIC FOR A MULTIPLY DISABLED GIRL

Barbara Crowe

INTRODUCTION

Tammy is a severely, multiply disabled teenager. She is nonverbal and cannot tell us herself what the music therapy experience means to her. In an effort to describe her experience, I write about her reactions in one session and then in the last section of this narrative, I speak for Tammy, giving her voice from my own understanding of her. I use many sources of information to speak for Tammy. I interviewed her mother (who asked that I use Tammy's real name) and a music therapist, Jane Price, who had worked with Tammy. I also reviewed professional records, particularly music therapy, audiology, and psychology reports. I use insight into Tammy's experience with music therapy based on my own observation of her weekly music therapy sessions over 3 years. As the professional supervisor working with the student music therapists, I help plan sessions, guide their therapeutic approaches, and watch each session carefully. In these sessions, Tammy enjoys familiar games and songs.

TAMMY'S SESSION

Tammy's excited cries are heard as the elevator opens and echo down the long hallway of the former hospital that now houses the music therapy clinic. Tammy has made this trip many times. Her mother reports she gets excited when they turn into the parking lot, and she believes Tammy knows exactly where she is going—to music therapy, her time of fun and socialization. Tammy has had music therapy since she was 3 years old. Now that she is 16, her sessions are a familiar part of her life and an anticipated part of her weekly routine.

After her mother's difficult pregnancy, Tammy was born severely, multiply handicapped. She is moderately to severely cognitively delayed. She has mild cerebral palsy that affects all limbs, a seizure disorder, and cortical blindness. From her infancy, her parents noticed Tammy's strong, positive response to music. She would shut out all external environmental stimuli, pushing away touch, crying at unusual sounds, and even rejecting food. Music was the exception. Music grabbed her attention, soothed her, entertained her, and coaxed her to reach out into the world. She would eat only when music was playing, would calm enough to sleep only to music. Music was the only external world Tammy knew and could tolerate. At 3 years of age, Tammy attended a special-education preschool program. Once a week, an amazing thing happened—music therapy, the purposeful use of the music Tammy had responded to since birth. Reports from these sessions show she responded to the music interventions with slow but definite changes in her responses, ability to use her hands, and general awareness.

As Tammy's wheelchair is pushed into the clinic, her high-pitched squeals, increased movement, and giggles tell us she is happy and excited to be here. Though nonverbal, Tammy does express herself through sound-making, and her mother reports the squeals and giggles appear when she is happiest. This is her music place and her response tells us she knows it. The student music therapist begins with a familiar "hello" song. Tammy looks toward her therapist and makes some excited sounds. She throws her head back, trying to see from the lower portion of her peripheral vision. She continues to respond to the therapist, making the soft "ah" sound that is reported from many sources to mean greeting and recognition. Now the familiar routine of the session begins. A variety of rhythm instruments are presented to Tammy while familiar songs are sung or favorite recordings are played. Tammy pushes the instruments away or tries to throw them across the room. Since birth, she has been reluctant to hold objects. According to the neurology reports, Tammy's nervous system is underdeveloped, making it confusing and unpleasant to touch objects. In this session, Tammy holds a drumstick and a maraca for up to a minute. She uses these to play briefly with the music. She has improved since the last session, holding these objects longer and using them appropriately.

Tammy is now wheeled to an electronic keyboard, and a lively rhythm track is played. She reaches out and begins to explore the keys. She tentatively presses several keys. At home and in other therapy situations, Tammy is reluctant to interact with people or objects. Tammy's mother says she herself uses music to encourage her daughter to explore her surroundings—to crawl, to play with toys, and to eat. Reports from many years of music therapy sessions show she responds longer to the keyboard than to most other music activities. Today she presses keys, moves her hand to different positions, and responds to the student therapist's requests, staying with the keyboard for 5 minutes.

The student music therapist now brings out her violin. As she plays, she moves to different spots in the room. This is musical tag. Tammy must follow the sound and find her therapist. Tammy turns her head in the direction of the sound and squeals with delight when she visually connects with the music therapist. Musical hide-and-seek follows. The therapist places a scarf over her face and, as she sings "Where, oh where is Susan?" Tammy reaches up and pulls off the scarf. Tammy moves out into her environment, exploring the world that is a frightening place to her and acknowledging other people. Now the scarf is put on Tammy's face. Her startled growl and big frown indicate she does not like the feel of this. It is hard for her to tolerate this sensation long enough to last out the song. But her love of this musical game helps her tolerate this tactile sensation for longer and longer intervals.

Now out of her wheelchair and supported by her music therapist, Tammy walks and dances to her favorite popular tune. Movement is difficult for her because her cerebral palsy makes her muscles stiff and her movement uncoordinated. But when rhythmic music is used, her mother reports, she moves for longer periods than at other times and her movements are smoother. This effect was noted in many music therapy reports and is observed during each of her current sessions.

The session ends with Tammy's favorite music playing on the stereo, usually a current popular hit. During this hour of music therapy, she has used her sense of touch, explored her environment, and socialized. Her smiles, intensified movement, and loud, enthusiastic cries tell us she's having fun, too.

TAMMY'S PERSPECTIVE

In this section, I speak for Tammy, projecting into words what music therapy means to her. Much of what is expressed here comes from extensive interviews with Tammy's mother. I have used her words and phrases to describe Tammy's experience of music therapy.

Thank God for music. It touches me gently and lets me reach out to the world when I'm ready. Music was my first bridge to the world outside myself. The other ways— touch, taste, and sight—frighten me. I can't understand these experiences. They are confusing and overwhelming. Music makes sense to me. It is regular, predictable, and safe somehow. Music never pushes me. It coaxes me out beyond myself and into the world around me. Music is my joy. It makes me feel alive. Music helps me be aware and alert. The real "me" is trapped inside a mind and body that hold me back. Music allows and encourages my real self to be expressed. Sometimes I even feel like a totally different person when I am surrounded by music.

Music therapy is my special time. I look forward to it every week. I am so happy and alive during this hour. I do the music willingly. My special friend, music, is all around me and so is a special person. The music lets me contact this person, my music therapist. It is safe and fun to play music with her. This is how I socialize, how I feel like the teenager I am.

Music therapy gives me chances to grow and change but only when I'm ready. The music makes it seem fun and easy to try new things. I never feel hurried or rushed to make a change in music therapy. Whenever I'm ready, the music is there for me.

Music therapy is my lifeline. It teaches me, encourages me, gives me a social life, and supports who and what I am. Thank God for music therapy.

Narrative 25

SOMETIMES THERE ARE NO REASONS: MARCO'S SONG

Mary Rykov

INTRODUCTION

I worked with Marco for 10 months during his admissions to the hospital. I present here the story of our first meeting, the song that became a means of expressing thoughts and feelings, and words from his mother, Nikki, about the song. Marco's parents wish to use their real names.

MARCO

Marco was sitting up in bed in his hospital room when I first met him in January 1996. He was 18 years old, the third and youngest child of his parents, Nikki and Martino Fragomeli. His brother, Tony, and sister, Cristina, were 13 and 10 years older than he, respectively. Marco was in the hospital receiving chemotherapy treatment for a recurrence of his brain tumor, an astrocytoma diagnosed in 1993 when he was 15 years old.

Marco told me that when he was first sick, he lost all of his functioning and couldn't walk or talk. He worked hard to get better and gradually regained his abilities. He was then in high school, involved in the sports he loved, and he had a girlfriend and a job. Life was good and everything was going well. Suddenly and without warning, the brain tumor came back. He kept asking, "Why?" and remarked he was too sad even to cry.

Marco's family meant everything to him. He talked fondly of how wonderful his parents were, that his sister recently married, and how much he loved his older brother. He frequently shook his head in shock and disbelief over his tumor's recurrence. Long silences punctuated his words and ideas as he struggled to talk despite the effects of the tumor.

Thoughts and feelings flowed freely despite his struggles with the mechanics of speech. He talked of many things that first session and decided to write a song the next time. I wrote the song for Marco, however, because of his word-finding problems and because he was discharged before another music therapy session was possible. The song was written literally with his content; the melody and harmony also reflected the essence of our interaction. The song lyrics and a tape recording were sent home to him. Marco expressed his approval of his song when next we met in the form of an enthusiastic thumb's-up. He declined offers to change any of the ideas, words, or music.

Marco and his parents participated in music therapy sessions off and on during his chemotherapy admissions until his treatment protocol was finished in October 1996. Marco and I did not engage in further songwriting because he was often not alone when we met and because the effects of his treatment made him sleepy. A second remission was not possible. Marco died March 3, 1997. He was 19 years old.

NIKKI'S PERSPECTIVE

When she first heard Marco's song, Nikki Fragomeli said, "It brought my emotions out to the surface. I felt sad and happy at the same time." Music therapy in the hospital "took my mind off our problems for the moment. It was nice to have someone bring us a little joy. I truly enjoyed the music therapy sessions." When Nikki was asked about Marco's experience of his song and music therapy sessions, she said, "Like me. He felt like me."

Marco's song now supports his family's grief. Five months after Marco's death, Nikki said she often listens to his song and reads the lyrics. She "took his song to work one day and played it for a co-worker. We both sat there and cried," she said. "I read the song words often and give copies to whoever I think will appreciate them. When I read the song words, I almost hear Marco saying some of the words to me."

Sometimes There Are No Reasons
(Marco's Song)

Refrain
Sometimes there are no reasons.
Some things we'll never know;
The whys and the wherefores, the hows, whats.
And so we hope for the best and take what we get,
And make of it the most that we can.
We hope for the best and take what we get,
And make of it the most that we can.

Verses
1. Yesterday I did it all. I played to win and didn't
   fall.
   I knew the plays and played by all the rules.
   I had speed, strength, and grace. I challenged any
   pace.
   Then a curve ball hit and I feel like a fool.
   (Refrain)

2. Now I falter and I stumble. I stutter and I
   mumble,
   And can't always find words for how I feel.
   I'm too sad to even cry, though I've tried and I've
   tried.
   What's happening to me seems so unreal.
   (Refrain)

3. But for all that has changed, I'm still much the
   same.
   Inside I'll always be the one you knew.
   I'm the little one who grew, the one who loves
   you.
   Remember this: my love will see you through.
   (Refrain)

Sometimes There Are No Reasons
(Marco's Song)

Figure A (Continues).

Figure A (Continued).

DISCOVERING MEANING IN KELLY'S NONVERBAL EXPRESSIONS

Suzanne Nowikas

INTRODUCTION

Kelly can be an affectionate and interactive child, yet also withdrawn and in her own world—all in the same session. She shows her many sides in the session I describe—her thirty-sixth session of music therapy. In order to compose the most complete picture of what Kelly's experience may be like in music therapy, I have interviewed two people who I feel are key in understanding her: Antoinette Lubrano, Kelly's co-therapist, and Barbara, Kelly's mother. Antoinette and Barbara watched a videotape of session 36 with me in separate interviews.

To get as close to Kelly's own voice as possible, I have created an inferred soliloquy (in italics) that is my interpretation of what Kelly's verbal expressions might be like if she were able to speak; these are based on my observations of her over several years of therapy. Her voice will be a thread throughout the chapter in a further attempt to relate my experiences of her as closely as I can to what a 9-year-old's perspective might be. The entire narrative is based on conjecture, impressions, assertions, and interpretations. I do not assume to be able fully to understand any person's experience in therapy. I do feel, however, that through piecing together others' experiences of Kelly, we may somehow be able to develop a fuller picture about who she might be. We bring our own personal expectations of her to this setting, but it is not the purpose of this account to identify one truism about Kelly.

In session 36, as in all our sessions with Kelly, the co-therapist and I work as a team; I create the musical themes at the piano to support, reflect, enliven, move, encourage, and motivate Kelly. Antoinette vocally, physically, and gesturally facilitates and supports Kelly's participation on the floor. We use improvised music in a variety of different styles and idioms, on the piano, with our voices, and on the guitar, to reach Kelly. Some of the musical ideas become themes that are brought back from week to week. The music is developed solely for Kelly and the hope is that she will begin to recognize and identify with the themes and know that they are "hers." Excerpts of the music from session 36 are included here.

KELLY

Barbara had a normal pregnancy and delivery. At 6 months of age, Kelly had her first seizure. She then underwent MRI (magnetic resonance imaging), which revealed that she was missing a portion of her corpus callosum. This is the portion of the brain that connects the right and left cerebral hemispheres. Her seizures continued, but it was not clear that she was physically or language delayed until she was 1 year old. At 1 year, she was not babbling and her seizures had increased. She began crawling at 2½ years old and worked with her mother and baby-sitter on developing walking skills for at least 1 hour a day (in addition to physical therapy sessions). Seven months later, she began walking. She was still not babbling at this time. Barbara commented in regard to controlling her seizures, "We have tried everything," referring to special diets and an assortment of medications and dosages. Kelly continues to have seizures one or two times a day. They are each less than 10 minutes long and they usually occur when she is waking up. Her head dips and shakes a bit. Barbara said, "They take their toll when they are that frequent."

SESSION 36

Early Moments

I am always struck each time I see her. She is angelic-looking—beautiful curly blond hair to her shoulders and a peaches-and-cream complexion. As she enters, I hear her hum. Yes! She wants to be here. She looks tired today and a little pale. I watch her sit down in a chair that is approximately 6 feet away from the piano. To see her, I must crane my neck and turn around while continuing to play. A little smile comes over her face, a cue for me to begin singing our greeting song [Figure A]. She seems to be anticipating something.

I'm happy to be back in music. Everything looks the same. Where is my chair? Hmmmmm. That song—when I hear that song, it makes me feel nice. Hmmmmm.

Figure A. Hello music.

I decide to hold out each tone of the hello song (emphasizing each note with my voice). I know she is warming up to the situation, but I feel she needs a little more energy from the music. I play in a livelier way, adding harmonic changes, and wait for little humming responses after I play very short phrases. She turns toward Antoinette as if noticing her for the first time; she is really listening.

Barbara* commented about these first few moments of the session:

> She is very aware that you both are there to give her pleasure. And that makes her feel happy. There is a moment [when] she is going to turn to Antoinette and seek her own sort of stimulation. But the music overtakes that [feeling] and it is so rich and enjoyable that the self-stimulation isn't necessary. She [is thinking,] "Oooh, I'm going to miss this. This is beautiful." She looks tired. The music is peaceful to her. It's peaceful and it's soothing.

Antoinette related her experience bringing Kelly into the therapy room:

> For a moment there, I felt she was on the border; she wanted to come in, but she didn't know how. She wanted to be a part of that welcoming, a part of the music. For instance, when she first walked in, she was slow; she went right to her chair. Then you played a faster tempo and she responded immediately. I think she was really absorbing it. And the way she was looking at me and looking at you. I really felt that she wanted to be part of it, part of your music. She was happy; she was in a really good mood. She was familiar with [the chair] and was comfortable. She was sitting up and she was ready for something, ready to be involved and engaged.

> *Where is Antoinette? She has beautiful thick curly hair like Mommy's. I want to touch it. It feels soft and warm. She doesn't pull away from me. I think she likes me.*

Kelly develops unique and separate relationships with each of us on the therapy team. Antoinette and I have cultivated strong and different relationships with her. Our differing roles, perspectives, and impressions afford us the opportunity to understand her better and to

---

* Throughout, both Barbara's and Antoinette's comments are indented (but not italicized).

appreciate more fully the complexity of her world and relationships with others.

To the Drum

I sing, "You want to play," and she signs, "Play." It is always a great feeling of assurance when I know she is understanding what I'm saying. Antoinette brings the drum closer to her and hands her the mallets. I encourage her to play, which she does in short bursts. The sleepiness is more apparent. Her eyes look glazed over and she puts the mallets down on the drum and turns to Antoinette to withdraw from activity.

> *Don't they understand that I'm busy listening? Sometimes I hear so many sounds together and it doesn't make sense. I'm so tired. Antoinette? Hmmmm. I'm so tired. I can't hold the stick anymore. I'll put it on the drum. Okay, now can I go to sleep, Antoinette?*

Antoinette discussed this moment:

When she came to me [this time, it was as if] she was coming to me for encouragement to participate in active music-making. When she backed up [away from the drum], I felt that she was ambivalent or not sure what she wanted to do. Each time she approached me (through the course of therapy), I tried to understand why she decided to come to me. Is it a way of avoiding music-making or does she really want physical contact from me? Or is it both at the same time?

Barbara had a slightly different perspective of what she believed to be Kelly's experience:

I don't think she is going to Antoinette for help. She is tired. She rises above [her sleepiness when she hears] certain tones. It takes her away from [her tiredness, sleepiness], just like the self-stimulation [does], because it is so pleasurable and she is drawn by it. And in general, more active music seems to get her going. It was an active moment, an active sound, and she connected to that sound. She is listening very carefully.

There are moments when she wants you [Suzanne] to restart, just by glancing. [These are] very passive indications, but definitely [her communicating that] "I want more of this."

Throughout our review of the video, Barbara clearly distinguished between Kelly's responses and interactions that were elicited by a relationship during a musical experience and her responses based directly on aspects of the music. Barbara said, "I think there is a pull between Kelly being connected and unconnected. Music can be both a personal and a shared (relationship thing) experience. I think she can be both active and passive when she is connected and enjoys experiencing music in both of these modes."

I like to bounce when I'm happy. Sometimes when I think of something happy, I begin to bounce. I think about Mommy and Daddy. It's fun to go up and down. Suzanne is looking at me. She is bouncing in the music, too. We are all having fun together. Maybe we can all dance together someday.

Antoinette and I agree with Barbara's statement that "Kelly is a complicated child. On the face of it, she is probably very simple to people, but I think she's complex and hard to understand." We have learned that she communicates choices clearly and definitively at times yet can also be ambivalent. How many of these changes are due to the medication she takes each day? We are not sure. Sometimes making a connection with her feels like a battle between the power of the music and the strength of our commitment to her and the potency of her medication.

Antoinette discussed her relationship with Kelly in reference to the drum work in session 36:

I'm sitting behind her and though she's not leaning on me, I sense that she wants and feels my support. I sometimes think that we are communicating on another level—maybe a sixth sense. I'm thinking, "Come on, play that drum," and I believe she is definitely sensing this even when I wasn't touching her. And the music you're playing is also saying, "Try." I think she was asking her-self, "Do I want to do this? Maybe I don't want to do this." She feels our strength and motivation. Here, I think she is trying to tell me, "No, I don't want to." She just wants to be held and loved. Maybe she doesn't want to work. She doesn't want to play the drum. I sometimes wonder if this is another wave of medication.

Antoinette, help me. I don't want to work on the drum. Let me hug you. Suzanne wants me to play; can you take care of me? You like it when I hug you, right? Oh no! You want me to play more, too? I'm seeing different colors; everything looks blurry. I feel air on my face. I hear voices and music. I like it, but I want to go somewhere. I feel far away. Where's Mommy? I feel sleepy. Everything is so soft, warm, and syrupy slow.

In her discussion of Kelly's musical life outside of music therapy, Barbara described her own use of music to enhance speech goals:

In the past couple of years, I made cassettes [about different objects] that we [would place] on a table. One was a ball, one was a can of blocks, one was a telephone. I [created] a song to go with each object. These were objects that she knows. I won't tell you what the speech objectives were because it's irrelevant. She experiences the objects in a different way with the song. She is more focused. There's more life to these objects. The music enriches the object. That's how I feel and she feels that.

Kelly withdrew from playing the drum in session 36. I asked Barbara what she thought Kelly was feeling. Was there something that we were doing that was making her want to cuddle? Barbara answered:

I think she is not connected to the music. And the music is not big enough to draw her out. I think generally that she is very tired at this point. It's completely obvious to me that she is not drawn into the musical experience at that moment, and so she is doing what she would when she is tired.

There are periods in Kelly's sessions in which she seems almost transfixed, intently listening and absorbing the sounds that she is hearing. Her responses to the music are sometimes manifested outwardly with flapping arms and jumping, but often it is more subtle. We hear little humming sounds and see half-smiles or notice more directed glances. This is the strongest indication we have that she is experiencing something that is moving to her. Barbara refers to the drum work when she begins to explain Kelly's responses and how they are demonstrated in this session:

> The moments that she is really into the musical experience, she doesn't [necessarily] want to [play] in a real active way. That doesn't mean that she isn't really getting a lot out of it at those moments. There are other times that I see her more active, but it's irrelevant. She's definitely into it at those times [when no activity is taking place]. I think you can participate passively. I wouldn't underemphasize the impact of what that does for her, even though it doesn't appear that she's really leading you directly. She's quite aware of the differences in the music, and some of it is more striking than others.

To the Cymbal

Sensing that she was no longer interested in the drum, I leave the piano bench and move the cymbal closer to her. She has been attracted to the cymbal in prior sessions. I'm hoping her interest in the sound will overtake her sleepiness and desire to withdraw. I tap it once after bringing it closer. She seems interested, leaves Antoinette's lap, begins to spin the cymbal with one hand. She hums and stands as I bring it over. I play a pentatonic theme lightly in treble register of the piano [Figure B]. The music has an almost mysterious quality to it; I leave spaces after each phrase, hoping she'll fill them with the cymbal. I occasionally return to thematic music for the drum, which is composed of pentatonic octaves [Figure C].

INTERLUDE
with Cymbal

Figure B. Interlude with cymbal.

PENTATONIC THEME
drum music

Figure C. Pentatonic theme.

Bright, shiny! I see me. It's cold and golden. Around and around, look what I can do! New colors each time it goes round and round again.

Barbara commented:

I think it became clear to you that she did not want to play the cymbal, but when she was spinning, it was enjoyable for her. [*Pause*] It was sensory for her when she was touching it, the movement was sensory. She was experiencing [the cymbal] with the sound. How she takes that all in, I don't know. Somehow it was very pleasurable, that sort of feeling, as opposed to banging the drum, sensory and pleasurable and seemed to match the [music]. Her movement was in agreement with the sound.

I ask Barbara if she thought Kelly's experience might also have been visual. I thought perhaps the lights were reflecting off of the cymbal and she could possibly see herself. Barbara said she could not tell from this excerpt, but that it might very well be the case. She said that some sort of shine or refection might be attractive to her. She also thought that the cymbal was cold and the texture of it might be pleasurable.

Antoinette pointed out something to me that I had missed during previous viewings of the videotape: She turns the mallet around so that the wooden part was striking the cymbal. Kelly reaches back and takes Antoinette's hand and moves it in a downward motion on the cymbal while she continues to spin it. This continues as Antoinette taps the cymbal repeatedly. Antoinette commented:

She doesn't do this often. She took my hand because I was holding the mallet. Maybe she recognizes [the music] you're playing. I don't know. Her relationship with the cymbal is a familiar experience from a past session.

Antoinette then offers Kelly the mallet in the same position, with the wooden side of the mallet within striking distance of the cymbal. Kelly bounces several times, accepts the mallet, hums, and smiles. She then strikes the cymbal a few times, looking over to the piano between beating. I reflect what she is doing by holding chords in the middle register of the piano. Kelly seems happy. She hums and smiles, turning the mallet around so that the soft side is striking the cymbal. I play with her on each beat that she plays. She stands with Antoinette supporting her back. Then she begins to bounce and I enliven the music by changing my articulation, returning to mostly the upper register of the piano.

> *Bouncing up and down* [Flaps hands, flaps hands]. *Keep going. It's fun, pretty. I hear that! More—more music!*

I play short phrases, leaving silences before repeating the phrase. I am asking her a question in the music and am waiting for a response from her. She seems awake and ready for action. Will she answer me? She has turned the mallet over and the wood end is facing the cymbal. When I leave a space in the music, she fills it, and a dialogue ensues, back and forth. I play a chord; she answers. She looks away in the distance. I begin to play a tremolo in order to refocus her. She begins the dialogue again. This continues consistently for several minutes. I begin to play with her, not only waiting for her to fill in the silences. I sense that she is tiring. She subsequently puts the mallet down on the drum and moves toward Antoinette.

Antoinette tries to characterize Kelly's experience:

> I heard the joy in her music. I wonder if she felt and experienced it as significant and meaningful. It seemed that way from her bouncing and playfulness. I wonder if she felt our joy that she was playing. She was bouncing and jumping. The music was in a higher register; it was light and playful. She was there!

From her own perspective, Antoinette described the nature of Kelly's interaction with me:

> There is a sense of awareness on her part when she plays and you follow her on the piano. She seems to know that you are with her. . . . Does she understand or is she aware of the dialogue/musical interaction? I think so.

Antoinette has a unique role as co-therapist, constantly deciding whether to actively assist Kelly. She stated:

I want to say something about sitting so closely by her [as opposed to moving away]. I really think that with Kelly, it is important to be that physically close to her. And even if I'm not holding her or doing hand-over-hand prompting in that moment, I know what I'm feeling. It's almost as if I'm saying in my mind, "I'm here." [I'm] passing my strength on to her. I think it comes across but yet it's not forced. . . . The feeling elicited when you're working and someone is behind you is "You can do it."

Barbara commented about Kelly's interactions with Antoinette and the difference between the drum and cymbal work:

That [drum work] was an example of [a time] when a lot of the leading by Antoinette was unsuccessful and Kelly didn't like it. And maybe it caused her to retreat all the more into something perseverative. But here with the cymbal, there was the moment that this was successful direction. There were moments when Antoinette tried to keep her going and was successful in keeping her connected to it. The time with the drum was so long that it was unsuccessful and the continuation of it was so long that it made her retreat and really get disconnected from the musical experience, whereas this time, there was some persistence in trying to direct her and she fairly quickly responded and it was successful. Had Kelly stopped with the drums sooner, she might not have retreated as much.

I was surprised by Barbara's next observation about the cymbal playing. It was quite contrary to my perception of the cymbal work:

She does not like the sound of the cymbal with the [wooden part] of the mallet. She likes the sound of the [soft] mallet side. She was hitting it, but she wasn't really into it. She might have started to get into the music, then she turned it around and got the [soft] mallet sound. The first time she heard it, she was really listening and she liked it and then she hit it a few more times. She liked the sound and it enhanced the music. [*Pause*] She was experiencing the instrument in a number of ways that were comfortable and pleasurable for her. One was with the mallet side and one was by touching [the cymbal]. [When] she hit it with the [wooden side], she didn't like it and even though she continued playing, she didn't like it; it disturbed her. Maybe I'll change my mind if I keep watching, but I felt that [*hesitation*] she's hitting [the cymbal] to restart [you]. She wants the music, but I don't think she likes that sound. Why did she [move her hands in a flapping motion]? Yes, she wants you [to play], but I don't think she likes the sound of the wooden side of the mallet.

We continued to watch the videotape and Barbara remarked as the dialogue between Kelly and me ensued:

I think she is tolerating it now. She was not tolerating it before. Is she so into responding and playing with you or is it the community feeling [she derives from] playing together? Is it that she's not focused on the sound? Is she tolerating it now that she's done it a number of times? When she first played, she hated the sound. Maybe the success, the noise of it, makes her more comfortable. I don't know. Now it's okay.

At this point in the session, I present a small communication board containing three laminated pictures of instruments attached with Velcro on a board. There is an additional "I want" symbol that Kelly's speech therapist has provided. Kelly consistently uses the chart that we have brought into the sessions. She usually makes a choice but sometimes does not follow through with the particular corresponding instrument that she chooses. This week, she chooses the tambourine. We usually ask her to choose two times to see if she will be consistent in her selection. She follows through this time with choosing and playing the tambourine.

They have a board for me where I choose what I want to play. The pictures are pretty. I have different boards wherever I go. I know how to choose. I want [she hesitates] the piano? The tambourine? I'll pick the tambourine. Here comes Suzanne with the tambourine; she is moving so fast! Sometimes I don't know what I want to play, but it is fun to touch the pictures.

To the Tambourine

Kelly hums before we start playing. She taps the tambourine
with the back of her hand. I begin a rhythmic improvisation in E-flat
major. She alternates playing with Antoinette. A melody develops in
the music [Figure D].

Figure D. Improvisation in E-flat major.

She seems to be listening and bounces in my direction. I begin to
sing nonverbally with the new melody. I add dissonance to give the
music a little more energy and spice. I again wait for her responses in
the music. She yawns and smiles at the same time. I increase the
tempo and intensity of the music. She smiles contentedly, although
she does not seem to have the energy to continue to play without
stopping. She hums and moves her head to the music. Antoinette
plays the tambourine for several beats, then gently touches Kelly's
elbow. It seems as if Kelly is finished with what she will do. She
moves to the piano bench and sits beside me.

Sometimes Antoinette and Suzanne play so fast on the
instruments. I can't do that. I wait till they are finished.
Oh, maybe I'll show them I can play fast too. [Tap, tap,

tap, tap] *Yes, see? Oh, they like that; the music sounds louder. Enough! I'm tired. Haven't I done enough? Can't I listen now?*

Barbara provided an example of how her 17-month-old son response to music differs from Kelly's experience:

He likes music a lot. He continually sways to the music. When he sways, though, he is swaying to show somebody. When Kelly jumps and flaps her hands, she is effervescent with joy. She is not necessarily moving to show someone else, like my baby. Kelly's flapping reflects personal joy and she would do it regardless of whether or not someone was present. . . . It's very personal for her. That was what she was doing with Antoinette at that moment. She doesn't sway; she cuddles. Even though it looks all the same, I don't think it is.

We discussed how Kelly uses instruments in order to get a musical response from me. Barbara stated:

She goes between [playing for herself] and using instruments to get you to play. It's merely cause and effect. [At those times,] she really doesn't want to play. She wants you to play. She's so focused on processing that sound that to be able to process that sound and play (this is sometimes, I'm saying) is difficult and not rewarding for her. There are other times when she does use the instrument for expression. And she's gone between [both experiences here] with the [tambourine playing]. I don't know why there are moments when she is real passive but clearly processing the sound and there are other times when she is enjoying [listening to] the sound versus [being] active in the sound. Is it too complicated for her to process? Is it too beautiful or is she just not inspired? When I watch ballet (I danced for 14 years), it doesn't inspire me necessarily to want to go up and do a pirouette.

I added that I thought there might be a delay in Kelly's processing, even with her smiles. It doesn't always occur at the exact moment that the sound is happening. I questioned whether when there is silence she is still hearing music. Barbara replied:

> The route for all auditory messages is very slow. So we would almost have forgotten the music by the time she is getting the message. Is she still getting the message? I don't know physiologically what the answer to that really is. Maybe the message has gotten up there.

When Kelly leaves her music therapy sessions, she often is happy and excited, jumping up and down, humming, seemingly very active. This is often contrary to the mood that she presents in the therapy room, especially on days that she appears very tired because of the effects of the medication. I questioned Barbara about this in relation to our discussion of how Kelly processes sound. I wondered out loud whether she is happy and relieved to be out of music therapy. Barbara responded:

> I don't really know [what that's about]. I don't think that it's that she is so happy to see me and I don't think it's that she is so happy to get out of the session. I don't know if I can answer.

> *I want to tell Mommy what we did; let me show her. I'll dance and move around the room. She tells me that she knows I'm happy. Yes! Antoinette and Suzanne are saying good-bye to Mommy. They are talking. I hear the good-bye music in my head. Mommy is putting on my jacket. We're going to school now.*

Barbara was careful throughout our interview not to go further than she felt comfortable in trying to interpret Kelly's experience. There were some topics that she addressed with a great deal of assuredness and certainty but other areas in which she did not even attempt to venture an answer or an explanation. This again reinforced the idea to me that Kelly could be mysterious and in some ways "unknowable" even to those closest to her.

This conversation about processing of information led us into a discussion about Kelly's overall experience in music therapy from Barbara's perspective:

This is presumptuous, too, but the motor planning [needed to play instruments] requires such effort for her. When I think that the goal of music therapy is to get her to participate . . . [*She hesitates.*] There are reasons to want her to participate. It's good to be able to motor-plan and do things, but that to me, to some extent, [may] take away from some of the pleasure she gets from it. It would take away from some of the experience itself.

I then asked Barbara how, from her perspective, music therapy helps Kelly.

I think it's a happy experience for her. I just have to be honest that when I drive down here (I tell my husband and my caregiver this all the time), it feels so good that I'm taking her here. I feel like I'm expanding her life a little bit. I feel like I'm giving her pleasure. . . . I could get technical about it. Just getting her to use her senses more is great, developing a relationship to sound and differences in sound is great. I could get technical about it, but I [won't]. I'm giving her something enriching and it's a lovely experience. It's just a lovely experience.

Antoinette compared session 36 to the other sessions in Kelly's course of therapy:

[Her responses] are subtle. There have been times when maybe she played more and we saw some of that. It's more subtle, but it is indicative of who she is. In this session, I think we are able to redirect her more. She is gently pulled out of the low energy, inactivity, spaciness, and wave of medications into active listening. I think I've seen her potential and what she can do [in earlier sessions] and even if the next session is different, it helps me say, "Wait, she can play that." And it can be that she does want to be here but doesn't want to work, or she just wants to listen. That's how I link the sessions together. Here's this child coming every week or every few weeks, and she's had these experiences. I think she holds on to them. I really do. I have to believe that.

Barbara questioned what a music therapy experience might be like for her other children:

> I have two other children, and I think, "Would this be nice for them?" They wouldn't experience it in quite the same way as Kelly does. It is uniquely beautiful to her and enriching to her in a way that it couldn't be for the other children. So many other people might say, "Well, those two kids could get more out of it." I disagree. Who are we in our world to say that it is more enriching for us? I would argue that it's probably more enriching for her. Compared to everything else in this world that we "normal people" take input from, other than a unique, select few like yourself [a musician], the input from a half-hour music session is likely to be quite small. But if you look at the odds, it's probably a much greater impact for [Kelly] than for most other people in this world. Her intake from the world is probably smaller than most people, but I argue, therefore, [that] her intake from music is probably greater proportionately.

To the piano

I see her interest in the tambourine is waning. Antoinette continues to present the instrument to her and taps it several times herself. Kelly moves away and sits next to me on the piano bench. I point to the picture of the piano on her board as she sits and wait to see what she will do. She gently touches a few notes. I reflect her touch very gently with light chords in a minor key. She plays clusters and some single notes. Barbara commented:

> I think she wanted more of you at that moment. And she didn't get it, and then she felt, "Oh well, that's it."

I tried to clarify Barbara's statement by saying that Kelly seemed to "check out." Barbara went on:

> You do have to be a mastermind to take all these messages from her because it's pretty difficult, but I suspect that she wanted you to [play for her].

I begin to play a melody [Figure E] that I have played in past sessions in a livelier manner:

PIANO THEME

Figure E. Piano theme in C.

Kelly occasionally reaches out and plays a note that is related to the melody. Since her early sessions, she has always had an uncanny ability to play the notes that corresponded to the key that I was playing in improvisations with the piano. Sometimes this occurs when she is not even looking directly at the keyboard. Antoinette and I do not have an explanation for this. We have tried to get philosophical about it. Perhaps she feels the music in a different way, without needing to think about it. This openness to the experience may enable her to connect in a way that we trained musicians find challenging to relate to. Her mother said, "I feel that it's beyond me to be able to comment on whether she can do that."

Kelly's interest in actually playing the piano wanes, yet she begins to hum along with the music. I vocalize with her and in response to her. It is a very special moment of connection in the session. She seems to be enjoying the vocal interaction and revels in her own ability to create musical sounds.

I asked Barbara what she thought about the quality of Kelly's vocalizations at this point in the session:

> I think it's lovely. Her speech therapist would [say], "Wow, is this possible?" It's far superior to anything we can get—to anything we do. I'm sure the speech therapist would just say, "Wow!" because I know this therapist so well and yes, Kelly's so happy. It just makes me beam. For me [what is so important] is that she's so happy, and it's coming out. It's outward expression, which we don't get [to see] as much.

Good-bye

Kelly moves back to her chair after this vocal interplay. I begin to play the music to the good-bye song [Figure F]. She listens intently, occasionally smiling and humming, but mostly, just listening. She waves good-bye in the air, not addressing anyone in particular, but letting us know she understands what is happening. In past sessions, she might begin to tug at the doorknob in anticipation of her exit, but in this session and other recent sessions, she waits patiently.

> *Suzanne knows I want to leave when I wave my hand. Sometimes we sing good-bye. I like good-bye. I know we'll be leaving soon when we sing good-bye. I like to hear this song lots of times. I like to sit and listen; sometimes I move up and down when I hear this song.*

Barbara compared the good-bye time to the beginning of the session:

> When she came in and now [during the] ending, it was so distinctly different from the rest of the session. It's almost as

GOOD-BYE

Figure F. Good-bye music.

if you're saying: "We're singing this good-bye song to you. We are singing this song to you." And like it was in the beginning, she sits there and is taking it in. It's almost as if she is saying, "I know you're singing this to me. I know it's not quite a shared musical experience, but I'm participating; I'm listening to the sound." It's like, "I know you're singing this to me and I like this and I like that you're doing this for me." It's the way she's sitting. She's very alert; she's very erect.

I explained that Kelly put herself in that position in the beginning and ending of the session. Barbara responded:

Did she? It just seemed like it was the exact same thing as the beginning. "You two do this to me!" So it was really nice, just really nice.

During the good-bye song, we sing to Kelly repeatedly and incorporate our own names. We continue with some embellishments and I play some harmonic variations. I am always curious, when she is away from the door at this ending point in the session, how long she will actually feel relaxed about continuing this song before wanting to leave. I eventually bring it to a close. The music stops. She gets up out of her seat and approaches the door. She tries to open it. Antoinette is right behind her and assists her in opening it, and she leaves first, heading in the direction of her mother in the waiting room, with Antoinette right behind her.

Narrative 27

EXPERIENCES
IN A PEDIATRIC NURSING HOME

Michelle Glidden

I think they experience joy. You just have to look at
them . . . it's all over their faces.
                    —Dorothy, teacher assistant

INTRODUCTION

All of the residents entered this pediatric nursing home as children
and will remain here for the rest of their lives. Some were born with
severe disorders, whereas others came to the nursing home because
of accident or disease contracted in childhood. Most are unable to
walk or talk or care for themselves in any way. They require nursing
care, wheelchairs, and other adapted equipment. Many are tube-fed.
Their developmental skills are measured at the 12-month level or
below. All of the residents attend school or a day program within the
nursing home 5 days a week. They are placed in groups of 8 to 10
residents according to age and skill level. It is within these groups
that I meet them, bringing songs and instruments adapted for each
student. The classroom staff are involved in assisting each group
member during the session. They help stimulate the students both
physically and with their own voices to enhance the effort and communication of each group member.

Since these children and young adults cannot speak for themselves in words, I have interviewed some of the staff at the residence.
We recognize that it is impossible to definitively describe another
person's experience, yet it is obvious to all of us that there are
changes in behavior and awareness brought about by experiences in
music. The following report represents a number of students' experiences, inferred by spokespersons who regularly observe their behaviors and are practiced in assigning meaning to the smallest physical
or behavioral change. The students' voices are heard through
descriptions of their actions and reactions to music.

THE SPOKESPERSONS

Alice works in the recreation department and assists in music therapy groups with adults who are in their twenties and thirties.

[Kids] who still don't respond to other things . . . respond to music. Music can get in [to a person's psyche]. It makes a difference to see something the [students] really enjoy. They're not just going through the motions; [they are not apathetic]. The live music gets their attention faster. They listen to piped music all day, but they probably tune it out. The minute they hear the first two notes on the guitar, they know; they react by smiling or laughing. Students who will not do independent tasks in the classroom will readily play an adapted instrument. The pride they feel is evident on their faces. [With some of the songs], the students will relax and appear to listen to the music.

Alice continues, talking about the progress one young adult in the group, Joan, has made. Joan came to this facility as a teenager after a riding accident and is now in her thirties. In observing Joan, Alice notices what seems to be unusual motivation during music.

When I first started working here, Joan had no motion whatsoever. I have seen the most [movement] from her in music. She enjoys having that control to be able to play the chimes by herself, and [playing] seems to have drawn her out even more. Music can definitely draw people out more than anything I've seen in the . . . 9 years I've been here.

Laura is the head teacher at the facility and currently teaches the youngest children.

In both the classrooms I've had—the older and younger— the children do more during that half-hour music therapy session than they do in any other session their whole week. As individuals, they just shine; there is no one [who] really holds back. It is the only group activity in which my students remain attentive throughout the session without reminders from the classroom staff. They respond much more consistently and at a higher level. . . . They stay focused on the music. The students will watch one another perform and they become excited when one of their peers is successful at independently playing an instrument.

She continues, talking this time about Jared, who came to the nursing home several years ago after an accidental near drowning.

Three years ago, Jared had no independent purposeful movements. He's shy and quiet; he's not going to let you in. It is necessary for the classroom staff to assist him in all activities which require the use of his hands; however, in music, he started playing the chimes. In every session, he consistently smiles and uses his fingers. This is a great achievement for him. Over the past year, he's become much more open and responsive than he ever was and that started out with music.

Laura also notes the unusual response of a new student, Ashley, one that has been seen in other children who were initially thought to be deaf:

I have a new student and part of her diagnosis is that she is deaf and blind; however, when the guitar starts to play, she immediately smiles and sings. She continues to smile and sing throughout the whole session.

Sharon is the speech pathologist at the nursing home. She notes the changes of one student in particular, Leslie. Leslie came to the nursing home just before she turned 22. She had been in residential programs most of her life. Leslie's care had been turned over to the state and much of her past history and skill level were unclear. The move to this new placement appeared difficult for her and she was initially very withdrawn. Sharon says: "Leslie has changed since she's been here . . . and music therapy has been the paramount thing in her life. By slowly building upon the music, she has made so many changes." Maura, Leslie's classroom teacher, agrees: "Music therapy has brought Leslie out of her shell so much. I [had] never [seen] her smile, [but] now more and more, [I see] the smiles, the reactions, and using her hands to play the instruments. It's just amazing."

Maura continues, talking about other students in her classroom:

> Sally begins to smile and vocalize as soon as she sees
> Michelle [the therapist]. That is the happiest anticipation
> I've seen her have for any person or activity. Robert laughs
> and smiles and enjoys himself. It is a wonderful experience
> to see and be a part of a group that is extremely [physically
> and mentally] challenged, yet the happiness, independence,
> and pride that is seen and felt is so very evident.

"I see the children really enjoying themselves," says Barb, a
classroom teacher. "[Their] body tone changes; they are vocal only in
happy ways. There is a [show] of happiness you don't usually see."
Andrea, a teacher assistant, adds: "They tend to come out . . . [and
show] more smiles and responses than you normally see in class."
Carol, another classroom teacher, replies, "Sometimes it's the only
time you see someone come out of [his or her] shell."

Mona, the parent of a 25-year-old young woman living at the
nursing home, says:

> I think that since Anne was born, the one thing that
> really soothed her and meant something to her was
> sound, music. For a long time, that was the only key that
> we had to access this child [who] could not speak or
> physically react to what was happening to her. Music has
> always been a part of our lives.

When Anne came to live at the nursing home after a difficult
hospitalization, it was traumatic for her at first. Her mother
brought along all of her favorite music and instructed the staff to
play it for her whenever she was uncomfortable or stressed: "At
this point in her life, if music is the thing that soothes her, gives
her some kind of inner peace, she should have it."

Mona is aware that because of Anne's physical handicaps,
Anne is often very uncomfortable and in some pain throughout
the day. Speaking to me about Anne's participation in music therapy now, Mona adds, "It's such a gift to have music, and it can be
so therapeutic, so peaceful. In children like these where it means
so much more, it may be the only door that's open. It may be the
only internal satisfaction they have."

Sheila, the teacher of the adolescent children, talks about students in her room. She mentions Sarah, who recently passed away.

She was so physically involved that for her to access those chimes independently just made her shine and was one of her great successes here. [The chimes] opened my eyes to what her capabilities could be.

She continues talking about Barry, another student: "Here is a kid who has seizures 90 percent of his life, but when he's on, it's usually in music. He can play [chimes] with either hand, and it's wonderful to see him shine like that."

Terry, teacher of the older adolescent students, notes the changes she sees in her students during music therapy:

The experience my students gain from participating in music therapy is one of increased levels of alertness and awareness. They seem more focused and in tune to what is occurring in their immediate environment. They smile, laugh, and vocalize more. They also turn their heads or eyes toward the source of people singing or playing instruments. Many students are proud of their ability to participate in music.

Terry comments on the added enthusiastic response of Bobby, a student in her classroom.

One student in particular is able to anticipate music therapy and becomes excited upon hearing the therapist come down the hall. During the sessions, he is very happy and excited, as demonstrated by the changes in his facial expressions and body posture. He is very motivated by music and moves his body to play instruments, which at times is difficult for him. He also moves his head and eyes and vocalizes (his way of singing and dancing) to music during these sessions, which he very rarely does in other settings. He experiences joy and pleasure from music and moves [his head and eyes] to be a part of the music and express himself.

The current education director, Karen, began as a classroom teacher with the youngest children when the music therapy program began 6 years ago.

I saw the changes in the kids, the alerting when they heard your voice [as you] started with your song. In music, they appear to know that they have control over whether they play or don't play. It's the one time I see the staff letting the kids do what they can do. What I've seen over the years is the attention the kids give you.

She adds a final note: "There is no one here who cannot be reached by music."

Narrative 28

LISA: THE EXPERIENCE
OF A CHILD
WITH MULTIPLE DISABILITIES

Barbara L. Wheeler

INTRODUCTION

Lisa is an attractive girl with long dark hair. She is a child with multiple severe disabilities, classified as being multiply handicapped. She is nonverbal, although she occasionally makes some sounds. Although she walks with no problems, she tends to lean to one side because of scoliosis. She occasionally drools.

I met Lisa in 1992 when she was 9 years old. She had been referred by her school district at her mother's urging for initial evaluation and then for music therapy which was written into Lisa's individualized education program (IEP). Lisa's mother brought her to each session, generally accompanied by Lisa's two younger sisters. Lisa's mother sat in on the first few sessions. Later, when we tried to have her mother go to a different room, Lisa became so upset that we decided that she should stay in the room. These sessions, in which we used familiar songs, movement, and percussion instruments, were continued for 2 years, after which I began working 1 day a week with Lisa at her school. I continued seeing Lisa there with a small group for 1½ years.

In an effort to communicate what might have been Lisa's experience of her 4 years of therapy with me, I report an interview with her mother, then I describe her behavior in sessions over the period. Since Lisa does not speak or communicate in a manner that allows me to know exactly how she experienced the music therapy, I write what I think she would say if she could speak her thoughts. I have put Lisa's thoughts in italics. Because of the large amount of speculation involved, I ground my statements about her experience in the behaviors that I observed and in my own reactions to her experience.

LISA'S MOTHER'S
PERSPECTIVE

I interviewed Lisa's mother to get her perception of Lisa's experience. Her mother is a teacher, doing only occasional substitute teaching during the time of the individual sessions, and homemaker. During the interview, we reviewed the chronology of the work with Lisa, including some significant sessions. We also listened to audiotaped portions of several sessions and looked at videotaped portions of sessions. With each, I asked her mother what she thought Lisa was experiencing and questioned her to develop her responses as fully as possible. What is presented here is a summary of what Lisa's mother said during that interview. She has also reviewed what I have written to be sure that it reflects her sense of Lisa's experience.

Lisa's mother first remembered Lisa's jumping with the recorded music and felt that she was reacting to the rhythm of the music. She felt, though, that Lisa generally responded to all aspects of music, not just the rhythm. She spoke of the variety of situations in which she had seen Lisa respond to all types of music; she described as an example Lisa's humming with a singer in church. Because of this general enjoyment of music, she felt that any response that Lisa made to music indicated some kind of pleasure.

She felt that Lisa was probably more responsive in music therapy than she had been in most other areas of her life during that time. She felt that music and tones appealed to Lisa and that I offered her an avenue of communication through my singing that appealed to her.

Lisa's mother was very aware of Lisa's enjoyment of the attention that she received from us and felt that this was an influence on Lisa's pleasure. She also felt that because the work with me was done individually, there were fewer distractions than there were at school and that this increased her responsiveness and pleasure. She said that when she would say, "It's time to go to Barbara's," Lisa would walk toward the car, although she would not do that in response to saying it was time to go somewhere else. She felt that this indicated pleasure as well as understanding.

In response to my question about the times that Lisa simply did not respond, Lisa's mother said:

> I think Lisa just "zones out" for some reason. I think something in her brain is just not clicking at certain times. I think that when she is tuned in, she always enjoys music. I think if she's not responding, it's just because she's not

tuned in, not that she doesn't like music or doesn't want to participate in some way with the music.

We spoke of some of the differences in the way that Lisa responded to music therapy when she had the individual sessions in my home compared to the later ones at the school. Her mother felt that she was more distracted at school and that this is consistent with Lisa's general behavior. Many things make her lose her attention, and those things were more plentiful at school.

She said that Lisa has continued vocalizing at a high level on the bus and at home. She feels that her vocalizing was and is generally a way of attempting to communicate and that now vocalizing may at times be a way of getting attention (such as when she vocalizes when she is supposed to be going to sleep at night).

She spoke also of Lisa's enjoyment of other children, particularly those of approximately her age. She said that Lisa, who is now 14 years 6 months, will at times hug a visiting child or lie on top of one of her sisters in order to hug her.

I kept Lisa's mother's perceptions in mind as I tried to understand Lisa's experience of the music therapy. In some instances, they changed my sense of Lisa's experience, as expressed in the remainder of the chapter.

LISA'S MUSIC THERAPY

Individual Music Therapy

THE FIRST SESSION. When Lisa first came to my house for music therapy, her mother helped her out of the car and held her hand as they walked to the house. In the assessment session, Lisa danced spontaneously and clapped, jumped, and swayed to recorded fifties music, with the latter responses being prompted. She used rhythm instruments appropriately, possibly because they were placed in her hands. As she was leaving at the end, she jumped up and down and made some sounds.

As I watched Lisa walk to my house before the first session, I was struck by the fragility of this child who did not speak and responded only minimally. I wondered what she might be feeling and what would evolve in our relationship. As she participated in the assessment session, showing apparent pleasure at some aspects and possibly doing some things mechanically (such as moving a tambourine that was placed into her hand), I wondered what was in this child's mind and how she experienced the session.

Here I am in this new situation. I wonder what it is about. There are instruments here and a piano. I like those things. And the lady is friendly. I am not sure. The instruments are okay, but I really like the recorded music, especially this fifties music. I love to dance to the music. I could do this for a long time. Now that we're finished, I'm excited to be seeing the rest of my family and be leaving, but this was an interesting new thing to do.

EARLY SESSIONS, 2–14. For the next sessions, Lisa's responses were somewhat inconsistent. This proved to be a pattern that would continue throughout her music therapy. As her mother said at one point, "If there's one thing we know about Lisa, it's that she's inconsistent." This seems to be primarily a neurologically based problem; something in Lisa's system does not seem to allow her to consistently process and respond to information. Her mother calls this "zoning out," and it was very much a part of working with her at times.

At other times her responses, particularly vocal responses and following directions, were consistent and exciting. She said something that sounded like "music" and at times sang it where there was a space in a song ("Lisa can make some music") or would say it when she wanted to use the recorded music.

After some of these sessions, I felt optimistic about Lisa's responses. After other sessions, when she responded very little, I felt very pessimistic. I believe it was later that I realized that these variations in response were part of what Lisa went through and I accepted them as part of working with her.

I like these music times. It is fun to come with my mother and my sisters and have all this attention. I especially like to dance with the tapes. Sometimes Barbara wants me to do things when I can't. Sometimes I don't even know what she's talking about. I just sit and don't really know what is happening. But other times, it is really fun to say "music" and dance to the music. And Barbara gives

*me lots of attention and helps make the music and gets
very excited when I do things. I like that.*

VOCAL SESSIONS, 15–65. During the next period of time, extending over the next year and 5 months, Lisa's vocal development was very exciting and was emphasized in our work. In the early months of this period, many of the vocalizations were around a song that had originally been improvised, "Me dance to the music," with which Lisa used hand signing as well as singing or filling in words when given a space in the song. I wrote the following session note after session 52 in November 1993:

> Near the end of the session, Lisa walked to the tape recorder and appeared to want to play the tape so she could dance. I asked her what she wanted, and she seemed to respond "music." We played the music a bit, then I turned the tape off and, in response to her look, said, "What do you want now?" She said (or appeared to say), "More music." I said, "Are you sure?" She said, "Yes." We repeated this routine or a similar one when she said "Dance" in response to my question as to what she wanted, approximately eight times. Her inflections were so clear and so consistent that, although the words themselves were not clear, there was no doubt in either my mind or her mother's that Lisa and I were having the conversation reported. It seemed so clear that it made me wonder how many other times Lisa is saying words but we simply cannot understand her.

During this same period, Lisa played instruments and continued to respond to commands. For a while, I encouraged her through a song to ask me for the rhythm sticks, then I would drop them on the floor when she said "yeah," indicating that she wanted me to do this. Unfortunately, throwing things on the floor generalized beyond this setting and became a problem in school; although it had led to good use of her voice to ask for things, the strategy could not be continued.

Near the end of this portion of Lisa's music therapy, she used her voice for extended singing and humming for approximately three sessions. I thought that this indicated increasing enjoyment of her voice and was very excited about it; however, shortly after that, her

vocalizations to approximate words or to indicate her wishes
decreased sharply, although she did continue the humming and
singing. They never resumed at the level that they had been, and I
never knew exactly why. It is possible that with increasing demands
for them, her vocalizations became less enjoyable to Lisa, or perhaps
they were simply something that changed for her or no longer provided an enjoyable outlet for her.

> *These have been really fun times in music. It has been so
> much fun coming to Barbara's and dancing. We've been
> doing all these fun songs where we dance and sing
> together and then Barbara gives me spaces and I get to
> put in my own words. Barbara gets so excited and I get
> excited and then we do some more! And we always get to
> dance. I love to dance!*
>
> *Then we got to throw the sticks on the floor. I loved
> that! I would just say "yeah" and Barbara would give me
> the stick, then I could throw it on the floor and we would
> laugh and sometimes I would pick it up. Sometimes Bar-
> bara would pick it up for me. I did the same thing in
> school, too. That was fun. But we don't do that anymore. I
> miss it.*
>
> *I really liked all that singing also. I just let my voice
> go wherever it wanted to. I did that in school also. People
> like it when I do that. I like it.*
>
> *There are still times when I just need to sit, though.
> But there haven't been so many of them lately. The music
> has been lots of fun. I love coming here!*

FINAL SESSIONS, 66–82. In the final individual music therapy
sessions, Lisa's vocalizations that approximated words or showed
her wishes decreased, although her humming and singing continued. She had more periods of not responding. During this time, I
dealt again with feeling discouraged when Lisa did so little, particularly since it was such a change from earlier sessions when
her responses had been increasing and I had been so excited.

The decrease of responses might have been due to its being
summer, when although she was involved in a summer program,
the expectations placed on her were much lower than during the
regular school year. My knowledge, beginning in July, that as of

September I would be seeing her in a different setting might have led me to respond to her differently. At any rate, there was less energy to the sessions and Lisa was less responsive.

> *Things are changing a little. I'm not sure why, but I don't like to do the same songs as much. And we don't get to throw the sticks down. I still like to sing and Barbara plays the guitar while I do that. We're doing other things that are fun, but it's not really the same as it was before. I miss those other times. Sometimes I just sit now and don't do anything. I just need to do that.*

Music Therapy Sessions in School

I was looking forward to Lisa's music therapy as part of her school program and hoped that some of the responses that she had made in the private music therapy sessions would carry over to her school environment. I also hoped that the new setting might help to bring back some of the energy that had been lacking in recent sessions. I especially wanted to see if her interest in music could help to develop her social skills, so I planned her music therapy sessions to be held with another child. I also wondered if she would be confused to see me away from my home and wished that I could help her to understand the change.

THE FIRST YEAR. There were many changes. First, Lisa was seeing me in a place where she spent much of her time, rather than in my home office. Second, she saw me with another child. Third, the move of her music therapy to her school coincided with her movement into a class of older children, where she had many more demands placed on her. Lisa was 11 years 9 months when the music therapy sessions at her school began.

The first part of the first year until after Christmas was a time of major adjustment for Lisa. Even small changes had always been difficult for Lisa and would generally lead to her being less responsive, so it was not surprising that the school changes were difficult. Not only was she adjusting to the change in her music therapy setting and having to share me and the music with another child, but she was adjusting to many more demands being placed on her. Her response was to withdraw.

Lisa's responses in all areas decreased during this time and she nearly stopped vocalizing. In addition, the room where the music therapy was held served other needs for teachers and students and there were frequent interruptions. These interruptions led to Lisa's being much less attentive; once her attention was diverted, she often remained distracted and unresponsive for the entire session.

I don't know what is going on here. There are a lot of changes and I feel very confused. Barbara is here, but I don't know why she's here instead of the old place. I don't understand. And we're not alone like we used to be; this other girl is always here getting some of the attention. I'm in a different classroom with different kids and a different teacher and they want me to do so many things differently. Then all these people come into the room while we're having music and I'd like to know what they're doing. I'm interested in them but don't know what to do, so I just look at them and don't do anything. I don't like this music like I used to when it was just Barbara and me and we were in the special room in her house. That used to be so fun. I really miss those times.

Later in the year, it seemed as though Lisa had adjusted to the changes and was ready to continue her development. She began vocalizing again and frequently made requests vocally, generally after being prompted. She seemed to enjoy the activities and the other child who was in the group as well as several adults who assisted with the group at times. She continued to be distracted by people coming into the room, although less so.

Some very nice emotional engagement occurred during this time. In one session in the middle of a song Lisa put her head down on my leg and hugged my leg. I thought it was a caring gesture; she may also have been wishing for my undivided attention, since it was being shared. This was just one of a number of emotional reactions during this time.

These music times have been fun. I got used to all the changes and to having someone else be in music therapy with us. Sometimes it's even fun having her there to do things with. Sometimes I still don't like it, though. One day I

*put my head on Barbara's knee just to sort of remember that
we have a special friendship. I've known her a lot longer
than anyone else has.*

 *The songs where we do things like stand and sit and
move around are fun. I'm not always so speedy on these, but
I get around to doing what they tell me to. It's kind of fun to
move around like that, and everyone is always happy when I
do what the song says. I like the instruments, too, and have
been playing them the way they want me to. And we still get
to dance. I always love to dance.*

SECOND YEAR. During this year, we could see the results of the
previous year's efforts to treat Lisa with the expectation that she
would respond more consistently. She showed progress in all areas
and responded more consistently than ever. She appeared very connected with me and the other child and seemed to respond in order to
get attention. She would laugh engagingly, particularly when someone dropped something or otherwise made a mistake. Her sense of
humor seemed to be more developed than many of her other
responses and made working with her very special.

 One thing that seemed particularly significant emotionally was
Lisa's attachment to a student teacher who assisted with the sessions.
This young woman shared many of Lisa's physical features, and Lisa
quickly seemed drawn to her. Lisa would stare at her and smile and
even reach out to her. On the student teacher's last day when we
spoke of the fact that she would be leaving, tears welled up in Lisa's
eyes and she appeared quite upset. This attachment seemed to reflect
her ability to experience deep emotions.

 *This has been fun lately. All of us have had so much fun
together. Playing the instruments and then letting someone
else play them is lots of fun. It's nice not to play alone all the
time, even though I used to enjoy it. Now sometimes we go
back and forth with the instruments and we laugh and move
and it's so much fun. And we've been doing some new songs
that have been fun. I like doing these new things, especially
when I catch on to them. I don't always do everything as fast
as everyone else, but I usually do it. It's fun to do these
things.*

 *I really liked that teacher's helper. She looks like me.
We have the same hair and are about the same size. I felt
like she was my friend. When she would smile at me and
hold my hand to help me, I just felt so wonderful that she*

was doing that. When they said she was leaving, I couldn't believe it! I felt so sad. I wish she would have stayed. I wonder why she had to go. I'll really miss her.

When I left the school in April of the school year, I told Lisa that I would be leaving and would miss her; it was never clear to me if she understood that I would not be back. My 4-year relationship with Lisa touched me in many ways. I have tried to reflect in this chapter ways that I hope it touched her as well as her other impressions of it. I hope that I have been true to her experience of the music therapy sessions, so that if she could read this, she would say, "Yes, that's exactly what I felt."

PARALLEL EXPERIENCES

Janice Dvorkin and Roia Rafieyan

JANICE AND ROIA'S INTRODUCTION

We use the concept of parallel process (a concept supported by research) to suggest what might have been the music therapy experience of Pat, a 30-year-old nonverbal man with pervasive developmental disorder. We compare the responses of his therapist, Roia (co-author of this narrative), in her supervisory sessions to Pat's behaviors during his concurrent therapy sessions and suggest that as Roia learned about herself in relation to Janice, her supervisor, Pat learned about himself in relation to Roia. It was difficult to assess Pat's feelings about or satisfaction with the music therapy experience. We made the assumption from observing Pat's behaviors that Roia's verbalized experiences of supervision were parallel to what Pat's responses about therapy would have been had he been able to report them.

Pat has been living in a developmental center since the age of 7. At the age of 5, he was found to have early infantile autism. Pat adheres to rituals, relies on routine, and has difficulty processing sensory information and developing relationships with other people. He continues to receive a variety of psychiatric and seizure medications for behavior and seizure control. Pat began individual music therapy 4 years ago, at approximately the same time that Roia began supervision. In the sessions, Pat and Roia use improvised piano to communicate ideas and feelings.

Roia sought clinical supervision because although she had been working as a music therapist for 6 years, she was experiencing limitations in her way of working and felt she was underestimating the abilities of her clients. Supervision provided her with mentorship from a more experienced professional, Janice. In supervision, Roia was guided to examine her own behavior in the therapist role and to look at why she might be reacting to Pat in certain ways. At the same time, she was encouraging Pat to develop a greater awareness of his own behavior in relation to the music and to herself.

PAT'S EXPERIENCE
AS SEEN THROUGH ROIA'S

Both Pat and Roia were eager but hesitant to begin their individual sessions. Both struggled to adjust to a new way of working that emphasized looking at how each of them was experiencing the relationship. Pat's expectation, based on the learning model at the developmental center, was that Roia would provide the "right" answer or give direction to their interactions. Roia had the same expectation of Janice. This became one of the first issues that was addressed by both pairs. Roia found it difficult to adjust to a mode of supervision in which she was encouraged to problem-solve rather than be provided with answers to her questions. Janice guided her through this process in much the same way that Roia learned to model for Pat. In his sessions, Pat was observed waiting expectantly for direction from the therapist. (His previous experience with her had been in a much more directive style of group music therapy.) When he realized no direction was forthcoming, he would pace and make ritualistic movements. Following Janice's model, Roia helped Pat learn to make choices on his own and to initiate musical expression. As his tolerance for interaction increased, he was able to sit for longer periods of time and to be more engaged in the relationship.

Both Pat and Roia attempted to demonstrate their initial eagerness by pleasing the therapist and supervisor, respectively, to ease some of the anxiety they felt when taking part in unfamiliar experiences. Roia's discomfort was expressed in her desire to increase her clinical skills, and she demonstrated her uncertainty and doubt by preparing a number of questions for the supervision sessions. Pat's eagerness and anticipation of the music therapy sessions was evident in his behavioral responses: he gradually moved from simply approaching Roia on her arrival in the cottage and accompanying her to the therapy setting to taking her hand and pulling her to the door.

Gradually, Roia became comfortable with Janice's nondirective yet empathic responses. Roia was able, in turn, to develop a more empathic and nondirective stance with Pat in his music therapy sessions. She improvised music and singing to mirror and show understanding of Pat's behaviors, to which he responded by making eye contact, by decreasing his pacing, and by approaching her more frequently to stand or sit close to her. As Pat began to demonstrate interest in communicating with Roia, she became more confident in her ability to reflect and interpret his behaviors. At one point early in therapy, Pat initiated the action of tapping two cards together. Roia responded to this by tapping back to him on a drum, reflecting and acknowledging his action (a nondirective stance), encouraging him to use this method as a way to begin to interact on a musical level, and showing him how he might begin to interact with her. Pat recognized and responded to this intervention, and they began to engage in nonverbal dialogues in which Pat and Roia took turns tapping the drum and the cards.

The parallel process was further demonstrated in both Pat's and Roia's wish for longer sessions. Pat would act this out by consistently going to the bathroom on hearing that the end of the session was near, thus extending the time spent in therapy. Roia would verbalize her desire for more frequent or longer supervision sessions.

In supervision, Roia began to explore the relationship between herself and Janice and how she felt about it. She struggled with her discomfort with regard to the sharing of difficult issues with Janice (such as her emotional responses to Pat) as well as her concern with regard to her ability to use music effectively as a therapeutic tool. Eventually, she developed enough trust in the supervision process and in Janice to feel safe and to know that she would continue to be supported and not rejected for trying something that she perceived as being new and frightening. The relationship between Pat and the Roia was similarly played out in the music therapy sessions. Initially, Pat avoided the piano, refusing to sit near the instrument or to touch it at all. Although he had begun to establish a rapport with Roia, his behavior clearly indicated some anxiety with regard to the introduction of this new musical element into his sessions. Roia noted Pat's apparent trepidation, acknowledging how difficult it seemed to be for him to try new things and at the same time modeling for him how he might use the piano to express some of these feelings. Thus, Pat began to approach and explore the piano, often looking to Roia for guidance and approval after he made an attempt to play the instrument.

As Roia increased her self-awareness and was able to bring these insights back to the therapy session, Pat began to increase his musical expression, using the piano with greater range of dynamics and engaging in musical interactions with the therapist. Because Roia developed the ability to self-reflect, she was able to be more "present" during Pat's sessions. As Roia began to be more comfortable using improvised music to communicate emotional meaning, she in turn helped Pat to match her comfort in expressing feelings through music. It was this level of comfort within the therapy relationship that also allowed Pat to begin to express resistance and anger during his sessions. These new facets in the therapy were exhibited by changes in his affect, in the way he used music, in his occasional refusals to attend music therapy sessions, and in requests to leave early.

A final parallel step was noted in the growth of Roia and Pat. After several years of supervision, Roia gave a presentation at a conference about her work. This step was possible because of her increased feelings of confidence as a therapist. Likewise, Pat seemed to be more confident in his new relationship skills, using the ways of interacting he practiced in his therapy sessions in social settings. For instance, he was more able to tolerate developing friendships and he demonstrated a desire for continued participation in these relationships by his ability to maintain socially appropriate behaviors and in his willingness to take part in outings.

HENRY'S TRANSITION THROUGH MUSIC*

Rika Ikuno

INTRODUCTION

This narrative explores the music therapy experience of an 8-year-old boy whom I will call Henry. Henry has pervasive developmental disorder (autism). For several months prior to the session described in this study, Henry had been experiencing tumultuous episodes of panic characterized by uncontrolled bouts of crying, palpable frustration, and loud negative verbalization. According to his mother, this behavior began clearly on a single occasion. One day, Henry was not allowed to participate in the opening session of his school's summer swimming class because he was suffering from a slight fever. Henry had always enjoyed swimming, but after this episode, he would not swim at all. He would say, "I'm going," and indeed he would go to the pool; however, he could not bring himself to get in the water and instead would begin to shout and cry uncontrollably. Since this episode, Henry has panicked selectively at his favorite activities, including music.

Since the age of 6, Henry has participated in a music therapy group that consists of three or four autistic boys. Henry's music therapy group meets for about 40 minutes. In this group, familiar songs provide a context for one-on-one or group communication activities. A year ago, piano-playing was introduced as part of the session. In this activity, each of the four or five children has a 5-minute individual piano activity sitting on the piano bench with me, the therapist. In Henry's piano activity, he invented a game that might be called "make the therapist play." He would sing his own melodies and allow me to copy his song on the piano with added harmony. Henry does not use words precisely. He often uses memorized phrases, inserting

* I thank Henry's mother, Henry himself (not his real name), co-therapist Akiko Mizuno, and Eric Myers, who helped with editing the English.

them into situations so that they sometimes seem appropriate and sometimes seem nonsensical. The melodies he sings seem to be refrains from television or video games; he hums them in precise pitch and wants to hear them repeated on the piano exactly as he has sung them.

Here, I report Henry's piano activity from session 15. I break down the 8-minute activity into units of less than 1 minute. I report observations of his behavior (from studying the videotape of our session), and since Henry is not capable of commenting on his own internal processes, I interpret his state of mind in the form of a soliloquy (I assume Henry's voice) based on my observation of his behavior and facial expressions and my knowledge of him during 2 years of therapy. I report each unit of approximately 50 seconds in three paragraphs: (1) a thorough documentation of Henry's outward behavior and activities; (2) an imaginative soliloquy by me, and (3) an interpretation by me with the help of Henry's mother and the co-therapist, Akiko, in response to their review of the videotape of the session. The three levels of analysis are laid out in the following manner: (1) the objective documentation is presented in the present tense and describes Henry's (and other participants') observable activities during the short time units; (2) Henry's soliloquies are presented in italics; and (3) the interpretation is presented in the past tense.

I have translated Henry's verbal phrases into English but have left in Japanese the few phrases that are incorporated into our music. During the part of session 15 reported here, I sit at the piano and Akiko moves among the boys, facilitating their participation.

HENRY IN SESSION 15
(8 MINUTES)

Unit 1

Henry stands away from the group, and Akiko is with him. Henry says, "No, no!" Akiko gently answers, "I know." Henry says, *"Ka-e-ro!* [Let's go home!]," with tonal intonation [Figure A]. He says, "[I] don't want; [I] don't want." Guided by Akiko, he walks in the direction of his seat. As Akiko touches his hand, Henry shakes it off and stops walking. Avoiding Akiko, he goes around to his chair.

Henry says, "[I] don't want." Akiko says, "I know, you don't want it at all." He passes by his chair, stands at the opposite side of the group, and cries out loudly. Akiko adjusts Henry's chair closer to him and says, "Here; please sit down." Akiko repeats it clearly, "Here—sit down."

> *I can't; I don't want; I hate to join the group! I don't want music! I just wanted to grasp that instrument and play by myself. Ah, I want to go home, but I can't because I want to join the music, too. Okay, I will go to the group seats and sit. No, I can't. I don't want Akiko to touch me! It is painful and sad. I can't do anything and I don't know what I want!*

Henry appeared to be confused, wanting to join the music session and yet wanting to reject everything. He was desperate and tried to ease the frustration with such behaviors as inappropriately grabbing for the instruments, crying out, and disrupting the group activity. Akiko gently sympathized with Henry's desire to reject everything but encouraged him to do what he really wanted to do—music.

Ka - e - ro!

Figure A. Henry's tonal intonation—music #1.

Unit 2

Henry coughs and sobs and then sits down, holding Akiko's hand. He repeatedly grasps her hands, strikes out at them, and shakes them off, crying all the while. Henry shakes his legs.

> *Ah, I finally sat down. I don't know how to get out of this frustration, but my loud voice seems to get people's attention. Take care of me, because I need help. But don't disturb me, because I hate it.*

Henry seemed slightly less confused once he felt the stability of his sitting position, but he was still ambivalent about Akiko's presence. Henry's shaking and crying was not a well-articulated "call for help," but he clearly seemed to be showing others his frustration.

Unit 3

I play a tender song to comfort Henry. Another member of the group stands up on his chair and expresses his irritation. I respond to it by saying, "Please sit down" and stopping the music. While my attention is directed to the other group member, Henry stops making the crying sound and wipes his nose with his shirt. He exhales, calms down for a moment, and wipes his tears. Suddenly Henry pushes Akiko, who has been squatting beside him, and she falls on the floor, laughing. The other group member sits down. Henry says, *"Ka-e-ro* [Let's go home]," pulls his shirt down to wrap up his knees, and cries loudly.

> *What's happening? People are not looking at me. Is that boy being scolded? The music stopped and the atmosphere changed. Wait—it was I who was in trouble. What a painful situation I was in. Hey, I am mad, so I'll push Akiko away! Give me your attention! Yes, I have sat down, but I still can't accept this situation!*

It was interesting that Henry's maladaptive behavior decreased when the other boy pulled people's attention away from Henry. This suggested that Henry's crying out meant at least two things: the releasing of emotion, such as anger or frustration, and a call for help or attention from others. Even in his panic fit, Henry was conscious of other people, including therapists and other members of the group.

Unit 4

Rika turns her body to the piano and says, "Henry, come here." Henry says, "[I] don't want!" and cries with a loud, hoarse voice. He scratches his shirt roughly. Rika starts to play a melody [Figure B]. Henry continues to cry, burying his face in his shirt and stomping on the floor. At times, he looks in the direction of the piano and starts to listen.

> *I am angry at being here and I am angry at everybody here who can't solve this problem! I won't go! Oh? I realize there is a song, a song I have never heard. What's that?*

Henry had became more attentive to the environment than when he was standing. He was still conflicted but also had begun to listen to the new music.

* Words used only during unit 12.

Figure B. Music #2: *Ka-e-ro.*

Unit 5

Rika continues playing Music #2. Akiko approaches Henry from his right, but he pushes her away, crying loudly. Henry shakes his right hand at Akiko, crying "Eh, eh, bye-bye!" Akiko holds the boy next to Henry. Then Henry holds Akiko's arm and pulls her toward himself. As she comes close, Henry pushes her away again, saying, "Bye-bye!" Akiko distances herself from Henry, and he pulls her back again, saying something inaudible. Akiko says, "Which is it? Okay, bye-bye—is that right?" and leaves him.

*Don't touch me! Don't control me! Leave me alone! But don't
ignore me. Don't be nice to the other boy. Be with me!*

Henry demanded to be left alone and to be cared for at the same
time; thus, there was very little Akiko could do to help him. He
needed to be left to himself; Rika and Akiko could do no more. At this
point, all was quiet except for Henry's occasional verbalization and
Music #2 that Rika was playing.

Unit 6

Henry listens to Music #2 and intones, *"Ka-e-ro* [Let's go home]"
twice. To match this, I emphasize the melodic theme *"Ka-e-ro"* at the
piano. Henry says, "Ah, ah . . . ," sounding scared of something. He
rubs his shirt, is still for a moment, and then moves again, scratching
his elbow and shaking his legs. Finally, he says something inaudible
with a calm voice, touching his ear.

*Now I am safe; nobody touches me or disturbs me. Where
does this music go? It is kind of sad. Now I have a space
to listen in. After all the shouting, I am a little tired, too.*

The way Henry said *"Ka-e-ro"* this time did not sound like the
rejection it had earlier. It seemed that he was focusing on the music
and was verbalizing a sound to respond to it. Gradually, this sound
(*ka-e-ro*) began to match the flow of the music. Less perturbed now,
Henry was drifting in a space supported by my music.

Unit 7

I continue playing Music #2. The next moment, Henry cries out
loudly again, "Waaaaa! Ba, waaaa," as if he is threatened by something. He pulls his shirt down to his ankles. Then he listens to the
piano, making short sounds like "Wa, wa."

*Ah, pain, pain, what a pain! And what a loud voice I
made! And that music still continues. Where is it and
where does it go?*

Henry felt an impulse to panic again and cried out. This crying out, however, seemed to signify more clearly an attempt at communication. He knew that he was making a loud noise, and by making it, he seemed to expect a response from people and the music. Henry's mother suggested that he might make noise to involve people in what he is doing; thus, the noise could be interpreted as a primitive way of calling for help.

Unit 8

I continue to play Music #2. Henry's hands touch the front of his pants. Another group member gets irritated, hits Akiko's hands, and calls out. Henry looks in that direction. Suddenly, Henry shows interest in the inside of his pants and rubs his penis strongly. He cries out, "Don't touch!" with a woman's high intonation. He takes his penis out of his pants and starts to play with it. I keep playing the piano and I say, "Henry, pull up your pants" in a calm, firm voice.

Here I've found a new thing that can help me escape from this pain. I shouldn't be touching it, but stimulation calls for stimulation. How can I stop? No, I can't stop

It was possible that Henry's sudden masturbation was aroused in part by the stimulating voice of the other group member. It was also feasible that Henry simply found a convenient way to escape his conflicting feelings.

Unit 9

I continue Music #2. Akiko approaches Henry from the back, helps him to pull up his pants, and holds his arms. He cries out, "Aaaa, haaaaa!" Akiko grasps him by the upper body, directs him firmly to the piano, and helps him to sit down on the piano bench.

Ah! Don't touch me! I've already said that, and you had left me once! Why do you come to me again?! No! Don't touch me; don't hold my body; don't push and control my body!

After seeing Henry become more agitated, Akiko decided that it was time to help him get in the direction of the music. He rejected her verbally but allowed himself to be guided to the piano.

Unit 10

Henry continues to cry but sits down on the piano bench. He looks at my face while I continue playing Music #2. He cries louder, his face distorted. Akiko sits at his back. Henry notices it and pushes her back but holds her hands. He says, "No!" as he cries and continues to play with Akiko's hands.

What's this?! What's this?! You told me that you would leave me alone, and now you take me to the piano and surround me like a wall! I won't have it; I don't like you. But the scenery from this bench is different from the group seat. It feels a little better.

Henry was shocked by being put at the piano so brusquely, but he stayed. He expressed his tentative shock in his voice and his face, but he was slowly digesting this new (and positive) environment. The way in which he treated Akiko's hands reflected the ambivalence within him.

Unit 11

Henry says, *"Daijobu, daijobu* [It's okay, it's okay]," with a totally different, gentle tone. Akiko and I immediately repeat it with comforting intonation: *"Daijobu."* I continue to play Music #2. Henry wipes his nose with his shirt, scratches his elbow, and looks at me. He turns to Akiko and says, *"Ka-e-ro!* [Let's go home!]" and cries. Akiko vocalizes with the piano.

I really want to stop being irritated; I want to be relieved. I want to be okay, and is this [daijobu] the word for that? Am I okay to be here? What I really want is not to panic and to stop this confusion. I just want to be okay. Maybe it

would be better if I went home. But this music is not bad.
What's that? Akiko is singing in a sad but soothing voice.

Amidst the many contradictory feelings within him, Henry
reached out and grasped the word *"daijobu* [it's okay]." It was possible
that his sense of self shifted from needing to cry out and upset the
environment to accepting that things were "okay."

Unit 12

Still crying, Henry says, "Oh, that's bad!" His voice is soft and
secretive. He wipes his nose and looks at me and at the keyboard
in turn. I continue Music #2 and start singing the word *"Ka-e-ro!"*
Akiko joins in. Henry says, "Oh, that's bad!" and scratches his leg.
He puts his left leg on Akiko's knee; he is now facing Akiko and
me, looking at us in turn and listening to the music. Now Akiko
and I are singing, *"Ka-e-ro, ka-e-ro, daijobu* [Let's go home, let's go
home; it's okay]."

> *This is a bad situation; I am to be blamed and you are to*
> *be blamed. This is bad. But what's this music? It brings*
> *me to the place where it is not bad. It's also accepting my*
> *confusion. Let me connect my body to Akiko. It is comfort-*
> *able. These two people are playing this music for me.*
> *What are they trying to say? I really need to know.*

As he calmed to a more stable emotional state, Henry briefly
returned to displays of negativity. According to his mother, "Oh,
that's bad" is the phrase that Henry habitually uses before falling
into a bad mood, but in this case, the negativity was only superficial, and he appeared already to be guiding himself to a calmer
place. Finally, he connected himself physically to Akiko. During
these moments, Henry appeared to be using the music to help
settle his feelings.

Henry's mother suspected that he was simply forgetting his
panic in concentrating on the beauty of the music. She felt that by
focusing on the music, Henry was losing sight of his previous bad
mood and changing to a new emotional state. According to her
view, Henry was not capable of using the music to resolve feel-

ings. Instead, he simply moved from emotional state to state rather easily because of his limited short-term memory.

In talking about this, Akiko and I decided that it is impossible to determine exactly what happens within Henry when he is profoundly listening to music. We agreed, however, that Henry's facial expressions and body language while listening to Music #2 suggested an internal state that was very different from that of any previous occasion in his therapy.

Unit 13

I continue improvising using Music #2. Henry asks, "Who are you?" His facial expression becomes stable, and he is seriously listening to the music. Suddenly he shouts, "Excellent!" and calms down. I respond, "Thanks."

> *What are you trying to say? What is the message? Anyway, I think it is something not bad. I like it. Keep on playing. This is good, whatever good means.*

It was hard to determine how precisely Henry used language. It was possible that he asked a kind of existential question—"Who are you?"—of the people he was struggling to understand and with whom he needed to communicate. Following this question, Henry might have been expressing his liking and gratitude for my musical communication with the word *excellent*. He probably used a line from a television program, compensating for his own language deficiency; his choice of words was reasonably appropriate.

Unit 14

I continue playing Music #2 and ask, "Why don't you play the piano, too? Will you play?" He ignores the question and continues to intone the *"Ka-e-ro!"* tune (Music #1). Then Henry whispers, "It hurts," touches his hair, and wipes his nose. Akiko and I include the words *it hurts* in the song. Henry repeats *"Ka-e-ro"* several times and listens to the song. He is very still and looks at me and the keyboard, in turn, with a calm facial expression.

*I need to be in this music, so let me drift in here. I am
calming down and the things around me and in me are
clearer. This music is safe and it protects me. I can connect to you with the word* "Ka-e-ro."

The utterance "It hurts" seemed out of place in this context.
In response to my suggestion to play the piano, Henry insisted on
continuing with the refrain *"Ka-e-ro."* It was as if he were saying,
"I am not ready yet, so continue prescribing the same medicine."

Unit 15

I transform Music #2 into a slow version of Henry's favorite
tune. This new music [Figure C] has a motif similar to Music #2 but
with the additional words *"O-wa-ta-ka ka-e-ro* [When the music is
over, let's go home]." Henry listens to it carefully. The second time, I
increase the tempo, and the third time, I move to the higher register
with a sharper touch, omitting the words *"Ka-e-ro."* Henry still listens
to the music, touching the piano cover.

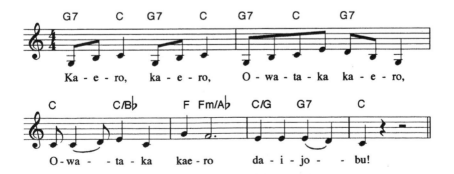

Figure C. Music #3: *O-wa-ta-ka ka-e-ro.*

Well, what's going on now? I know this melody, and it is positive but slightly different from the last one we were playing. Rika is still singing our word "Ka-e-ro," but the message from the music is not the same. I have to be very careful.

Here, I was pushing Henry along because the other boys were waiting. He accepted these variations for now, even though he must have noticed that it was different music.

Unit 16

I stop playing and ask, "Will you play, Henry?" and show my finger to him. Henry glances at my face, holds my finger, and pushes it back to the keyboard, singing, *"Ka-e-ro"* (Music #1), with a dark voice. I repeat Music #3 with the words *"Ka-e-ro, ka-e-ro, o-wa-ta-ka ka-e-ro* [Let's go home, let's go home, when music is over, let's go home]." He sings, *"Ka-e-ro!"* (a combination of Music #1 and #2) loudly and slowly to erase my music. Then Henry says, "Ghost" and sings, *"Ka-e-ro!"* again.

What is she saying? It is really hard to get. No, don't start a new thing. No piano-playing. What I need now is your "ka-e-ro" song. No, not that one. Slower, darker, sadder, I say—like a ghostly sounding "ka-e-ro!"

I pushed Henry further, hurrying him to come out from the darkness and to be a "good, cheerful boy." He tried to understand the situation but insisted on the dark, slow, and minor-key *"Ka-e-ro"* music. He communicated this need first through his singing and then with the word *ghost*. It was amazing that he found this word from his extremely limited vocabulary; I assumed he was asking for slow, literally low-key music.

Unit 17

I go back to Music #2 with a slow tempo, lower register, and minor key. Henry listens to it, looking at me and the keyboard in turn. He wipes his nose. I end the music with the word *"daijobu* [it's okay]," slowing down. After a moment of silence, Henry whispers with a very gentle voice, *"Daijobu-ne-e* [It's okay, isn't it]?" Akiko and I respond, *"U–n, daijobu* [Of course it's okay]." Henry repeats, *"Daijobu-ne-e,"* with a peaceful face.

> *This music really makes me feel relieved. Yes, I should be okay. I can feel it now. I am pretty convinced.*

Henry was satisfied to be going back to the dark, rich music and to be taking the time he needed. He smoothly accepted this sudden ending. It was as if Henry preferred to conclude his inner transformation with this quiet music (Music #2) rather than the cheerful one (Music #3).

Unit 18

A sad expression comes to Henry's face, and he says after a long sigh, "But, but," with sobs in his voice. I fill in the word *sad.* Henry continues his sentence with the same sobbing voice "sad, I, I." Then he adds, *"Ka-e-ro* [Let's go home]," with a sad, weak voice. He is touching Akiko's hands with his left hand.

> *But I remember how difficult it was a while ago. I was— let's say -sad! That's the word! I wanted to say, "I am sad. Listen: I was sad." I wanted to go home. Ah, I am becoming sad again!*

This time, Henry's emotional swing did not express itself through a display of crying out or maladaptive behavior. Rather, he expressed it—with my help—through his words. Voicing the word *but,* he connected and verbalized his contradictory feelings. By speaking to and physically touching Akiko and me, he seemed to be trying to share his feeling of instability with us.

Unit 19

Henry changes to a hoarse, almost comical voice and says slowly, "Wait a moment, wait a moment!" and then rapidly, "Wait a moment." I respond, "Okay, I'll wait." Henry says, *"Ka-e-ro,"* with a merrier voice than previously.

> *No, I shouldn't; I don't want to go back there again. I am fine now. I don't know what the word is for this feeling, but I can say, "Ka-e-ro"* [*in this cheerful way*]!

Where the phrase "Wait a moment, wait a moment" came from was somewhat of a mystery. It might have been the line that followed the phrase "I am sad" in a television program, and Henry simply drew that from his memory, or perhaps he constructed different memorized phrases into a longer phrase simply out of the blue. Perhaps he found that these were the words that would express his newfound cheer. The tone with which he uttered *"Ka-e-ro"* right afterward might have been a reflection of this. In any case, this line seemed to help prevent him from falling back into a bad mood and allowed him to complete the transition to a state of emotional well-being.

Unit 20

Akiko stands up and moves Henry's chair to the group seating area. She points to it and says, "Yes, let's go back to your chair." Henry watches Akiko's actions and moves to his chair quickly, with a calm face.

> *Okay, I am done. I'll go back to the seat where I should be. This is the what I should do.*

Henry seemed to be simply satisfied; he accepted the transition.

Part V

Client Words
About Experiences
Are Gathered by Researchers

In these three narratives, qualitative researchers
compile studies of client experiences of music therapy
by presenting client words. The researchers organize
the words to clarify the experiences. In two of the narratives, researchers interviewed multiple clients. In
the other narrative, the researcher made ongoing
analyses of videotapes of client sessions and of the
client's self-reports, reporting back to the client and
therapist; the researcher presents transcripts of the
client's words in sessions and the self-reports. Two of
the researchers present the verbatim words of their
clients, then synthesize or distill the meaning contained in the words.

Narrative 31

TALES FROM
THE THERAPY ROOM

Dorit Amir

INTRODUCTION

A few years ago when I was doing graduate research in the United
States, I interviewed music therapy clients and asked them to tell me
about some of their experiences in music therapy. The following are
stories that were told to me by three people: Ben, Karen, and Lyn.
Each of these three experienced different ways of using music and
different therapists. Ben's main activities in his music therapy sessions were song-writing and singing; Karen experienced Guided
Imagery and Music (GIM), in which, with the help of her therapist,
she produced imagery from her deep unconscious while listening to
music in a relaxed state; Lyn improvised with her therapist on piano,
percussion instruments, and with her voice. In reporting their interviews, I have arranged their words under the topics that emerged as
meaningful. I introduce the interviewees before I present their words.

BEN

> When I* met Ben, he was a 21-year-old man who had
> received music therapy for 1 year while in a rehabilitation
> center. Both of Ben's legs were paralyzed as a result of a car
> accident that had happened a few years before. He had some
> movement in his hands, arms, and upper body. Ben moved
> around in a wheelchair, although he was very slow in man-
> aging daily living activities. Ben had participated in indi-
> vidual, dyadic, and group music therapy with Tania, his
> music therapist, three times a week for 1 hour each.

---

* Dorit's comments are indented here and throughout the rest of this narrative.

Well, since I was in rehabilitation in the hospital, music therapy was a way to forget all of your problems—you know, just have fun, try to reach your creativity and see if you can adapt to certain situations, try to cope or overcome, and overall just to have fun with what you are doing. Music therapy is basically just trying to look at things in a lighter way. . . . Music therapy was a place where you [could] go, converse with other people in the same situation, or be creative and just write something that might have something to do with what you feel, you know, [and] which [could] identify with your situation. . . . Being creative is just sitting down and really feeling certain things, certain feelings you get, and trying to write a song as good as possible, you know; that's where creativity comes in. It's really to dig in and to see if you really have it, not to let your shyness keep you back. It's where you can really let yourself go and say and do things that ordinarily you wouldn't say or do.

"We All Were in the Same Spirit"

One session that I recall very clearly is a session held on the Fourth of July. I was soon to be released from the rehabilitation center and a few people gathered together: me, Tania, Jacob [a friend who was in the same condition as Ben], and you. It was one of the best sessions we had. We sat down and sang some gospel songs; we made up songs, you know. Everyone took a part in putting this song down. And my friend Jacob, he dedicated a particular song to me, spontaneously. He just sang this particular song [that] he made up on the spot, and it was a nice session, a session where we all were loose, everybody was in the same spirit, and we all left feeling good. So I can see that was one of the special times in my life. It wasn't, like, just a song you were singing. It made sense; it sounded real good. It was a song you can listen to. It wasn't . . . like the guy just singing anything just for me which sounds like he just wants to say something [nice]. It sounded really good, the lyrics matched up nicely, and you could tell that it was about someone going away and you were wishing him well.

"How Soon You Forget"

I would sit in the shower and something would come to me. . . . The warm water feels nice on your body; it is soothing, makes you loosen up and feel kind of relaxed, and it's kind of joyous. So I guess when you are happy, you sing. Since the lyrics of this particular song were especially meaningful to me, I decided to keep the song in my head and to work with Tania on it. We would sit down and work on it, and we picked up the melody. She was playing the acoustic guitar, and we finished the work off and we taped it; it was falling tightly, and we kept it as a finished product. I named the song "How Soon You Forget." It related to a relationship that I had with a certain girl. We broke up and I was singing how soon you forget, you know, all the times, the fun that we had . . . we were off from that. It was, like, a real first time I really tried to see if I could put a song together, so I worked hard on it. I tried to make it as professional as possible and I feel I like this one better because I really worked hard on it. It felt nice that it was finally done, and you get a sense of accomplishment because you started, let it go, and finished it the whole way through. It's a nice feeling, now that we have a song.

"We Start with Nothing and Come Up with a Good Song"

I loved to improvise songs. I remember one session where Jacob [and I] worked with Tania. Tania started to play a few notes on the guitar and whatever came to mind came out of it and so it was building and building and building and building. . . . It starts from nothing, then the song that you are singing starts to mean things. . . . Good lyrics are coming out; they are rhyming or they are falling in the proper format. You just pull it out from nowhere, you know; you are just coming out with it. It's the first time and it's just going right down, as speaking is coming out of this tape. And I can feel this kind of joy to know I can do this; you can actually just sit there [and] say something that sounds good, you know. You can sit there and sing a song and say, "Let's try this," and boom! You just come up with something. And the more you sing, the more it sounds good and it sounds better and better and better and better.

KAREN

When I met Karen, she was 48 years old and working as a music therapist in a nursing home. She had experienced music therapy as a client and had been doing GIM work with Beth, her music therapist, for 3 years. Karen said: "After many different experiences with [verbal] therapists, I always walked away feeling that I was a failure because I didn't know how to do it. I didn't know how to do the verbal therapy thing, and I was always so self-conscious and tense and battling my silence, even with some very nice, good therapists." In GIM therapy, Karen experienced deep imagery while listening to classical music in a relaxed state.

Karen's goal in her music therapy with Beth was to have a successful experience and to increase her self-esteem. "I wished to feel okay about myself. A tendency to downgrade myself crept into almost every aspect of my life. . . . My feelings about myself were too often colored by worries, doubts, and apologies about not being good enough."

My experience in GIM work is of rich and varied imagery. The most striking imagery has been beautiful golden light, which has made such a change in my life, in any and every moment, whether I am thinking about it or not, and I am talking about beauty. . . . It's been that way from the beginning; that's my sense. Not that every session has it, but the light endures. It has been an extraordinary experience—aesthetically, humanly, emotionally, in every way. It's just amazing. In some sessions, I had moments in the imagery in which the image that I saw resolved a traumatic experience in my life. Just seeing the image and immediately having an understanding of it . . . which in an instant integrated whatever had been the experience with a new way of viewing it, transformed the negative or the worried part I had carried with me for years. It was gone!

The GIM process consisted of an initial talk at the beginning of the session when I discussed something that had happened that was difficult or sad. Sometimes the discussion revealed an image that Beth used to begin the imagery work. This image was introduced to me. I was, with my eyes closed, lying on a mattress, following a relaxation exercise. Then a specific tape was chosen by Beth and I would travel to the music and share my inner process with Beth, who sat right next to me.

"The Golden Light"

One session, I experienced an inner struggle. There was darkness and confusion in the imagery and in my feelings. I was lying on my back on the bottom of a boat, a rowboat or canoe, and moving slowly along in very peaceful water. . . . There were trees on both sides of the stream, and the trees' branches reached over the water from both sides and formed an arch. And in the middle, directly above me, was the Hebrew word *chai,* [which] means "alive." And when the boat went under the arch, there was light. As I went under this arch, light shown down on me. It was like a gift to me; [*she hesitates*] it was a blessing. This heavenly golden light was shining on me and being given to me, to absorb into my whole self. That moment was of beauty, shining on me and being offered to me and going into me. It was [*she hesitates*]—it was the most powerful but very quiet blessing. That's how it felt. I'm just [*she hesitates*] trying to think of good words for it. It was extraordinary. It was so moving. I never consciously thought about color, light, and beauty as elements I related to. I am almost crying telling you this and it's really extraordinary to me. I feel that connecting with light was a beginning of having light to see by, to work on issues for myself.

"All of a Sudden, the Dread Was Over"

At some point very early in my childhood, I often saw an image of a little kitten whose hind legs are yanked apart. A red shiny ball springs from somewhere between the kitten's legs. I think that this daytime image had to do with fear of rape. Very early in my life, my mother, out of concern and maybe also out of some experiences she had, [warned me to be careful and not to talk to strangers and she] scared me. . . . And this was a recurring image to me for many years, until adulthood. During one session, suddenly I had an image of a sort of stick figure. . . . It was this tall, skinny figure of someone skiing up the hill. And somehow I knew it was me, although it didn't look like me particularly. And it was wearing gray, this figure, but it had a red scarf, floating in the wind [*she hesitates*], and there was a red ball sort of bouncing along in the air next to this figure. . . . What happened was that the waving, carefree scarf sort of reached out and encompassed this red ball. The ball got transformed; it didn't exist anymore. As I saw that image, my experience, in a flash, was: Here is this alive, healthy, active person climbing this hill, and the red ball that represents terror and dread and probably also doubts and worries about my own sexuality, my own body, my own essence—whatever this red ball struck me as—was just transformed into part of this lighthearted healthy person in becoming the scarf. It was the most astonishing thing. That dread was over and it felt fantastic. Since then, I don't have this daytime image anymore. . . . It was like an integrative, instantaneous healing in a way.

"What a Relief!"

When I was 20 years old, I graduated from college and my parents gave me a trip to Europe and Israel as a graduation present. I was in a very bad shape emotionally, very depressed and withdrawn and not very aware of what was going on around me. After the trip, I was very ashamed ever to say that I had been in Europe [*she hesitates*] because it would have been very hard for me to say what I had seen, where I had been. I felt like a total idiot, uncultured, stupid, and, in fact, at the end of a day, it would have been very hard for me to tell where I had been. And so for years, I really hoped that I wouldn't get into a conversation and be asked if I had ever been in Europe. In one of the sessions . . . [I had an image that] I was on a train that was speeding ahead. The train was not like a closed train. I am using the word *train* because it seemed like a train to me, but it was sort of open on the sides, so I was inside and outside at the same time, which was very beautiful. There were dark green trees, a very lush feeling, and somehow I knew I was in France. There was no sign, no French language, and I can't tell you how or why I knew it, but I knew that I was in France. The instant meaning for me, without any thoughts, without any mental activity, was of letting go of the old worry. Somehow, in that moment of the train ride, I didn't feel bad about it anymore. It was just over, that's all. And it was such a relief, such a relief. It didn't mean that I wanted to go with a megaphone and announce that I had been in Europe! But I guess it's all about self-acceptance. That's what had happened. I had been a mess, it was a big waste of a great present, but that's what happened. So it was a release from the self-hatred, from the self- recrimination and shame.

LYN

Lyn was 50 years old when I met her. She was a private client in individual music therapy with Adam for 4 months. At the time of the interview Lyn had been divorced for many years and was about to get married again. She worked as a secretary doing administrative work. What brought Lyn to music therapy was a combination of physical sickness, emotional discomfort, and a need to deal with her own creativity. She explained that she was not feeling well last spring. She had bronchitis and respiratory complications that caused her to wake up a lot in the middle of the night, coughing. Once awake, Lyn would sit and draw and write things that were coming to her: "It's almost as though as I was coughing, I was coughing out some very old stored memories." At the same time she said that she was feeling a tremendous urge to get in touch with her creative self. "I knew that I had certain creative potential, but I never really took it seriously, so after dealing with all the traditional medical community and the alternative-health community and diet, I decided to give it a try." Lynn experienced improvising at the piano (she was not a musician), vocalizing, and creating imagery accompanied by Adam's piano.

Well, music therapy is really the concept of having the freedom to explore and play. . . . It's strange, even though I have had a number of wonderful experiences, it seems like every time I go in there, I have no idea of what's going to happen. It's not as though I have something I am working on or thinking of [*she hesitates*], so it's very strange to me. Now I have realized that something will happen when I get there even if I don't know what it might be, and it's usually the most spontaneous amazing things that come out.

"I Have Become Me"

In this particular session, Adam [and I] were standing in front of each other next to the piano. We were breathing and vocalizing, making one sound at a time. Adam would sing a note and I would sing with him. I felt confused. I did not know how to follow him, and he said that I should just look at him and follow him. As he sang a note, I sang it. . . . He kept taking me down lower and lower and lower and lower. He felt that I am always up here—in my head, my forehead, my nose, all this area—and he wanted to bring me to a sense of myself in a much lower, deeper place. . . . I thought that I could not go any lower, but Adam encouraged me to try, and I was surprised. I could feel it; I could feel it in an emotional way. When I got all the way down, I said I couldn't imagine that was a space that could be me down there. It's [amazing] hearing that sound of me in the world, the me that I have become. I have become me, this is me, and this is the sound of me.

"Playing the Piano Felt Like Being a Playful Child"

Since I was a child, I have not played the piano. As a child, I took piano lessons, and every time I made a mistake, my teacher was upset with me. He would tell me, "No, it's wrong; you have got to do it this way; you've got to practice." It was so much of a turn-off. In one of my sessions, I told Adam that I wanted to play the piano, but I did not want to be told if I was doing right or wrong. I just wanted to play it and I didn't really want to take piano lessons. I just wanted to have a sense or feel of the piano. We both were sitting next to the piano. I was sitting next to the upper notes and Adam was sitting next to the lower register of the piano. He gave me a couple of notes to play and he accompanied me with those notes. [He told me] just to play them any way I wanted, these two notes, which I did. And then [he told me to play] a couple of extra more notes, and then just to go back and forth on those notes or to play a couple of chords and so on, and, somehow, whatever rhythm I created, he filled in with. So he kind of worked around me and created a melody, and I had the rhythm and the two notes [*hesitates*] and this beautiful thing came out and it was wonderful. It was just wonderful, because the biggest thing for me was to be allowed to just play the piano without being told if I was right or wrong. And I thought to myself that it would be a lot of fun to have a piano or to have a keyboard. . . . I mean at some point, I might want to play the piano again and take lessons or to just explore it.

"It Was a Very Spiritual Experience for Me"

One time I came and discovered a number of new instruments; there were a gong and new drums. In the beginning of this session, I discussed my fears of getting married and my own personal needs and wants. Toward the end of the discussion, Adam went to the piano and asked me to talk about my present needs and I just got into a fantasy. My fantasy was like going to the depth of the ocean and to the heights of the sky. It had to do with dolphins and swimming and flying. It was like seeing a movie [*she hesitates*], and as I talked, he was accompanying my fantasy on the piano. For example, I was on the edge of a stream, so he was playing music which was streamlike. The fantasy was tying up some ancient things that I don't even understand so much; [they were,] you know, soul connections, connections to people in worlds that are beyond. . . . I don't even remember what I said. . . . I cried; I let go of certain emotions. At the end of the fantasy, Adam asked me what else would I like to do. I wanted to play the gong. What happened was I didn't end up playing the gong; we didn't have too much time and what he did was he played the gong for me. . . . That was one of the most incredible times that I spent there. I felt like parts of me that I wasn't even in touch with [started] resonating again. Toward the end of the session, Adam played the tuning forks for me. It came toward the end and it kind of just quieted me down. He kind of tuned me up; I felt whole. I was very much at peace with myself, and just like the whole fantasy started by the water, I almost felt like I was the water. It was just like I was still. This is what I was yearning for, to come to a still, quiet place. It was a very peaceful feeling. Because I am planning a wedding [and] I am working full time and I have no place to run to, I can't get away from it [*she laughs*], so the only place that I can really go to is to a fantasy or a dream kind of thing. . . . I realized that this experience permitted me to approach some deep issues with my fiancé. I feared getting married again and starting a new life. I was divorced once. All this creativity and what I want to do [and] how I view life and the intuitive way that I experience things [are different]—my fiancé is not like this. I mean, we get along well, but he is much more matter-of-fact, although he appreciates it if I tell him some of these things. Part of the whole thing was that I needed to be alone, but, see, this part is hard for somebody to understand. It's only alone in my mind, but when somebody is trying to get closer to you and you are scared of being swallowed up, that's the emotional component. So I worked out a lot of that, too, because I did share some of that with him, and he really enjoyed it. He enjoyed hearing about it; he could understand what I told him. I [had] thought he would never understand!

Narrative 32

FEELINGS OF DOUBT, HOPE, AND FAITH

Henk Smeijsters

INTRODUCTION

I am a qualitative researcher reporting on Ingrid's experience of music therapy. In her sessions, Ingrid's music therapist, José van den Hurk, suggested music improvisations on the piano, splitdrums, fiddle, and congas and with voice to help Ingrid express feelings and strengthen her personal identity and self-esteem. Ingrid had felt depressed since her husband died 3 years earlier. Sometimes she said to herself: "Who am I? I'm in the habit of acting as though on a stage. I have lost myself." Ingrid was referred to music therapy after 21 sessions of verbal psychotherapy; while in music therapy, she continued psychotherapy on a less frequent basis.

After each session, Ingrid and José independently wrote self-reports for this research project, and I made a detailed report from the videotape of the sessions, transcribing Ingrid's words verbatim. Ingrid's self-reports were also typed out in transcripts on which I commented in memos. The transcripts and memos were checked by Ingrid and José. I analyzed the transcripts, using qualitative research techniques: I developed diagnostic themes, gave feedback on the treatment process, and made suggestions for goals and techniques. During this process, there was repeated feedback between José and me. On several occasions, there were talks between Ingrid, José, and Ingrid's psychotherapist.

I present Ingrid's statements during the music therapy sessions (3 through 22), her talks with José and the psychotherapist, and her written self-reports, all of which describe the therapy experience from her perspective. I follow Ingrid's words with my own analysis from a phenomenological point of view (Smeijsters, 1997); this is called a protocol analysis (Colaizzi, 1978; Giorgi, 1985). Phenomenology tries to "understand what meaning . . . the music therapy intervention has for those who experience it" (Forinash, 1995, p. 372).

INGRID'S STATEMENTS

Session 3

SELF-REPORT. My first thought was, "How will it be?" How is it possible to use music instruments without being able to read a single note? I was very surprised that I felt pleasure in just making sounds. I liked searching for some sort of a melody. José made me even more enthusiastic. How will it be the second time? Now everything is new and surprising. I will wait and see what the next session will bring. I have faith.

Session 4

DURING THE SESSION. How can music therapy help me? It feels as if I'm acting as though I am a handicapped person. . . . When José intensified the music, I said to myself, "Don't go any further." I won't let myself hurry up. But sometimes it feels as if I have more energy.

SELF-REPORT. Contrary to the previous session, there was a need to make music of my own. When José started playing loud, I thought, "You can do it." But I kept to my own tempo and loudness. I did not want to attune to José's playing. My experience was very different from the previous session. I wanted to explore sounds myself.

Session 5

DURING THE SESSION. I feel fine. I like to do gardening at home. Why should I come to music therapy? Why am I digging in the past? . . . What I am doing completely lacks melody. In the beginning, I thought that this was stupid. If I could not succeed immediately, I stopped it. But when you [José] asked me to give it another try, it worked out. . . . I don't want to be soft. . . . It is impossible to say how I feel. Something is missing. . . . Is there a need to come next time?

SELF-REPORT. Searching for notes that make a whole—make a harmony—with notes played by José on the piano gives me a pretty feeling. Whenever I cannot find the right tones, there is disharmony. When we are playing against each other, I don't like it. . . . When José told me afterward that she had felt contact, I could not understand what she was saying. I cannot feel it that way. The statement made me nervous, and I felt as if I was going to hyperventilate. I guarded against it by not giving way to it. I think I become frightened when people come too close. Sometimes I get angry because I want to decide myself when there should be closeness. Why am I afraid of closeness?

TALK WITH JOSÉ AND PSYCHOTHERAPIST. I did not feel any contact with you [José] and thought, "What are you talking about?" Do I want this with a stranger? Do I have to become even more sensitive? I am afraid when you talk like this. . . . Does music therapy have any effect on my daily life?

Session 6

SELF-REPORT. I hesitated to write this self-report. Why? Because I found it so difficult. Everything is so close again, but I shall try to write down what I felt when I was looking at the videotape from the improvisation. . . . I was watching with a lot of concentration and with a critical attitude. I don't know what I felt while watching. But I know what I felt afterward. I was moved and sad at the same time: sad because I am a sad person but also because I cannot accept myself. I look very rational, but this attitude gives me a bad feeling. Often I think that I am doing and saying things all wrong. Deep inside, I feel very insecure. I would like to change, but how?

Session 7

DURING THE SESSION. What I am doing is stumbling. . . . The moments when we played together were nice. . . . If you [José] play loudly, I do not understand it at all. . . . I wonder whether making contact is the same as playing together. When I say I felt contact, I become anxious. Crossing hands with you on the piano is weird.

SELF-REPORT. When you [José] were rubbing the congas, this was irritating, as if somebody were petting over my body. But when I kept on playing on the piano and surrendered to the sounds of the piano, it became less frightening. Later on, for the first time I felt sorrow about the death of my mother [a long time ago]. When I remembered my childhood, I felt the lack of cuddling by her. She gave me a lot of care, but at a distance. There was a lack of warmth. My parents never gave me compliments and this took away my enthusiasm. I believe, therefore, that my self-image did not develop. I hope that in music therapy and psychotherapy, it will be possible to develop my self-image. I want to become cheerful and relaxed.

Session 8

DURING THE SESSION. I ask myself why I write the way I do. Why is it so restless? Why can't it be quiet? Always, I am hewing things down. It resembles my behavior in music. Playing the piano is like my life. . . . In music now, I try to let it merge, but saying to myself that I am playing on the piano is so strange. Is it really playing the piano?

SELF-REPORT. I have no self-report because it is always the same. Why am I so negative? Is this the process?

Session 9

SELF-REPORT. During piano-playing, a lot of memories came up. But they are just memories. I don't feel any pain. Negative experiences belong to life, and one should try to guard against these experiences in the future. I want to work on the future; I want to strengthen my ego, accept myself.

Session 10

DURING THE SESSION. Using my voice costs me a lot of effort. It is oppressive; my voice is so locked. It only comes out stumbling. . . . I am afraid. There is a lot of energy that is not coming out. . . . Humming is spasmodic; it is not spontaneous. But I have to try because I want to break down my façade. If I put away my frustrations, I will never find rest.

SELF-REPORT. When I am playing with José on the piano, I am searching for balance and for a melody. I want to make a consonance, a fluent whole. When I succeed, it gives me a nice feeling, although it still is melancholic. I feel sorrow. In the beginning of music therapy, this feeling had to do with me; now it is linked to others. Today, I know that I need to release myself from something, but I don't know what it is. I also feel anxious and insecure when I manifest myself in sounds. I need to have less pride. Reluctantly, I started walking on thin ice. In past years, I built an immense façade, looking tough and communicating "Don't come close; I can do it all by myself." As a result, I cannot handle important feelings. In the last few weeks, I have learned to have more insight into these things. Some time ago, I didn't know what others were talking about. I had only one thought: "I don't want to be soft." Now, this is totally different. Cognition and feeling are in contact; they are balanced now. Because of too much pride and fear of making errors, I was very tense. Now I want to listen to my feelings. It is a very slow process. There still are many blocks—for instance, in my voice. Nevertheless, I want to do my best. I must show and accept myself.

Session 11

DURING THE SESSION. Putting feelings into words, saying things without defense, is difficult. I become angry. . . . I have to stop suppressing my feelings. . . . Whenever there is some melody, I enjoy it. . . . I am growing up. . . . I liked the improvisation, but it is very difficult. . . . I need to accept myself. There is nothing that gives me the feeling that this is what I am good at. I really want to be able to do something very well, not just play like in kindergarten. Immediately, there is the feeling that what I am doing is of no value. . . . I am searching for the reasons.

SELF-REPORT. There is no self-report because I am always writing the same things. This is boring. Things are moving too slowly.

Session 12

DURING THE SESSION. I am still in a melancholic mood. I feel sorrow and resignation that I can hear in my voice. I am unable to write things down on paper. I can make a sound, but this is not feeling.

SELF-REPORT. While singing, I felt a block, which made me feel peevish and angry. The feeling of anger disturbs me and increases tension. I think it is because of the death of my husband. Maybe it will last for years. I cannot accept this, but I cannot change it either. Pain and anger are present very often, especially during music therapy. I feel pressure; I feel a heavy burden and a sorrow about a lot of things. I don't want it that way. It makes me angry, as if I need to account for everything.

Session 13

DURING THE SESSION. I can't think of an instrument [I want] and I don't want to bang on an instrument to express my anger. Nobody can force me to do it. Banging, being temperamental, does not help at all. . . . My helplessness can be expressed on the violin. . . . I have the feeling that music therapy cannot bring me any further.

SELF-REPORT. Since the last music therapy session, I have felt very depressed, tired, and lonely. José asked me to make an evaluation report, but I am inclined to postpone it. Writing down feelings on paper feels like stepping over a high threshold. I have the same feeling during music therapy. Inside me, something blocks my feelings. . . . But I will try to continue writing because it is necessary to make progress in music therapy. I am on a good track. In psychotherapy and music therapy, processes have begun. Especially in music therapy, my feelings are evoked, and then I can feel a block. Because I have been very aware of this block during the last days, I am depressed. . . . At the start of music therapy, I said to José that I want to work on the future. My childhood and education were very normal. There were no traumatic experiences; however, now I know that there is a period in my life that I think about frequently. When I remember this period, I become very angry and feel helpless again. One of my sisters was favored above others. She was a troublesome girl, disobedient. One time she attacked my throat. Previously, I could not shake off these memories. Sometimes an immense fury came over me. I always had to be the wise girl who did not hit back. Thus I learned to keep silent, to suppress my feelings. I felt misunderstood but was too helpless to fight for my own rights. . . . I think because of this period in my life, I have been blocked and have lost my spontaneity and self-confidence.

TALK WITH JOSÉ AND PSYCHOTHERAPIST. I feel anger. What am I doing? What is the reason I am doing this? There are positive aspects, too. I am putting my life upside down, quarreling with my family. What is the profit of this? I was depressed last week. I feel there is a block. . . . I also feel a lot of anger against my sister, who was hysterical [and] stupid but smart enough to get what she wanted. I think about those moments, but I don't know if it makes any sense to bring up these memories. What should I do? My brother is the same story. If he hurts me, I will hit him. He is a son of a bitch, always telling me that I am worthless. . . . What is the value in all this? I am not the one I used to be. I feel depressed and chaotic and am unable to sleep at night. When I sleep, I dream a lot of new things. . . . I am no expert. I don't know where the limits are. I don't want to quarrel. At the same time, I tell my brother, "If you talk like this to me, you no longer can count on me.". . . I want music therapy to help me to be less depressed. But please, don't come too close. I don't want to evoke problems that are not real.

Session 14

DURING THE SESSION. Not everything is negative. During music therapy, negative things surface. I am frustrated that I am doing nothing with the negative things. I get sad about my anxiousness, my hesitation to speak of things. [*While looking at the videotape of the previous session, she says to herself*], Come on, sing with more certainty; let's hear yourself. [*After she starts singing while watching, she says,*] Do it like this. What are you doing? It can be much better, more energetic.

SELF-REPORT. Looking at the videotape is fascinating and makes me feel good. I am not humiliating myself but telling myself to go on. Although on the videotape there was much hesitation and I was thinking how laborious it was, I had no negative feeling. I said to myself, "Carry on." I felt very lonely, but I want to continue, to become less tense. Will I ever succeed?

Session 15

DURING THE SESSION. Things are going fine, but writing them down is very difficult because then everything looks so negative.

SELF-REPORT. It was my task to write down how I feel when I have to make decisions. From this I learned that when someone asks me to do something I don't want, I am unable to say no. Afterward, I have a bad feeling because I didn't react at the right moment. . . . This week has been very quiet. I stayed at home the whole week and tried to become conscious of my feelings, not knowing yet how to handle them. I have decided to go on with it.

Session 16

DURING THE SESSION. I reacted very impulsively last week when somebody told me rubbish about other people. I became very emotional and felt it deep inside me. I don't want it that way. . . . I realized when I looked at the video that for the first time, I have been not humiliating myself. Now as I remember, I feel that I am not completely free because there is pressure in my chest. . . . When I use my voice, I come very close [to expressing something]. I have to jump over a rock, but I don't want to run away. There is almost no variation when I am singing. You [José] have much more variation. If you are not playing the piano, my voice completely breaks down. When you were playing the conga, I said to myself, "Now throw it out." There is not yet joy, but there is no more depression. It is not easy.

SELF-REPORT. During the improvisation, I was not satisfied; I could not get started and again felt the block. While driving home in my car, I said to myself that I should try to sing now. Then it came out much more spontaneously. . . . During the session, I felt the same loneliness I felt when looking at the videotape. How lonely I am. When I left church on Sunday and when I saw families around me, I had the same feeling. How sad it is. I need over and over again an affirmation to help me to build self-confidence. I need to tolerate being lonely. . . . I try to get over my blocks or to accept them. I also want to discover new ways of living outside music therapy, by taking courses; however, I think my goals are too high. I always want to reach goals quickly. I need to be more quiet; then I will succeed.

Session 17

DURING THE SESSION. It doesn't work. In my car, I can sing along much better. In the car, I am much more relaxed. During the music therapy session, there are too many thoughts. Being lonely feels so bad; I get angry about it. It is possible to learn, isn't it? I am so lonely; everybody else has companionship. Inside me, there is a lot of pain.

I had to blow my nose, but I didn't want to stop playing. I wanted to sing through my grief. Being together is beautiful. If you sing along with me, my grief fades away. When it sounds beautiful, the grief disappears. I feel less lonely, but grief has not disappeared completely. . . . Things are going much better.

SELF-REPORT. During the improvisation, I felt a lot of grief about my deceased husband. After some time, the grief faded away. Then there was rest. I consciously tried to use my voice. I felt that I wanted to go through this. Sometimes I tried to sing loudly. I didn't like the pain I felt. In the beginning of the improvisation, it was so deep. It was a very fine experience when, later on during improvising, the peaceful feeling came. I hope this will stay and grow in the future. I show my vulnerability, which still is not easy. With little steps forward, I will succeed.

Session 18

DURING THE SESSION. I want to sing through something. What is this? Is it aggression, pain? It happens every time when I am in music therapy. I just want to sing a simple melody without feeling anything, and then strong feelings come up. . . . I will try to use my voice as I do in the car. Why is this so difficult in music therapy? In music therapy, there is no singing—just screaming for my husband. It hurts. Why does this grief not come to an end? . . . The grief blocks my spontaneity. Music therapy evokes very strong feelings.

SELF-REPORT. I feel there is stagnation; I want to sing, but my voice is blocked. Is there something else we can do? The transcripts of the sessions were fascinating and astonishing. I would like to talk over some of the points with the psychotherapist to reach more insight.

Session 19

DURING THE SESSION. In the transcript, it seems as though the aspects of my life have been well organized. I am unable to write it down this way myself. It looks nice, but in real life things are mixed.

Several things I do not understand yet. Is it possible to live without a pressure to achieve? What I wrote about myself is difficult to read. Feelings come up. . . . Today I don't want to sing. Using my voice is linked to being free, but there still is no freedom.

SELF-REPORT. There is a conflict in me. I feel lonely; I want to meet people and at the same time I don't. I know that I can be a complete human being only together with others, but it is so difficult to be open. I want intimacy, but at the same time, I revolt against it. . . . Often, I think that I don't have any creativity, that I hold on too much to the well known. But I also long for something new. . . . I have a mass of feelings. Again and again, I search for self-acceptance and identity. In the last weeks, I have been close to hyperventilation; my chest became tight. There also are a lot of good things.

Session 20

DURING THE SESSION. In church, I have been singing with a trembling voice, fighting my grief. I felt as if I had to surrender [to the grief]. I was anxious. It [the improvisation] went right through my soul. My chest became tight; I don't know what it is. Am I straining myself too much? . . . There is a wish to make contact but with a clear limit. When you [José] played on my instrument, I felt this to be intrusive. Being very close is not pleasant; I don't want to surrender. When the music gets loud, I don't like it, but I also say to myself, "Let it happen; stand up for yourself." I don't know exactly how I feel. Is there an unconscious anxiety? Is it because of my fear of being rejected?

SELF-REPORT. During the session, there were a lot of mixed feelings. But most of the feelings were fine. I liked it when contact came up spontaneously, when it did not intrude on me, and when we were carefully touching each other in music and creating something beautiful. When someone else comes too close, I feel resistance. Loud music is not pleasant either. It makes me insecure; then I lock myself up. . . . I have decided to cancel my holiday trip; this decision felt good. But I am still insecure and hope that I will feel better. I feel lonely and I don't like it. I don't know how to continue.

Session 21

DURING THE SESSION. Playing loudly is aggressive. I don't like it. I don't experience the intimacy you [José] feel while we are playing. But I like it. I have a long way to go.

SELF-REPORT. Writing down my feelings in the self-report takes a lot of effort. Is it because I don't want to show my weak sides? . . . Our contact in music was very nice, but for me, this is not intimacy. Body contact—when José touched my hand during playing—I don't like. Playing together is wonderful. I felt very fine when I drove home. There was rest, balance, complete harmony, no tension, no nervousness, no questions, and no negative feelings. Last week, I tried to stay connected with this feeling. It is so important to make contact with my own feelings. Each time when I become insecure, I say to myself, "Stay close to your feelings. Don't try to be someone else and don't press yourself. Attune to your feelings." When I attune to my feelings, I learn to accept myself. My negative self-image is changing. Now I can meet difficulties without losing self-confidence. It still is difficult to be assertive at the right moment. Processes have begun that take time. Not everything can change at once. Last week, this came to my mind: "Life is like an expansive garden in which you are walking, sowing, planting, and trimming, where plants are flowering and dying. But all the time, one takes a walk, during rain and sunshine. Again and again. Life is good to live! It is good to learn how to live!"

Session 22

DURING THE SESSION. I want to love somebody, but there is no feeling of love for anybody. I am very clumsy, challenging someone else and then withdrawing. What do I want? . . . Today I can't sing, I am blocked. [*Nevertheless, after some time, she spontaneously starts singing.*] I said to myself, "Come on." Today it came out very well.

SELF-REPORT. I look back at the session with much pleasure. The music-playing was beautiful; I was involved in it and there was no anxiety about coming too close. The alternation between loud and soft was beautiful. It was fragile, and I felt completely there as a personal self. I experienced life going up and down with highlights and setbacks. In the music-playing, I experienced being moved as in life but without the big discrepancies between hills and valleys. In the subtle passages, I found a part of my inner self that is deep feeling, tenderness, and love. . . . I also felt vulnerability and a lack of self-confidence. . . . In my contacts, I try to transform the indifferent woman into a feeling human being. I try to listen; I try to be patient. I feel engaged and feel love for someone else—not like love between man and woman; however, not everybody notices that I am changing. Last week, someone said to me that I am dictatorial, that there is no love inside me. When I heard his words, I cried. It hurt me deeply; there was real pain. Then I realized that my self-confidence is still weak. I doubt myself. I am getting tired of this, but I want to continue and I will try it over and over again.

SELF-REPORT PREPARED FOR TALK WITH JOSÉ AND PSYCHO-THERAPIST. My self-confidence, self-worth, and assertiveness still are weak. I have to work hard on it. I say to myself, "Continue; make transformations from negative to positive feelings." Is it because I cannot yet find an activity that I can master, like when I am playing subtly on the piano? I will try gardening and drawing. . . . There is progress, too. At the time, I feel much more relaxed and less depressed. I stay close to my feelings, as if I have to pull down first before I can build up again. In summary, I can say that several changes have been initiated and that I need to continue. Perhaps the time has come to stop therapy now and continue on my own.

FINAL TALK WITH JOSÉ AND PSYCHOTHERAPIST. I am still weak; I get frustrated when somebody says I am dictatorial. Yes, I am firm, but I am helpful, too. I think when I am firm, I say things in a way that people don't like. . . . I have changed. I feel relaxed, less nervous, and less depressed. I stay close to my feelings, but I am not yet satisfied. I am in the stage of pulling down and building up, like in gardening.

Now I don't say anymore, "You are playing like a child"; I say, "Continue." In music, things have changed already. In daily life, change is not yet spontaneous; each time, I need to think about how to behave. . . . There should be fewer hills and valleys in my life and more self-confidence, self-acceptance, and positive assertiveness. When I am stable, then I will be creative. I will continue with gardening, without the pressure of high standards. I will put my feelings in colored drawings. When I draw, I say to myself, "I am who I am; I will use the blue color because I want it.". . . On the one hand, I want to continue music therapy; on the other hand, I want to stand on my own feet. I will search for something I can do on my own, into which I can put my feelings and find self-confidence and pleasure.

HENK'S THEMATIC ANALYSIS OF INGRID'S STATEMENTS

Theme 1: "Why Am I Doing This?"

Ingrid was suspicious in the beginning about music therapy and about her playing on musical instruments. She asked herself how this could help her because she had no formal music training. Throughout the course of therapy, she doubted the value of expressing negative feelings. She kept asking why negative feelings had to be expressed. When the music therapist asked her to express her feelings on instruments, she said she could not find the right instruments and she was resistant to banging on an instrument to express her anger. In her opinion, banging on instruments did not help at all. She had doubts about digging into the past. She had the impression that she was turning her life upside down. Remembering past experiences made her upset and depressed. She felt chaotic and was unable to sleep at night. At those kinds of moments, she would say that music therapy could not help her any further.

Ingrid wanted to become less depressed and decided she did not want to evoke problems that she thought were not real. She had the impression that especially in music therapy, negative experiences became manifest.

When improvising with her voice, Ingrid felt blocked, whereas she said that in her car, she could sing spontaneously. Each time she wanted to sing a simple melody, strong feelings were evoked. Many times, she asked herself why singing in music therapy was so difficult. Singing was like screaming for her husband. At times when she recognized that this grief had not come to an end, she felt stagnated and resigned. It was burdensome to her that her personal process was a very slow one.

When, at the end of therapy, Ingrid started to make decisions and change her relational behavior outside music therapy, not all her relatives noticed the changes in her. Because of this, she again felt her insecurity, vulnerability, and lack of self-confidence. This made her cry and filled her with doubts about herself. It made her tired.

Theme 2:
"Will I Ever Be Creative?"

When playing with the music therapist in the beginning, Ingrid forced herself to find the right notes. Not finding the right melody upset her. At those times, she felt stupid and handicapped and stopped the improvisation. She felt she wanted to do something well. In music therapy, she felt as if she were playing in kindergarten.

She complained that there was no variation in her singing and that her singing completely broke down when the music therapist stopped playing the piano. When Ingrid started to experiment with free melodic lines, she doubted whether she could ever be creative. In her opinion, she stayed too much with the expected. She expressed a strong wish to change this situation. She longed for something new, and whenever she found a new melody, she enjoyed it.

At the end of music therapy, Ingrid no longer felt as if she were playing in kindergarten. She now communicated a personal wish to be more self-confident, self-accepting, and assertive in activities without feeling she had to fulfill high standards. She decided to put feeling into activities, to give way to her wishes, and to be who she is.

Theme 3:
"I Want to Make Contact My Way"

When Ingrid was playing with the music therapist, she was searching for balance and consonance. When she succeeded in doing this, it gave her a nice feeling. Although Ingrid liked playing ensemble, she was unwilling to imitate or synchronize with the music therapist's increase of tempo and dynamics. For Ingrid, this felt like an act of aggression that made her insecure and made her close up; however, there were moments when she reacted to this by saying to herself, "Let it happen; stand up for yourself."

Several times, Ingrid said she could not understand the music therapist's playing. She did not feel any contact in the music and was afraid of the music therapist's talk about contact. When the music therapist rubbed the congas, she said that it was as if somebody were petting her body. When the music therapist played on Ingrid's [part of the] instrument and accidentally touched her hand, it felt intrusive.

Ingrid told how in the past she had built a façade that communicated to everybody not to come too close. There was a wish to make contact but with clear limits. When someone else passed her limits, it felt as if she would surrender. Because she didn't want to surrender, she expressed resistance.

In the final sessions, Ingrid liked it when contact came up spontaneously, when it did not intrude on her. When she and the music therapist were carefully touching each other in the music, they were creating something beautiful. Although she didn't experience intimacy as the music therapist did, she said it had been wonderful. When driving home (after session 21), she experienced rest, balance, complete harmony, no tension, no nervousness, a lack of questions, and no negative feelings.

Theme 4:
"I Need to Cry It Out from My Soul"

Ingrid was frightened to express feelings. When feelings came up, it was difficult for her to say how she felt. She told the music therapist that she looked very rational on the outside, but that deep in her heart she was very insecure. Her anxiety and her hesitation to tell things made her feel sad. On the other hand, she wished to release a lot of energy. At some moments, this wish manifested itself in impulsive reactions, which upset her. She expressed a wish to change but did not know how.

She experienced her voice as being blocked and was afraid to express herself in sound. For her, this felt as if she were walking on thin ice. When she became aware of the vocal block, she became depressed. She realized that she never had been able to understand and to handle feelings.

Although at the start of music therapy Ingrid had told the music therapist that she had had no traumatic experiences as a child, during music therapy she admitted that she had. Pain and anger about her life were present very often during music therapy. When remembering her childhood, she felt a lack of warmth and caring by her mother. Because one of her sisters had been very difficult, Ingrid had been forced to control herself and to suppress her own feelings all the time. Now she felt furious about this. She expressed anger because of what her sister and brother had done to her. She concluded that because of these past experiences, there had been no development of her self-image and self-confidence and that she had lost her spontaneity. This, in her opinion, now became obvious in music therapy. She said she did not feel completely free in music therapy. She used her singing to counteract her grief but at the same time felt anxious. She told the music therapist that the vocal improvisations went right through her soul and made her chest feel tight. Ingrid's negative feelings forced her again and again to search for self-acceptance and identity. She also was aware that there were many fine feelings.

Theme 5:
"The Music—That Is Me"

Ingrid talked about her restless writing and way of relating. She compared these behaviors to her music-playing. These she thought were identical. Playing the piano, she said, was like her life. Using her voice was like an expression of freedom. On the other hand, she had doubts whether playing together on musical instruments is the same as making contact. Inside and outside music therapy, Ingrid experienced an inner conflict about social contacts and the wish to meet people.

In the final session, she experienced the music improvisation as fragile. In it, she said, she found a part of her feeling self. She described how during improvisation she experienced life going up and down, with highlights and setbacks. In the improvisation, she experienced being moved as in life but without the great discrepancies between hills and valleys. She said that while in music therapy she had changed already, in daily life her changes had not yet occurred spontaneously.

Theme 6:
"Just Look at Me"

Looking at the videotapes of several sessions was fascinating to Ingrid and gave her a good feeling. She was aware, when she saw herself on video, that she was not humiliating herself by telling herself to go on.

Although writing her feelings down in the self-report cost her a lot of effort, Ingrid told the music therapist that the transcripts of her self-reports, the music therapist's self-reports, and the researcher's observations were fascinating and astonishing. She expressed a wish to talk them over to reach more insight.

Theme 7:
"I Hope I Can Change;
I Want to Change"

Ingrid expressed the hope that by means of music therapy and psychotherapy, it would be possible to develop her self-image, to become less insecure, more cheerful and relaxed. When grief for her deceased husband had turned into a peaceful feeling, it was a very fine experience for her. She expressed hope that this feeling would stay and grow in the future.

In the first music therapy sessions, Ingrid was surprised that it was possible to make music, and this experience stimulated her to explore her musical possibilities further. The experience gave her faith. In the final session, she was pleased that when playing she did not have anxiety about coming too close.

Ingrid felt as if she was growing up and learning. Her negative self-image was changing and her self-confidence was increasing. Although she knew that her self-confidence, self-worth, and assertiveness still were weak and that she had to work hard on them, she knew there had been progress already. She said that she had become more relaxed, less nervous, less depressed, and was closer to her feelings. She felt that she was on a good track and that she had begun to make progress. She became confident that she would succeed little by little.

During the course of music therapy, Ingrid became convinced that she needed to release herself from something and she expressed a firm wish to express her energy because she thought this would be the right way to break down her resistance. She expressed a wish to listen to her feelings, to lower her pride, to show herself vulnerable, to take the risk of making errors, to strengthen her ego, and to accept herself.

By singing, she tried to get over her blocks and to express what was inside her, to sing through her grief. Several times, she overcame her resistance to singing. She showed her strong will when she continued improvising. Although sometimes as a result of her experiences in music therapy she felt depressed, tired, lonely, blocked, and unable to write her self-report, she continued writing because she wanted to make progress. After looking at the videotapes, she expressed a strong wish to continue.

Outside music therapy, she tried to stay connected with feelings of harmony and rest. Sometimes she stayed at home the whole week to become conscious of her feelings. When she became insecure outside music therapy, she trained herself to stay close to her feelings, not to try to be someone else.

Ingrid used several metaphors that expressed her will to change: a rock she had to jump over, a garden that time and time again needed care, and a building that had to be pulled down first before it could be built up again. She knew that the process takes time, and that not everything can change at once, but she was willing to keep trying. At the end of music therapy, she expressed a wish to stand on her own feet.

EPILOGUE

José and I were deeply moved by Ingrid's will to change. We observed a very brave woman who, knowing that the road to health was a rough one, nevertheless decided to take the path. It was moving to observe how she gradually let go of her perfectionistic goals, how she became more open to her feelings, and how she allowed herself to experience her inner self in the music.

PIVOTAL MOMENTS IN GUIDED IMAGERY AND MUSIC

Denise Erdonmez Grocke

INTRODUCTION

I prefer the term *pivotal* to describe moments of insight or under-standing in therapy. These moments are turning points in which a client understands an issue or problem from another perspective. Clients in Guided Imagery and Music (GIM) therapy experience these moments in different ways. GIM involves listening to prere-corded classical music in a deeply relaxed state so that a sequence of images that symbolically represent aspects of the client's life experi-ence is evoked; the therapist keeps verbal contact as the client nar-rates the ongoing imagery.

In my study of pivotal moments in GIM, seven people who have been involved for differing lengths of time in GIM therapy have been interviewed. I interviewed four people who were clients of another GIM therapist, and a research assistant interviewed three clients of mine. An open-ended interview procedure was used so that the flow of the interview followed the person's experience. The primary ques-tion was: "When you look back over your GIM sessions, does one stand out for you as being pivotal?" At some point during the inter-view, the people were asked if they recalled the music during the piv-otal moment, if they recalled the therapist's interventions during the pivotal moment, and whether the pivotal moment had had any impact on their life.

The participants volunteered for this study by responding to a letter explaining the research. Each participant gave informed con-sent for the interview to be tape-recorded, and in accordance with phenomenological research procedures, they have been involved in validating the analysis, or "distilling" the interview material. The participants tell their own stories; their words are direct quotations from the interviews. In the last section, I analyse and distill from the content of the interviews "meaning units" or categories of experience and report these to clarify what is experienced as pivotal moments in GIM.

PIVOTAL MOMENTS IN
GUIDED IMAGERY AND MUSIC*

Sarah

Sarah identified a session that had occurred 3 years earlier.

> [There was] a lovely experience of a wise old man in a cave, of me sitting there holding his hand and being affirmed. The old man said, "What you're doing is good work; do it with confidence."
> [The second pivotal image was] being in the lion's den. The lion smoothed out the floor where I could lie down. He respected me and treasured me and prepared a place for me. He had a piano there and I played the piano. I played well, with confidence, and felt affirmed. I made friends with the lion, combing his mane, stroking his face, and resting with him.

As Sarah described these images, she developed further insight into their meaning.

> The cave and the den are feminine images and inside them both is the masculine—the wise old man and the lion. It feels like coming to know the masculine; I knew I was safe with both. I felt I belonged, like a home place where I can be myself.

Sarah didn't remember very much of the music of the session, just the first chords and the sense of marching and the heavy rhythm of the music. She was aware that the music "really moved me along."

> The lion is the symbol of strength and courage. Meeting him 3 years ago has helped me in developing more masculine qualities in my own life. And in the last 12 months, I have found a wise old man to continue my therapy work.
> [The session was prophetic for me because] the wise old man has appeared in my life.

---

* In this section, Denise's comments are indented to distinguish them from those of clients.

Bernadette

[My pivotal session was] the one where I found my voice. The music started. I was sitting at the piano in an orange dress. I have always hated orange. It was a strong dress. The orchestra and I were working together. They were giving me a sense of identity. I was able to play what I wanted to play, and this was a powerful experience.

I had a wonderful feeling in my body, a tingling in my hands. I felt the stiffness in my body going—my body was starting to loosen up. My mouth was very, very dry. I felt like running. I wanted to be free. It was a feeling of wanting to grow up. There was a feeling of strength in my body, of wanting to be in control, and I felt this [was] the moment to do it.

There was something choking me in my throat, like something had to get out. The therapist said, "Can your throat make a sound?" It was a feeble sound to begin with, but the strength came into my voice. I remember just letting it come. It was a feeling of knowing "I do have a voice." It was a freedom in my throat, a physical change. It was an incredible moment because I've always felt so powerless over my voice. I did not want to say anything for the next selection of music. I pictured myself with an orchestra and choir and I was the lead singer. It was a brilliant experience. I could stand out there in front and have enough faith in myself that I could do it. The beauty of it was that it went on for a while. It was not a fleeting thing. I was really living the moment and I could stay with it.

My next image was being at a victory ball. I was able to celebrate finding my voice. An image of an old man said, "Well done."

Bernadette found that this session had a very significant effect on her life.

Since the session, I have made wonderful decisions in my life. It has given me confidence that I can do things, that I can say things, that I can make decisions, that I have my own voice, and I can go out and do what I want to do. It was life-changing, a turning point. I feel I have something to offer. I don't think I will ever lose that image. I still feel the strength of that session in my body. It is right in my body, in my heart, in my soul, in every part of me.

The singing voice in the music held me there and helped me really live the moment. In the imagery, I was asked to take the solo part, and I accepted. I was feeling, "Yes, I can do it." It was the strength of the music [that] made the session pivotal. The singing, to me, was expressing the very core of me.

Suzanne

Not all pivotal sessions in GIM are enjoyable. Suzanne—
and, in the next section, Timothy—described uncomfortable
experiences. It seems that the sessions were pivotal because
the uncomfortable images were resolved in some way.

[The pivotal session was] the one in which there was a bad,
negative memory of God as a pillar turning to rock. The pillar was a
negative image, an immovable, solid, faceless, shapeless image. I
didn't like the image. I chiseled away at the rock and exposed a gold
nugget. The nugget was beautiful, precious, and small.

The significant image was the rock turning into lava, flowing
from the pillar, and exposing a gold nugget underneath. The lava
flowed out of my body, and with it, all the negative images of God. It
was freeing, getting all the mountain of lava off. There was a feeling
of letting go, of being able to move. My whole body was freed. And
that freedom has stayed with me. I was able to breathe without a
weight on me. There was a breaking away from old feelings [and] old
ways of being, of needing more freedom in my life, a freedom of being.

[The pivotal moment] was a powerful, explosive moment. I felt
the awfulness of it and needed to feel the depth of that to break out.

Suzanne explained that the session had had a significant
effect on her life.

Recurring bad dreams have weighed heavily on me. The lava
flowing has changed that. I don't have as many dreams about it. I can
retrieve the memories without [their] destroying me.

The images leading up to the pivotal moment were important. I
need to have my body involved. The most powerful experiences are
the complete ones where there's sensation in your body and you are
physically involved. The more the body is involved [in the experi-
ence], the more powerful the experience is.

Timothy

Timothy's experience of pivotal moments in GIM was
described as a recurring image that reappeared in several
sessions. He did not think any one session stood out as being
pivotal.

There is an image that is significant: an image of a dead baby being carried on a barge in the underworld or underground. I am pushing the barge, [which is] like a Venetian gondola. There is a feeling of sadness. It relates to something which happened to me when I was younger. It is a recurring image. It lasts for different lengths of time. As the image comes back, it is a reminder that the issue is not resolved.

Timothy describes in more detail that the experience is not a pleasant one. "It isn't a happy experience coming to the image, and I don't enjoy revisiting it. But it is alive and I take it with me. It has its own life." The recurring image, however, transforms from one session to the next.

In recent sessions, there is a shift in the image. There are jewels imbedded in the boat and surroundings. A baby son, which is alive, is now in that image, on the boat with the dead baby. There is a shift in emotion. There is always a feeling of loss and sadness. But in the recent image, there is a lighter feeling, like an acknowledgment.

The image stands apart from other images in that it recurs. It is deep inside me. The image is experienced emotionally, physically, and intellectually. It draws together all the images of the session up to that point. It stands the test of time.

Pamela

Pamela's pivotal session was a childhood memory of isolation, loneliness, and not being cared for, at a time when the family house had been destroyed by fire.

I almost relived it. I remember the physical feelings of being sick and crying. I was right back inside the experience, not as the little girl but with the insight of an adult. There were feelings of loneliness, fear, feelings of dislocation, that nobody understood what was happening for me. I was [an] isolated, terrified little girl, and my mother was preoccupied with so many other things.

In her GIM sessions, Pam feels she is engaged with the music.

It's like being on another level. If the music is something I love, I just enjoy the music. Other music I may not recognise, but I'll tune in to it; if I think it's superb, I'll say, "That's beautiful, I'm going to listen to this." [Yet] it amazes me that after a session, I often cannot remember any of the music at all.

David

David's pivotal session was an experience of healing following the recall of traumatic experiences.

It was a meeting of myself before I was traumatised. I was a happy, vibrant, chubby child. I felt proud that this 3-year-old boy was attractive. There was a feeling of coming home, of discovery, wonder, and recognition. [There was] a feeling I had discovered this vital part of me and that it hadn't been destroyed after 30 years. I had found something that was lost.

I felt something happening in my body; my body became active. There were noises in my abdomen as if something was moving. My breathing changed; warm breath filled every part of my body.

The impact of this session had influenced many aspects of his life.

There is an opening up of my mental horizon. There is future. I have put on weight; I stand differently, taller, more physically aware. In a situation where I was very nervous, I called to my mind the image of the boy, imagined holding his hand, and I felt powerful. My disposition has changed; I can let go of anger.

Ken

Ken could not identify any one GIM session as pivotal for him; instead, he mostly remembers the music, not the imagery of the session.

The meaning is in hearing the structure of the music, hearing it as a whole and having the emotional experience. In the Brahms

Requiem (part 1), I was struck by the cooperation between the singers. It was a very, very, very powerful image; how beautiful it was and how uplifting. It was a strongly emotional experience. It sent shivers up and down my spine. There was strength and gentleness; it was controlled yet beautiful and powerful.

In the Brahms *Piano Concerto*, number 2, slow movement, I felt the expression of passion and feelings and their resolution—an expression of joy, yet gentle and embracing. The pianist was having a ball and sounded as though he was really involved in it.

THE SIMILARITIES AND DIVERSITIES OF PIVOTAL MOMENTS

Pivotal Moments Are Recalled in Vivid Detail

All seven participants recalled in vivid detail the pivotal imagery, feeling, or body sensation of the experience. The colours and shapes of visual images were recalled in detail, and the feelings and body sensations were described in graphic detail. Some also described the mandala they had drawn from the session.

The Image Lasts and "Stands the Test of Time"

Sarah identified a GIM session that was pivotal for her and had occurred 3 years prior to the interview. For others, the pivotal session had occurred between 18 months to 3 weeks prior to the interview. It was Timothy who stated that the pivotal image "stands the test of time." Bernadette said, "I don't think I will ever lose that image."

Pivotal Moments May Be Unpleasant or Uncomfortable

The session or moment within a session may involve imagery that is in a disliked colour or may be an unpleasant, uncomfortable, or a horrible feeling. For David and Bernadette, the pivotal moment had emerged after feelings of being uncomfortable, but their pivotal experience itself was quite wonderful. For Suzanne and Timothy, the experience itself was not at all comfortable and not enjoyable, yet the meaning of the moment affects their life in a very positive way.

Pivotal Moments May Involve an Embodied Experience

For many of the participants, the pivotal moment was experienced as body sensations or changes within the internal organs of the body. David, Ken, Suzanne, and Bernadette all experienced strong body sensations and emotions during their pivotal experience. They commented that the more the body is involved in the experience, the more powerful the experience is. The whole body may be involved, physically, emotionally, and intellectually.

The Experience of Pivotal Moments Is a Lived Experience

Bernadette and Timothy described how the image is a lived experience. Bernadette said, "It was not a fleeting thing. I was really living the moment and I could stay with it." For Timothy, the image "has its own life. It is deep inside of me."

Pivotal Sessions Have a Significant Effect on the Person's Life

There can be feelings of "coming home" (Sarah and David) and feelings of freedom, of room to move and grow, of expanding, and of growing up (Bernadette and Suzanne).

Images Are "Building Up" Toward the Pivotal Moment

Most participants wanted to describe the images and feelings that led up to the moment in the session that was pivotal, as if the pivotal moment comes out of the accumulated experiences from the beginning of the GIM session.

Recurring Images May Be Pivotal

For one of the participants, the image was a recurring one that appeared over several sessions and transformed itself. In this sense, the pivotal image seemed stored in a symbolic process, whereby it was reactivated in a further session but underwent change.

Music Is an Important Aspect of the Pivotal Moments

All the participants were invited to describe the experience of the music during the pivotal moment or pivotal session. For some, the music sustained the pivotal moment so that it could be felt fully. Sarah mentioned that the music moved her along. For Bernadette, the music helped to build up strength and to hold her in one place so that she "lived the moment."

For Ken, being with the music was like being on another level. He remembered the music and not anything else, and the meaning of the moment lay in the structure of the music and the emotional experience of it. In her GIM sessions, Pam felt she was engaged with the music. She said, "If the music is something I love, I just enjoy the music. . . . If I think it's superb, I'll say, 'That's beautiful; I'm going to listen to this.' "

Suzanne did not remember the music at all. The imagery or emotion of the pivotal moment took all of her attention, so there was nothing left for the music.

Clients' Perceptions of the Therapist During the Pivotal Moments Vary

Pam described the therapist as being there "only for her and for no one else." Pam said her therapist is a symbol of survival for her because during the fire that destroyed her family's house as a

child, she had saved her doll, named Anna—and her GIM therapist is also named Anna.

Ken found the therapist supportive when he was feeling very
distressed and very guilty about something. "I felt bad about it. It was
significant for me because the therapist was nonjudgmental. She was
supportive of how I was feeling; she let me have the feeling. I was
touched by her response." He also said, "I feel I am with a kindred
spirit, sharing the music."

Suzanne's experience of the therapist was that she was quite
directive in inviting Suzanne to search and explore the imagery that
led to the pivotal moment. David described a strong positive transference to the therapist: "I felt safe with her. Allowing someone into the
space is precious to me. I am not as guarded—I give over."

Therapists Surmise Clients' Pivotal Moments

The second part of this study (not fully reported here) was to
interview the two therapists of the participants, to ask them about
their perceptions of the pivotal moments or sessions described,
and to ask if they would have selected the particular sessions
identified as pivotal to the participants' therapy work.

Suzanne's pivotal experience was that the rock (representing
God) turned into lava and flowed away. Suzanne's GIM therapist
assumed that the pivotal moment was finding the nugget of gold.
In the interview, the therapist then said, "The process [of the rock
disintegrating] was obviously more important to her than the
reward [of finding the gold nugget]."

Timothy had recurring images of the dead baby in the barge.
Timothy's therapist had expected that images from ancient times
would have been the pivotal moments for Timothy, because he
drew a lot of strength from those images. The chosen image, however, came from different sessions altogether, ones in which the
image of the baby in the barge was transformed.

FINAL DEPICTION OF PIVOTAL MOMENTS

Pivotal moments in GIM may be unpleasant, uncomfortable, and
disliked experiences, but they open up mental horizons and influence

change in the person's life. The experience of the pivotal moment is remembered in vivid detail over time. The more the body is involved in the experience, the more powerful the pivotal moment is. The embodied experience is felt as physical, emotional, and spiritual. The therapist may be a kindred spirit in this experience and the music may sustain the moment, giving it strength and moving it along. The imagery of the pivotal moment may take all the person's attention so that the music and the therapist's interventions are not remembered. The experience stands the test of time, and there is a sense the moment will never be lost.

REFERENCES

Aigen K (1997). *Here We Are in Music: One Year with an Adolescent Music Therapy Group*. St. Louis, MO: MMB Music.

Colaizzi PF (1978). Psychological Research as the Phenomenologist Views It. In Valle RS, King M (eds): *Existential-Phenomenological Alternatives for Psychology*. New York: Oxford University Press.

Ely M, Anzul M, Friedman T, Garner D, Steinmetz AM (1991). *Circles with Circles: Doing Qualitative Research*. New York: Falmer.

Forinash M (1992). A Phenomenological Analysis of Nordoff-Robbins Approach to Music Therapy: The Lived Experience of Clinical Improvisation. *Music Therapy* 11:120–141.

Forinash M (1995). Phenomenological Research. In Wheeler BL (ed): *Music Therapy Research: Quantitative and Qualitative Perspectives*. Gilsum, NH: Barcelona Publishers.

Giorgi A (1985). Sketch of a Psychological Phenomenological Method. In Giorgi A (ed): *Phenomenology and Psychological Research*. Pittsburgh: Duquesne University Press.

Jordan AP, Cloninger C (1979). You Gave Me Love. Recorded by Thomas BJ. Jack and Bill Music Co. & Word Music.

Lee C (1996). Aspects of Improvisational Music Therapy for People with HIV and AIDS. *Music Therapy International Report* 10:24–29.

Norbet G (1972). *Wherever You Go*. Weston, VT: Benedictine Foundation.

Smeijsters H (1997). *Multiple Perspectives: A Guide to Qualitative Research in Music Therapy*. Gilsum, NH: Barcelona Publishers.